SOVEREIGNTY IN POST-SOVEREIGN SOCIETY

This book provides an important reconstruction of theories of sovereignty and an original discussion of their position in current legal and political realities. It contains a distinctive argument in a generally crowded field of research, and it shows how systems-theoretical approaches, placing emphasis on semantics and self-description, can be applied to illuminate theoretical constructions in law and politics.

Christopher Thornhill, Manchester University, UK

For my parents

Sovereignty in Post-Sovereign Society

A Systems Theory of European Constitutionalism

JIŘÍ PŘIBÁŇ
Cardiff University, UK

Routledge
Taylor & Francis Group
LONDON AND NEW YORK

First published 2015 by Ashgate Publishing

Published 2016 by Routledge
2 Park Square, Milton Park, Abingdon, Oxfordshire OX14 4RN
711 Third Avenue, New York, NY 10017, USA

First issued in paperback 2016

Routledge is an imprint of the Taylor & Francis Group, an informa business

British Library Cataloguing in Publication Data
A catalogue record for this book is available from the British Library

The Library of Congress has cataloged the printed edition as follows:
Přibáň, Jiří, 1967– author.
Sovereignty in post-sovereign society : a systems theory of European constitutionalism / by Jiří Přibáň.
pages cm.—(Applied legal philosophy)
Includes bibliographical references and index.
ISBN 978-1-4724-6087-5 (hardback)
1. Sovereignty. 2. Constitutional law—European Union countries.
3. International and municipal law—European Union countries. 4. European federation.
I. Title.
KJE5078.P75 2015
341.26—dc23

2015002218

ISBN 13: 978-1-138-70149-6 (pbk)
ISBN 13: 978-1-4724-6087-5 (hbk)

Contents

Series Editor's Preface

The objective of the Applied Legal Philosophy series is to publish work which adopts a theoretical approach to the study of particular areas or aspects of law or deals with general theories of law in a way which focuses on issues of practical moral and political concern in specific legal contexts.

In recent years there has been an encouraging tendency for legal philosophers to utilise detailed knowledge of the substance and practicalities of law, and a noteworthy development in the theoretical sophistication of much legal research. The series seeks to encourage these trends and to make available studies in law which are both genuinely philosophical in approach and at the same time based on appropriate legal knowledge and directed towards issues in the criticism and reform of actual laws and legal systems.

The series will include studies of all the main areas of law, presented in a manner which relates to the concerns of specialist legal academics and practitioners. Each book makes an original contribution to an area of legal study while being comprehensible to those engaged in a wide variety of disciplines. Their legal content is principally Anglo-American, but a wide-ranging comparative approach is encouraged and authors are drawn from a variety of jurisdictions.

Tom Campbell
Series Editor
Centre for Applied Philosophy and Public Ethics
Charles Sturt University, Canberra

Preface

This book is an outcome of many debates and polemics with a number of excellent intellectuals and scholars working in the fields of social theory of law, constitutional theory, sociology of constitutionalism, European law and governance. Their comments, criticisms and advice helped to shape my theoretical position and particular interpretations of developments in the systems of European law and politics. I especially want to thank Petr Agha, Loic Azoulai, Nehal Bhuta, Paul Blokker, Michal Bobek, Hauke Brunkhorst, Monica Claes, Adam Czarnota, Roger Cotterrell, Gareth Davies, Bruno De Witte, Kenneth Dyson, Alberto Febbrajo, Peter Fitzpatrick, Jo Hunt, Poul F. Kjaer, Dimitry Kochenov, Jan Komárek, Martin Krygier, Martin Loughlin, Neil MacCormick, Mikael Rask Madsen, Hans-W. Micklitz, Panu Minkkinen, Richard Nobles, Dennis Patterson, George Pavlakos, Andreas Philippopoulos-Mihalopoulos, Isobel Roele, Ralf Rogowski, Michel Rosenfeld, Wojciech Sadurski, Giovanni Sartor, David Schiff, Angelos Sepos, Daniel Smilov, Stijn Smismans, Chris Thornhill, Kaarlo Tuori, Neil Walker, Thomas Webb, Joseph Weiler and Dan Wincott.

During my writing, I enormously benefited from the institutional and research support of Cardiff Law School and several research fellowships and visiting scholarships, especially the visiting professor fellowship at the Centre for Interdisciplinary Studies of Law, University of New South Wales in 2008, the visiting scholar fellowship at the Center for the Study of Law and Society, UC Berkeley in 2011, the visiting professorship at the University of San Francisco in 2011, the Franz Weyr Fellowship at the Czech Academy of Sciences in 2013, the visiting professor fellowship at the International Institute for the Sociology of Law in Onati in 2014 and the Fernand Braudel Senior Fellowship at the European University Institute in 2014. I want to express my gratitude to all people working at those institutions for their incredible help and assistance without which I could never successfully complete this book.

I also would like to express my gratitude to all students in my courses on the sociology of law, legal theory and comparative constitutionalism who so intelligently commented on my preconceptions and critically contributed to my ideas and views.

Finally, I want to thank my family for supporting me during this long period of research and writing.

Acknowledgements

This book accommodates some substantially revised, modified and expanded research and parts from the following previously published articles and chapters:

'The self-referential European polity, its legal context and systemic differentiation: theoretical reflections on the emergence of the EU's political and legal autopoiesis', *European Law Journal* 15(4) (2009): 442–61.

'Multiple Sovereignty: on Europe's self-constitutionalization and legal self-reference', *Ratio Juris* 23(1) (2010): 41–64.

'Legal Flexibility, Governance and Differentiated Integration: on functional differentiation of EU law and politics', in *Which Europe? The Politics of Differentiated Integration*, eds K.H.F. Dyson and A. Sepos (New York: Palgrave Macmillan, 2010), 24–38.

'Self-reference of the Constitutional State: a systems theory interpretation of the Kelsen-Schmitt debate', *Jurisprudence* 2(2) (2011): 309–28.

'Constitutionalism as Fear of the Political? A comparative analysis of Teubner's Constitutional Fragments and Thornhill's A Sociology of Constitutions', *Journal of Law and Society* 39(3) (2012): 441–71.

'Desiring a Democratic European Polity: The European Union Between the Constitutional Failure and the Lisbon Treaty', in *The European Union After Lisbon: Constituitonal Basis, Economic Order and External Action*, eds H.J. Blanke and S. Mangiameli (Berlin: Springer Verlag, 2012), 71–91.

'The Self-Referential Semantics of Sovereignty: A Systems Theoretical Response to (Post)Sovereignty Studies', in *Constellations* 20(3) (2013): 406–21.

'Asking the Sovereignty Question in Global Legal Pluralism: from "weak" jurisprudence to "strong" socio-legal theories of constitutional power operations', *Ratio Juris* 28(1) (2015): 31–51.

I want to thank the publishers for permission to use parts of these texts in this book.

Introduction

Yet another book about sovereignty?! Every year, hundreds of academic studies and scholarly articles dealing with the problem of sovereignty are published around the world. Different theories and philosophies of politics and law and social science approaches tackle various issues and themes traditionally associated with the concept of sovereignty. They examine operations of political power, including its legal form, yet also specify what the relations between public authorities and their subjects should be like. Theories of sovereignty can address both legitimate origins and uses of power, the criteria and conduct of public authorities and conditions of obedience of their subjects. They can be realistic encounters of politics as the realm of power and decision-making, yet equally explore the notion of the common good and political virtues as preconditions of the maintenance of political and social order. The coercive state power is impossible to exercise without legitimacy of the power's origin and use. No wonder Michael Walzer, for instance, states that 'sovereignty is a permanent feature of political life'[1] and notes that the most important political question concerns the boundaries within which sovereignty operates and the ideology or doctrine legitimizing those boundaries.

Sovereignty, together with democracy and legal constitution, forms the conceptual trinity of modern legal, social and political theory. Despite the quasi-theological imagination associated with the general will and sovereignty, these concepts are profoundly linked to the historical emergence of legal and sociological positivism. Jeremy Bentham's reductive and inadequate, yet simple, seductive and notoriously quoted definition of law as the sovereign's command has made the concept of sovereignty a pillar of modern analytical jurisprudence drawing on the positivistic methodology of social sciences. As if sovereignty in its primitive social structure of commands and the general habit of obedience were an indisputable social fact constituting the normativity of positive law and integrating society in general.

Bentham's notion of sovereignty obviously cannot grasp complexities of modern political and legal reality. Nevertheless, sovereignty remains one of the constitutive metaphors of modernity and its persuasive force still profoundly affects theoretical discussions of the last three decades, reflecting the social transformation of modernity into post-modernity with its recent conceptualizations

1 Michael Walzer, *Spheres of Justice: A Defense of Pluralism and Equality* (New York: Basic Books, 1983), 318.

of 'post-sovereignty',[2] 'late sovereignty',[3] 'plurinational democracy',[4] 'post-democracy'[5] and 'post-constituent'[6] politics. It seems as if the paradigmatic leap required to analyse the increasingly more globalized (and, within the European context, Europeanized) post-modern societies cannot materialize without using exactly the same – arguably superseded – concepts of sovereignty, constitution and democracy.

Sovereignty is thus questioned and examined within the context of transnational, supranational, international and national politics and law.[7] Academic discussions and internet blogging on sovereignty and post-sovereignty are booming to the extent that one wonders if recent announcements of the post-sovereign era have some informative value beyond the banality of 'post-everything' remarks. No wonder some scholars warn against a naïve depiction of a brand-new globalized world of governance and insist that popular sovereignty and democratic legitimation need to be revitalized at both nation state and international levels to oppose encroaching forms of global economic and administrative domination.[8]

However, the current rapid expansion of the sovereignty and post-sovereignty discourse and its associated conceptual confusions in itself clearly indicates that the modern nation state and national polities are increasingly globalized and therefore

2 Neil MacCormick, *Questioning Sovereignty: Law, State, and Nation in the European Commonwealth* (Oxford: Oxford University Press, 1999), 123; William Wallace, 'The Sharing of Sovereignty: The European Paradox', *Political Studies* 47 (1999): 503.

3 Neil Walker, 'The Idea of Constitutional Pluralism', *Modern Law Review* 65 (2002): 317.

4 See Michael Keating, *Plurinational Democracy: Stateless Nations in a Post-Sovereignty Era* (Oxford: Oxford University Press, 2001), 12–28.

5 See Colin Crouch, *Post-democracy (Themes for the 21st Century)* (Oxford: Polity, 2004); see also Richard Rorty, 'Post-Democracy', *London Review of Books* 26(7) (2004), 1 April 2004.

6 For instance, Neil Walker calls the European Union's emerging constitutional domain as 'post-constituent constitutionalism'; see Neil Walker, 'Post-Constituent Constitutionalism? The Case of the European Union', in *The Paradox of Constitutionalism: Constituent Power and Constitutional Form*, eds Martin Loughlin and Neil Walker (Oxford: Oxford University Press, 2007), 247; see also Lawrence Lessig, 'Post-Constitutionalism', *Michigan Law Review* 94 (1996): 1422–1470.

7 In this study, I differentiate between supranationalism and transnationalism by emphasizing the EU's structure of supranational organization with powers primarily negotiated and delegated by its Member States, yet establishing their specific multilevel governance and multiple hierarchies, rules and operations. Unlike supranationalism, transnationalism refers to processes of social communication, networks and organizations evolving independently of state power and boundaries in globalized societies. The EU's supranational structures typically go beyond the level of international delegation of power and international law monistic claims and even adopt specific forms of non-state transnational governance.

8 Saskia Sassen, *Losing Control? Sovereignty in an Age of Globalization* (New York: Columbia University Press, 1996).

go through profound structural and semantic political and legal changes.[9] It would therefore be far too simplistic either to dismiss all criticisms of the modern concept of sovereignty as just one of many intellectual fashions and trendy clichés, or to dismiss the concept itself as theoretically flawed and politically obsolete. Instead, the fundamental disputes and increasing discussions and criticisms of the concept of sovereignty should theoretically inspire us to reconsider the political and legal semantic and structural changes in global society.[10]

The primary aim of this study, therefore, is to comprehend the persistence of sovereignty as a political and legal concept in the post-sovereign social condition. The tension and paradoxical relationship between the semantics and structures of sovereignty and post-sovereignty are addressed by using the conceptual framework of the autopoietic social systems theory.

I argue that the modern question of sovereignty permanently oscillating between *de iure* authority and *de facto* power cannot be discarded by theories of supranational and transnational globalized law and politics. Globalization involves profound structural and semantic changes in the systems of positive law and politics. Nevertheless, this evolving post-sovereign global society is typical of the persisting political and legal semantics of sovereignty. In this respect, I want to emphasize that the concept of post-sovereignty employed in this study has no prescriptive or critical political meaning and does not suggest that the systems of globalized law and politics should abandon the concept of sovereignty. The social theoretical concept of post-sovereignty rather refers to the evolution of modern society impossible to comprehend in terms of nationhood or statehood and national or state sovereignty. It thus highlights historicity of the concept of sovereignty and signifies the contemporary complexity of functionally differentiated society in which the nation state and sovereignty have ceased to play a central role in political and legal communication and lost their status of ultimate metaphors of societal unity and integration.

While primarily engaging in social theoretical interpretations of the concept of sovereignty, this study, nevertheless, has one important consequence from the perspective of normative political and constitutional theory, namely the impossibility to perceive sovereignty as a 'thing' constituting society in the existentialist sense. In other words, there is no 'real life' or concrete societal order in the form of a nation or any other social group which could constitute its politics as a sovereign entity. Criticizing quasi-theological conceptualizations of political sovereignty and its juridical form, I reformulate the problem of sovereignty and its persistence and persuasive force as part of the self-referential communication of the systems of positive law and politics. Drawing on the recent revival of social theoretical and sociological perspectives of constitutionalism and their advantages

9 Gerard Delanty, *Social Theory in a Changing World: Conceptions of Modernity* (Cambridge: Polity Press, 1999), 61–70.

10 John W. Meyer, John Boli, George M. Thomas and Francisco O. Ramirez, 'World Society and the Nation State', *The American Journal of Sociology* 103(1) (1997): 144.

against traditionally normativist and decisionist theories of sovereignty and constitutional democracy, I argue that *sovereignty is thinkable of as part of functional differentiation* between the autopoietic systems of positive law and politics of modern society.

Sovereignty marks the boundary between politics and law, highlights the legal context of politics and the political context of law,[11] and thus contributes to the internal dynamics of both political and legal systems. Furthermore, the autopoietic social systems theoretical view makes it possible to reformulate the question of constitutional sovereignty as the constitution *in* society rather than the constitution *of* society. No political or legal conceptualization of sovereignty can guarantee moral and value integration of modern society and operate as the unifying force ultimately determining the political and moral foundations of society and its inside/outside border distinctions. Functional differentiation of modern society requires rethinking and redefining the concept of sovereignty as part of the differentiated systems of politics and law beyond the classic image of Leviathan and its socially integrating force.

Paradoxes of Sovereignty in Post-Sovereign Society: the State, the Popular Will and its Constitutional Form in the Globalized World

State sovereignty became a central category of national and international jurisprudence in the second half of the seventeenth century and continued to dominate European legal and political thought for the next three centuries, especially in the form of the sovereignty of the modern nation state. Modern systems of international politics and law historically emerged as systems where sovereign states mutually coordinated their actions, settling their disputes and establishing institutions of international cooperation. In this context, sovereignty was commonly defined as 'the highest power of command'[12] over a particular territory and over those who live there – the subjects of a sovereign. It was associated with the sovereign's externality and transcendence.[13]

However, the absoluteness of sovereignty is a modern idea associated with the popular will which is the general and ultimate source of all laws and thus serves as the only legitimate law of democratic society. In modern society, sovereignty ceased to be an attribute of the Prince exempt from the laws and became an abstract and independent political entity.[14] The sovereign will is absolute because

11 Neil Walker, 'Late Sovereignty in the European Union', in *Sovereignty in Transition*, ed. Neil Walker (Oxford: Hart Publishing, 2003), 20.

12 Jean Bodin, *On Sovereignty* (Cambridge: Cambridge University Press, 1992), 1.

13 Michel Foucault, 'Governmentality', in *Power. Essential Works of Foucault 1954–1984, volume 3*, ed. James D. Faubion (London: Penguin, 2000), 204–205.

14 Bertrand de Jouvenel, *On Sovereignty. An Inquiry into the Political Good* (Indianapolis: Liberty Fund, 1997), 218.

the exemption from the laws paradoxically became the first law – the general will can never be wrong! In Rousseau's political and moral philosophy, the general will is always right and desires the public good and, more importantly, knows best what it is.[15]

In modernity, sovereignty particularly signifies tension and conflicts arising from attempts to legally define, limit and regulate political will and the decisions of specific political bodies. However, sovereignty also means the possibility of increasing political will and enhancing decision-making power by legal means.[16] It means power to both make and suspend the law and declare the general political will as the ultimate law to exceed all positive laws. This legally unbound sovereignty, nevertheless, has the exclusive form and legal force of a constitution in modern society. Sovereignty's conceptualizations thus continually oscillate between the normativity of a legal constitution and the unrestrained political will of the commanding sovereign.[17]

Sovereignty is a relational and paradoxical[18] concept with both legal and political dimension: it is constitutive of politics but escapes the regulatory logic of political institutions and often gets associated with the domain of 'real life' with all its excesses; in modern constitutional rule of law it is both defining and defined by positive law and thus both outside and inside the juridical domain. Sovereignty means both the power that enacts laws (the political sovereignty of *pouvoir constituent/constituent power*) and the law that restrains and regulates the constituent power of the people (the legal sovereignty of *pouvoir constitué/constituted power*).

Sovereignty thus has had its explanatory value as a concept formulating the complexities of modern attempts to legitimize political commands, obedience and civic bonds between the governed and those who govern them.[19] The modern state became the nation state legitimized by the sovereignty of its people. The historical transformation of the state sovereignty into sovereignty of a nation and the nation state has been part of the canon of political theory and modern politics.[20] Popular sovereignty, manifesting itself within the institutional constraints of the

15 Jean-Jacques Rousseau, *Discourse on Political Economy and the Social Contract* (Oxford: Oxford University Press, 1994), 66.

16 Daniel Philpott, *Revolutions in Sovereignty: How Ideas Shaped Modern International Relations* (Princeton, NJ: Princeton University Press, 2001), 143.

17 For further comments, especially regarding the revolutionary power see, for instance, Ulrich Preuss, 'Constitutional Powermaking for the New Polity: Some Deliberations on the Relations between Constituent Power and the Constitution', *Cardozo Law Review* 14 (1992–1993): 643.

18 See, for instance, Martin Loughlin, *The Idea of Public Law* (Oxford: Oxford University Press, 2003).

19 John Jackson, 'Sovereignty-Modern: A New Approach to an Outdated Concept', *The American Journal of International Law* 97(4) (2003): 801.

20 Bernard Yack, 'Popular Sovereignty and Nationalism', *Political Theory* 29(4) (2001): 517.

democratic constitutional state, gave rise to modern constitutionalism and all its productive paradoxes and differences between the constituent power of the people and the constituted power of the democratic state.[21]

Modern constitutional democracy's legitimacy rests on two main pillars: popular sovereignty and the civil-rights-based rule of law. A political system is democratically legitimate if it is imposed by the sovereign people on itself, and political power can be exercised either directly by the people or through their elected representatives. The system itself needs to be constitutionally legitimate in the sense that its principles, rights, rules and procedures are expressed in legal form and public officials and their actions are subject to the law. Democratic practices are governed by the rule of law and, at the same time, the legal rules are open to democratic change.[22]

Because of sovereignty's ambivalence and the paradoxes associated with it, the sovereign's constituent power allegedly 'offers lawyers nothing but problems',[23] and current legal and political theory is typical of numerous attempts at demolishing the generally accepted interpretation of nation state sovereignty and international law history as a 'myth'.[24] Interpretations of the Westphalia international treaties as the beginning of modern international politics and of the state as the organization of social, political and juridical modernization are criticized by many different schools of historical, legal, political and social thought. The reasons for these criticisms are methodological and epistemological but also ontological and instrumentally political. For instance, Morgenthau's famous statement that '[B]y the end of the Thirty Years' War, sovereignty as supreme power over a certain territory was a political fact ...'[25] is increasingly challenged by a 'global village' of human rights[26] and other ideological projects of globalized democracy and cosmopolitan ethics.

Sovereignty as the supreme ordering power of a particular polity subsequently becomes increasingly challenged in the globalized world[27] because state

21 Martin Loughlin and Neil Walker, eds, supra n. 6.

22 For one of the most illuminating exchanges of views regarding constitutional and democratic legitimacy, see Jürgen Habermas, 'Reconciliation through the Public Use of Reason: Remarks on John Rawls's Political Liberalism', *Journal of Philosophy* 92(3) (1995): 109; John Rawls, 'Political Liberalism: Reply to Habermas', *Journal of Philosophy* 92(3) (1995): 132.

23 Martin Loughlin, supra n. 18, 99.

24 Stephane Beaulac, *The Power of Language in the Making of International Law* (Leiden: Nijhoff Publishers, 2004), 71.

25 Hans Morgenthau, 'The Problem of Sovereignty Reconsidered', *Columbia Law Review* 58(3) (1948): 341.

26 See, for instance, Richard Falk, *Law in an Emerging Global Village: A Post-Westphalian Perspective* (Ardsley: Transnational Publishers, 1998).

27 For one of the most opinionated arguments against the concept of sovereignty, see, for instance, Stephen D. Krasner, *Sovereignty, Organized Hypocrisy* (Princeton, NJ: Princeton University Press, 1999).

authorities are unable to regulate and order the flow of capital, environmental crises, migration, security policies and so on. The globalization processes establish new forms of social domination and control.[28] Power is ever more fragmented and diffuse. The territorial nation state is increasingly decoupled from globalized law pushed forward by a variety of global agencies, transnational private corporations and their regulatory bodies and supranational governmental or non-governmental organizations.[29] The state legislatures of 'hard law' are bypassed by the networks of 'soft law' usually defined as a set of rules of conduct without directly binding legal force but with a potentially strong force of persuasion and practical effects. Sovereignty has moved beyond its territorial state form, and is now shaped by multifaceted and polycentric forms of globalization.[30] Even the domain of international law and politics, which used to consider the notion of state sovereignty as one of its conceptual pillars, familiarizes criticisms of state sovereignty and calls for giving a more important role to the international community as a whole.[31]

The Pluralism Argument: Toward a Sociological Understanding of Sovereignty and Constitutionalism

Many theoretical and philosophical innovations, from the jurisprudence of legal pluralism and political theories of global governance to critical theories of governmentality[32] or the global 'Empire',[33] divided and shared (pooled) sovereignty,[34] and sovereignty and its discontents[35] have been introduced to cope with the complexities, paradoxes and antinomies of political sovereignty and power in global society. Nevertheless, recent theoretical debates of sovereignty often

28 Saskia Sassen, supra n. 8.

29 Hendrik Spruyt, *The Sovereign State and its Competitors: an Analysis of Systems Change* (Princeton, NJ: Princeton University Press, 1994).

30 David Held, *Democracy and the Global Order: From Modern State to Cosmopolitan Governance* (Stanford, CA: Stanford University Press, 1995), 62.

31 Among many collections of essays, see, for instance, Howard Hensel, ed., *Sovereignty and the Global Community: The Quest for Order in the International System* (Aldershot: Ashgate, 2004); see also Stephen D. Krasner, ed., *Problematic Sovereignty: Contested Rules and Political Possibilities* (New York: Columbia University Press, 2001).

32 Jean Francois Bayart, *Global Subjects: A Political Critique of Globalization* (Cambridge: Polity Press, 2007), 287.

33 Michael Hardt and Antonio Negri, *Empire* (Harvard, MA: Harvard University Press, 2000).

34 Though the notion of shared sovereignty primarily has been adopted by scholars of EU law and integration, its meaning is general. See, for instance, Stephen D. Krasner, 'Sharing Sovereignty: New Institutions for Collapsed and Failing States', *International Security* 29(2) (2004): 85.

35 William Rasch, *Sovereignty and Its Discontents: On the Primacy of Conflict and the Structure of the Political* (London: Birkbeck Law Press, 2004).

surprisingly replicate a number of arguments and polemics related to the problems of legal theoretical methodology discussed in the beginning of the twentieth century by Kelsen, Schmitt, Heller, Smend, Ehrlich and other legal scholars. These debates often continue to be illuminated by the triadic structure of 'Will' (*Wollen*), 'Norm' (*Sollen*) and 'Fact' (*Sein*) which informs the semantics of sovereignty. The typically modern differentiations between the state and civil society, society and community or living law and legislated law also find their specific uses in recent sociological theories of non-state law and societal constitutionalism.

It is fascinating to see how some classical conceptual differences are being reinvented and reconceptualized in the context of contemporary global society, its politics and law. As Kaarlo Tuori observed, legal and political theories and philosophies draw on the tension between power and norm, respectively will and reason from the ancient times to the post-modern globalized systems of transnational politics and law.[36] The law's normative coherence depends on its capacity to manage the intrinsic tension between law's *voluntas* and *ratio* and it remains unimportant whether the legal system couples with political institutions of the nation state or supranational and transnational organizations.[37]

Classic legal positivist definitions of sovereignty as power impossible to be limited by law may emphasize the modern state's ultimate and final decision-making capacity and political will. Constitutions as normative foundations of politics, however, predetermine political will and establish limits of its legitimate use. Legal positivists may brand it a logical contradiction,[38] yet the functionally differentiated systems of positive law and politics make productive uses of this contradiction well beyond the sovereign state. The paradox of constitutionalism operating between the unrestricted will of constituent power already restricted by legal norms of the written constitution is a general paradox unconstrained by the state organization which needs to be further examined and explained by a general theory of the systems of positive law and politics.

Despite these historical reminiscences, the revival of social theoretical and sociological perspectives against traditionally normativist or decisionist theories of sovereignty and constitutional democracy indicates a significant methodological and paradigmatic shift. The *pluralism argument* equally enhanced by sociological perspectives and rejected by the decisionist and normativist theories becomes a focal point for the variety of sociological, constitutional and general legal theories. The pluralism argument also profoundly affects theoretical conceptualizations of sovereignty in the post-sovereign social condition.

---

36 Kaarlo Tuori, *Ratio and Voluntas: The Tension Between Reason and Will in Law* (Aldershot: Ashgate, 2010).

37 Ibid., 287.

38 For a critique of this legal positivist claim in particular and analytical jurisprudence of Bentham and Austin in general, see Massimo La Torre, *Constitutionalism and Legal Reasoning: A New Paradigm for the Concept of Law* (Dordrecht: Springer, 2007), 15–17.

Globalization represents the functional differentiation of modern society on a worldwide scale[39] and shows how concepts and communication patterns established by societies organized into nation states, such as sovereignty, constitutionalism and democracy, evolve into their new supranational and transnational forms. Sovereignty may be shared and divided and thus replicate social plurality and horizontal communication between different social systems of globalized society. It can be located in a number of political bodies other than the state.[40] The protection of the state against other states is no longer sovereignty's ultimate function. Instead, it functions as another form of societal organization at the transnational, supranational, national and regional levels.[41]

The sociological metaphor of the constitution of society mainly signifies the unity of social plurality and differences. Sociologists and social theorists, therefore, do not mean by it a political constitution overarching and accommodating all social domains but a unifying pattern of social dynamics and the structuring of a multiplicity of highly differentiated social subsystems. For instance, Edward Shils claimed that every society is constituted by a number of societies.[42] Similarly, Anthony Giddens states that the structural constraints on human action, although they always operate via actors' often diffuse and convoluted motives and reasons, are institutionalized features of differentiated social systems stretching across time and space.[43]

The epistemological argument of social plurality and diversity is often adopted by normative political theories to strengthen various forms of politics of identity and recognition. Unlike the homogenizing state constitutionalism, theories driven by the logic of diversity emphasize the role of 'hidden constitutions'[44] in contemporary pluralistic and culturally fragmented societies. The classical sociological distinctions, such as official/unofficial law, law in books/law in action or legislated law/living law, thus achieve the problematic status of a normative ground shaping the political argument against liberal constitutionalism and reformulating the democratic conventions of social recognition, political consensus, cultural identity and continuity of a constitutional polity.

Nevertheless, the paradoxes of sovereignty and constitutionalism at any stage in the evolution of modern society can hardly be resolved by normative and

39 Niklas Luhmann, *Theory of Society. Volume 1* (Stanford, CA: Stanford University Press, 2012), 91.

40 Neil MacCormick, 'Sovereignty, Democracy and Subsidiarity', in *Democracy and Constitutional Culture in the Union of Europe*, eds Richard Bellamy, V. Bufacchi and Dario Castiglione (London: Lothian Foundation, 1995), 98–100.

41 Niklas Luhmann, *Die Politik der Gesellschaft* (Frankfurt: Suhrkamp, 2002), 221.

42 Edward Shils, *The Constitution of Society* (Chicago, IL: The University of Chicago Press, 1972), 59.

43 Anthony Giddens, *The Constitution of Society: Outline of the Theory of Structuration* (Berkeley, CA: University of California Press, 1982), 310.

44 James Tully, *Constitutionalism in an Age of Diversity* (Cambridge: Cambridge University Press, 1995), 99.

more critical answers or 'right' moral and political options. They rather need to be accommodated and further expanded by an epistemological constructivism.[45] Radicalizing the social constructivist perspective, we may recall an early claim of the theory of autopoietic systems: 'Do not avoid paradoxes, but make productive use of them!'[46] Taking this methodological and theoretical turn, sovereignty paradoxes can be perceived as a source of operationality and structural coupling between the systems of positive law and politics.

The Difference Between the Semantics and Structures of Society: an Autopoietic Systems Theoretical View of Sovereignty

The dissolution of once clearly defined boundaries between the territorial national state and the domain of international politics and law impels supranational and transnational developments which demand the adoption of a *dynamic* concept of sovereignty,[47] not only divided between different systems of governance but also adapted to dynamic processes of systemic change and functional differentiation. Sovereignty consequently may be seen as a network of dynamic procedures and activities exercised in different social contexts and not a set of institutions and norms.

These new distinctions and conceptualizations are semantic responses to structural changes and contingencies[48] of global society which lacks a common constitutional pattern and thus cannot channel information exchange between law and politics in the manner of the sovereign state. As Niklas Luhmann pointed out, 'the structural coupling of the political system and the legal system through constitutions does not have an equivalent at the level of global society'.[49] The modern territorial state's intensive coupling of political and legal sovereignty, part of which is the sovereign rule of law in the form of the state constitution, has not been evolving at the global level. Recent European and global developments, therefore, show a need to examine how specific *structures* and *semantics* of the legal and political systems couple with each other and how this coupling affects the meaning of sovereignty.

45 Gunther Teubner, 'How the Law Thinks: Toward a Constructivist Epistemology of Law', *Law & Society Review* 23(5) (1989): 727.

46 Ibid., 736.

47 This paradigmatic change precedes the current process of globalization and had already been typical of legal and political philosophy of the first half of the twentieth century. See James Marshall, *Swords and Symbols: The Technique of Sovereignty* (Oxford: Oxford University Press, 1939).

48 For contingency of practices and activities shaping constitutional meaning, see Richard Bellamy and Dario Castiglione, eds, *Constitutionalism in Transformation: European and Theoretical Perspectives* (Oxford: Blackwell, 1996).

49 Niklas Luhmann, *Law as a Social System* (Oxford: Oxford University Press, 2004), 487–488.

According to Luhmann's autopoietic systems theory,[50] society is a functionally differentiated system consisting of different subsystems, such as politics, law, economy, education or religion which are cognitively open but normatively closed.[51] It means that autopoietic social systems use information from their environment but this external reference between the system and its environment does not affect the systems' operations. Systems are autopoietic in the sense that they self-create their operations and their functioning is guaranteed by self-referential communication[52] using the system's binary code, such as 'legal/illegal' in the legal system and 'government/opposition' in the political system.[53]

The functional differentiation of society into autopoietic social systems operating concurrently without any hierarchical ordering replaces the Parsonsian image of specific social systems supporting the functioning of overall society. Systemic differences are more significant than societal unity and the concepts of self-reference, self-description, self-production and self-organization need to be employed to explain the level of interference and interdependence between the structures and semantics of different autopoietic social systems.[54]

Social structures and semantics are two coeval, profoundly intertwined, yet autonomous constructions of an autopoietic social system.[55] Different social systems, such as law and politics, construct their specific structures and semantics which coevally change as part of general systemic changes. New concepts emerge as semantic responses to the structural changes of a system. Self-descriptions of a social system equally require structural responses and adjustments. A recent example of such structural responses to the semantic change is, for instance, the growth of law-making and institution-building in the domain of international

50 For the legal and political contextualization and critical elaboration of Luhmann's theory, see, for instance, Gunther Teubner, *Law as an Autopoietic System* (Oxford: Blackwell, 1993); Michael King and Chris Thornhill, *Niklas Luhmann's Theory of Politics and Law* (Houndmills: Palgrave Macmillan, 2006); Andreas Philippopoulos-Mihalopoulos, *Niklas Luhmann: Law, Justice, Society* (Oxon: Routledge-Glasshouse, 2010); Jiří Přibáň and David Nelken, eds, *Law's New Boundaries: The Consequences of Legal Autopoiesis* (Aldershot: Ashgate, 2001).

51 Niklas Luhmann, *Social Systems* (Stanford, CA: Stanford University Press, 1995), 102.

52 Niklas Luhmann, supra n. 49, 437–477.

53 See, for instance, William Rasch, *Niklas Luhmann's Modernity: the paradoxes of differentiation* (Stanford, CA: Stanford University Press, 2000), 151.

54 Niklas Luhmann, *Essays on Self-Reference* (New York: Columbia University Press, 1990), 93.

55 Niklas Luhmann, *Gesellschaftsstruktur und Semantik. Studien zur Wissenssoziologie der modernen Gesellschaft*, vol. 1 (Frankfurt: Suhrkamp, 1980); Niklas Luhmann, *Gesellschaftsstruktur und Semantik. Studien zur Wissenssoziologie der modernen Gesellschaft*, vol. 2 (Frankfurt: Suhrkamp, 1981); Niklas Luhmann, *Gesellschaftsstruktur und Semantik. Studien zur Wissenssoziologie der modernen Gesellschaft*, vol. 3 (Frankfurt: Suhrkamp, 1989).

criminal law and public law triggered by the global proliferation of human rights arguments in the last two decades.[56]

Coevally constructing their structures and semantics, systems sustain their self-reference and external differentiation. For instance, the legal system's semantics of constitutional sovereignty and legal monism corresponds to the structural self-validation of legal rules by other legal rules which replaced former references to natural law and justice or the command of a political sovereign. Similarly, semantics of equal constitutional rights for all citizens makes it possible to establish general, abstract and externally independent legal communication necessary for operations of the modern legal system.[57]

Structural changes usually coincide with semantic changes, such as the semantics of rights and liberties with the rise of the nation state. Nevertheless, the semantic and structural constructions of modern law and politics are differentiated and often full of temporal asymmetries.[58] Structural changes thus may also precede semantic changes and vice versa. For instance, the modern political semantics of democracy, civil liberties and the nation state can continue to dominate both democratic and autocratic political structures and even try to make sense of global politics short of state structures, democratic procedures and public accountability. Similarly, the legal semantics of constitutional sovereignty, legal monism, the duality of international and national law and legal validity can continue to describe legal structures which correspond to neither international, nor national legal regimes, such as the supranational legal system of the EU.

The persistence of sovereignty in contemporary post-sovereign European and globalized politics and law is best understood as the difference between the semantics and structures of these social systems. The semantics of sovereignty coincides with the history and evolution of modern national and international legal and political systems. Nevertheless, the emergence of supranational and transnational legal and political structures has not resulted in the new semantics and self-descriptions which would make the concept of sovereignty redundant. In fact, the persistence of sovereignty in the post-sovereign EU constellation is powerful evidence of differentiation of social structures and semantics because it shows the continuing semantic importance of sovereignty even in the most complex post-sovereign structural settings of the EU and the relationship between the Union and its Member States.

The level of interference between the structures and semantics of modern law and politics as well as their systemic closure thus contribute to the self-referential

56 Beth A. Simmons, *Mobilizing for Human Rights: International Law in Domestic Politics* (Cambridge: Cambridge University Press, 2009).

57 Niklas Luhmann, supra n. 49, 482.

58 Jiří Přibáň, 'Multiple Sovereignty: On Europe's Self-Constitutionalization and Legal Self-Reference', *Ratio Juris* 23(1) (2010): 55.

semantics of sovereignty.[59] The complex interplay of social structures and semantics shows that sovereignty studies require the methodology and perspectives of the social theory of law and politics, facilitating study of the evolution and structural changes of sovereignty in modern law and politics and parallel semantic changes in their conceptualization in the field of legal and political theory.[60] The autopoietic social systems theory, therefore, is used in this study to examine the evolution, differentiation and self-reference of the concept of sovereignty and its theoretical reflections and normative expectations invested in them both within and beyond the modern state framework.

The Concept of Political Constitutionalism and Sovereignty Beyond the Sovereign State

In order to understand the process of constitutionalization of national, supranational European and any other society and the persisting role of the semantics of sovereignty in them, it is also important to keep conceptual and theoretical clarity and accept Luhmann's notoriously repeated understanding of constitutions as organizations – subsystems of structural coupling of law and politics. As a specific social system, this organization is not limited to the political institution of the modern nation state, yet it is misleading to apply the concept of constitutionalism and constitution-making to any societal process of systemic self-constitution and self-reference – a theoretical view often favoured by recent theories of global legal pluralism and societal constitutionalism.

According to Luhmann, the functionally differentiated system of politics has power as its medium of communication in modern society. However, politically organized coercive power is the subject of a secondary coding by the medium of legality. Political power is thus itself subject to the law and can amend the existing laws only through the legal process. This self-referential juridification of power is described as the rule of law which is purely defined by the secondary coding of power and its structural coupling with legality and thus may be distinguished from moral and ideological concepts of the rule of law of liberal and constitutional statehood.[61]

In fact, the self-referential juridification of power makes the rule of law independent of organizational constraints of the modern state and stretches the self-constitution and self-inclusion of mutual coupling between the media of

59 Samantha Ashenden, 'The Problem of Power in Luhmann's Systems Theory', in *Luhmann on Law and Politics: Critical Appraisals and Applications*, eds Michael King and Chris Thornhill (Oxford: Hart Publishing, 2006), 128–130.

60 See, for instance, Michael Fowler and Julie Marie Bunck, *Law, Power and The Sovereign State: The Evolution and Application of the Concept of Sovereignty* (University Park, PA: The Pennsylvania State University Press, 1995).

61 Niklas Luhmann, supra n. 39, 213.

power and legality to the level of European and global society and its multi-layered organizations, networks and regimes. The self-inclusion of power in the medium of legality makes it more efficient at the supranational and transnational levels because it is not referred to merely in terms of the success/failure distinction but also the compliance/non-compliance distinction.

Power subsequently cannot be treated as a universal medium of controlling global society but requires further juridical specification of its universal competence. The secondary coding of power by the medium of legality thus contributes to the functional differentiation of global society and both power and legality serve as catalysts for the differentiation of the functional systems of politics and law of global society and its segments, such as European society evolving through the structures and semantics of the EU.

Modern society does not have one moral or cultural 'super-medium' which could unify all social communication in all of its subsystems and both legality and power as fully developed symbolically generalized media of the systems of law and politics can perform only specific operations without any possibility of fully integrating and founding a global polity and/or a basic norm of global society.[62] Nevertheless, this *societal neutralization of moralism* looking for normative foundations of the systems of law and politics should not lead to the opposite conceptual and theoretical extreme which considers any form of secondary coding and structural coupling between different social systems a form of societal constitutionalism beyond politics and its medium of coercive power. Global law often does not evolve as spontaneously recognized and voluntarily upheld and negotiated contractual regimes and networks and actually draws on the secondary coding of power.

European and global supranational and transnational constitutionalism need to profoundly reflect on this structural coupling between politics and law and explore power structures evolving beyond the nation state and their various forms of constitutionalization. Any form of constitutionalism, therefore, needs to be constrained to the analysis of this secondary coding and hardly can be depoliticized by some forms of civil or societal constitutions.

A Critique of Political Existentialism in the Concept of Sovereignty as Polity

This book focuses on the semantics of sovereignty as a political and legal concept and its persistence in the post-sovereign social condition. The autopoietic social systems theoretical analysis of legal and political paradoxes associated with the concept of sovereignty captures both the persistence and productive uses of sovereignty within the systems of positive law and politics. However, it also explains historical evolution of the concept of popular sovereignty as the

62 Ibid., 214.

legitimation of power without recourse to the transcendental foundations of modern society.

The autopoietic systems theoretical view of sovereignty thus represents a powerful critique of quasi-theological conceptualizations of popular sovereignty as the general will of *demos* – the nation as a 'real' existing constituent power and the substance of the state and/or any other political organization of modern society. It contrasts the normative idea of popular sovereignty as polity representing the totality and cultural unity of society to the functionally differentiated legal and political procedures in which the people – *demos* – exercises its sovereignty only through self-limiting legal subsystems of constitutional rights and political operations of different branches of constitutionally codified and separated power.

Sovereignty as the pre-political substance of constituent power of *demos* establishing the normative foundations and legitimacy of the state as its constituted political organization can be described by the autopoietic systems theory of law and politics as part of collective symbolism and cultural communication evolving both within and beyond the societal imagination of nationhood and the modern nation state. Recent theories of European and global imagined communities of cosmopolitan values and universal humanity are strong evidence of the fact that *demos* as the sovereign nation is not the final and ultimate stage in cultural and normative imaginations of popular sovereignty.

Like any other images of society as unity, nations are merely historical constructs of social evolution and not the existential precondition of society defining its moral foundations and substance. In this context, conceptualizations and criticisms of European supranational *demos* may be critically analysed in the same manner like former theories of national sovereignty and the nation state.

Popular sovereignty is not the guardian of societal unity. It is part of the specific cultural function of collective popular memory which defines its normative foundations and collective images only by constant selection between remembering and forgetting. This cultural 'constitutive' moment of popular sovereignty as polity, however, does not have the integrative capacity in modern functionally differentiated society, whether national, supranational European or global. It rather enhances general operations of the systems of positive law and politics by incorporating the cultural images of non-political and non-juridical unity into their specific and circularly operating semantics of sovereignty.

*

The book is organized as a social theoretical treatise on sovereignty using a number of recent European examples, developments and paradoxes to demonstrate both semantic and structural challenges related to the concept of sovereignty and its persistence in the post-sovereign social condition. The opening part 'Cases and Concepts' starts by analysing the current state of EU legal and political integration and shows that this specific process of supranational societal evolution includes critical reflections on the typical modern concepts of legal and political theory, especially legal monism and pluralism, political sovereignty as the unity of will and decision, the basic norm and the ultimate rule of recognition. Classic legal and political theories of sovereignty, therefore, are examined in the current European and global context to put forward the central argument that the concept of sovereignty needs to be revisited and reconceptualized by the autopoietic social systems theory.

In the first chapter, I focus on sovereignty in the context of the Europeanization of the nation states, their politics and legal systems. The EU paradox of divided sovereignty shows profound semantic changes in the sovereignty discourse in contemporary national and post-national societies and the impossibility to apply classic legal and political theories and philosophies to the processes of supranational legal and political integration. However, European constitutionalism also reveals the persisting capacity of the sovereign nation state to operate in a supranational and transnational world and thus effectively questions the claim of governance theories that nation state institutions have become significantly marginalized, if not redundant in global society.

In the second chapter I engage in a historical, theoretical and conceptual analysis of sovereignty and highlight its persisting semantics in the social systems of positive law and politics. I use the autopoietic systems theory's distinction of social structures and semantics to redefine sovereignty as part of the self-referential semantics of both the legal and political system. Sovereignty, therefore, is not a concept signifying the unity of society integrated by fundamental values and ultimately governed and controlled by one power centre and its laws. The self-limiting and self-referential concept of sovereignty concurrently operates through the functionally differentiated systems of politics and law at national, supranational and transnational global level.

In the next part of the book entitled 'Concepts and Theories', I examine recent debates and critical reflections on sovereignty in post-sovereign society by revisiting some of the most important conceptualizations and arguments of modern political, legal and social theory. I especially focus on the concepts of legal monism and pluralism, political decision-making and the impossibility of both the value integration and ultimate depoliticization of functionally differentiated modern society. In the third chapter, I, therefore, examine conceptualizations and criticisms of the constitutional state and sovereignty by Hans Kelsen and Carl Schmitt as early reflections on modern legal and political self-reference and functional differentiation. Retrospectively interpreting Kelsen and Schmitt's theories as specific examples of legal and political self-reference, functional differentiation and the self-limitation of law and politics, I argue that the process of legal and political Europeanization and globalization discredits substantive theories of the sovereign state identifying its organization with metaphysical values and an ultimately self-validating collective identity and pre-political existence.

In the fourth chapter, I subsequently examine recently popular theories of legal pluralism, so heavily criticized by both Kelsen and Schmitt, as a theoretical response to the evolution of supranational and transnational law and politics. In particular,

Gunther Teubner's concepts of societal constitutionalism, global legal pluralism and constitutional fragmentation, inspired by Eugen Ehrlich's sociology of living law, radically reformulate the problem of constitutionalism and sovereignty in global law and politics. Unfortunately, the concept of societal constitutions and its assumption of post-sovereign global law and politics are typical of depoliticization of problems of constitutionalism. Contrary to these theoretical conceptualizations, I argue that the semantics of sovereignty persists as part of legitimation of power structures operating in the post-sovereign social condition.

In the fifth chapter, I, therefore, reformulate the question of sovereignty as a sociological problem of complex power operations communicated through the constitutional state's organization and reconfigured within the supranational and transnational legal and political organizations. Theories of global legal and constitutional pluralism cannot eliminate power politics. Sovereignty, therefore, is part of multiple power structures in modern society. The interplay between power structures and the semantics of sovereignty as a legitimation strategy opens the possibility of self-description and mobilization of modern polity which is not limited to the nation state but replicated through specific legitimation dilemmas of supranational or transnational organizations.

In the third part of the book entitled 'Theories and Systems', I return to the process of European integration as one of the most persuasive examples of the paradoxical constitution of polity beyond state sovereignty, yet constantly searching for its efficiency and democratization as two general forms of legitimation of power in modern society. Structural and semantic complexity of the current state of the EU persuasively shows that sovereignty is a concept internally constituted by the social systems of law and politics.

In the sixth chapter, I describe both the theoretical and practical emergence of self-referential European politics and law. The general theory of autopoietic social systems turns out to be the best response to the current European 'unity of conceptual contradictions' because it synthesizes the temporal, functional and self-referential aspects of European integration and avoids the epistemological trap to identify the particular concept of polity, its organizational restraints and institutional hierarchies with the general concept of society. Although the Union transgresses its nation state segmentation, the notions of statehood and democratic legitimacy continue to inform legal and political semantics of the EU and specific responses to the Union's systemic tensions, such as the policy of differentiated integration legislated by the EU flexibility clauses.

In the seventh chapter, I extend the previous chapter's argument by summarizing the concurrent democratic legitimacy and efficiency commitments formulated by the Lisbon Treaty and their impact on the character of European governance and European polity. The most recent EU attempts at democratizing its forms of governance are subsequently contextualized by outlining historical links between the EU's institutional framework and the notion of European polity.

Using the EU and other examples, the final chapter presents a critique of political existentialism. The concept of sovereignty is analysed as part of pre-political cultural communication of collective symbolism and moral value foundationalism in both the national and post-national European or global contexts. Following a brief systems theoretical analysis of modern nationalism and national statehood, the semantics of sovereignty as the 'real' democratic polity representing the whole society is criticized and described as mere part of the specific cultural function of memory. Political and constitutional references to 'foundations' and 'constituting' moments of a sovereign polity actually use memory as operation selecting between remembrance and forgetting which only supports and enhances general operations of the autopoietic systems of positive law and politics.

PART I
Cases and Concepts

Chapter 1

Multiple Sovereignty in the EU: On the Differentiated Semantics and Structures of European Law and Politics

In this chapter, I focus on sovereignty and constitutionalism in the context of the Europeanization of the nation states, their politics and legal systems.[1] The paradox of divided sovereignty and the European Union's differentiated constitutional domain are used as examples of profound semantic changes in the sovereignty discourse in contemporary society. Nevertheless, European post-national constitutionalism shows that political and legal institutions of the sovereign nation state continue to operate in a supranational and transnational world. Instead of sidelining those institutions and replacing them with purely supranational forms of governance, the self-constitution of European polity proceeds by introducing the concepts of divided sovereignty and internalizing state sovereignty as part of systemic operations of EU law and politics.

A Sort of European Prelude: on Sovereign Nations, Constitutional Nationalisms and the Nation States of the EU

The Euro crisis of 2010 revealed vulnerability of the EU's common currency, this most striking example of supranational limitation of state sovereignty by economic means, and prompted a series of vitriolic media attacks and a revival of extremely strong nationalist resentments among Greeks, Germans and other EU nations.[2] The system of European economy and its administrative supranational governance thus became responsible for an avalanche of modern nationalist prejudices,

---

1 Constitutionalism is not identical with the body of constitutional laws and usually involves an academic and public critical discourse on constitutional law. See, for instance Paul Craig, 'Constitutions, Constitutionalism, and the European Union', *European Law Journal* 7 (2001): 125; Richard Bellamy and Dario Castiglione, eds, *Constitutionalism in Transformation: European and Theoretical Perspectives* (Oxford: Blackwell, 1996).

2 For the German media's stereotypical portrayal of the corrupt Greeks contrasted to the hardworking German citizens, see, for instance, Hans Bickes, Tina Otten and Laura Chelsea Weymann, 'The *financial crisis* in the German and English press: Metaphorical structures in the media coverage on Greece, Spain and Italy', *Discourse & Society* 25(4) (2014): 424–445.

once again proving that modernity evolves as a parallel growth of instrumental rationality and what Max Weber referred to as a 'new polytheism' and 'the coming wars of the gods'.

The acrimonious Belgian constitutional crisis, devolution politics and persisting nationalisms in parts of the United Kingdom, traditional nationalism and recent terrorist campaigns in the Basque country and Corsica also show that the typically modern claim to national sovereignty has not disappeared but often reinvented itself as a politics of identity, self-determination and self-government in the post-national and post-sovereign EU constellation.

The self-limitation of nation state sovereignty within the EU does not necessarily weaken collective aspirations for some level of, if not full, sovereignty over historically and ethnically defined territory. The weakening of state sovereignty is accompanied by a reclamation and redefinition of sovereignty beyond the nation state. Sovereignty and identity politics continues to be an important vehicle of formulating new sets of goals, interests and public demands but also different forms of social and political inclusion and exclusion.

Traditional ethnic and national divisions acquire new importance, force and political or constitutional settlements. For instance, the Act of Autonomy granted significant autonomy, especially in taxation and judicial matters, to Catalonia within the Spanish state in 2006. Following this constitutional reform and the subsequent judgment of the Spanish Constitutional Court in June 2010, which declared a number of the Act's articles unconstitutional and ruled that there was no legal basis to recognize the Catalans as a nation and no reason for the Catalan language to take precedence over Spanish,[3] a million-strong crowd protested in Barcelona in July 2010 calling for even greater autonomy, if not independence for Catalonia. The Euro crisis and its devastating effect on the Spanish economy subsequently increased tensions between the Catalonian and central governments and the tide of both economically and culturally driven nationalism has been translated into the most serious constitutional crisis of the Spanish democratic statehood further escalated by the unofficial referendum of 9th November 2014 and subsequent tensions between the Catalonian and central Spanish governments.[4]

More examples of the persistence of nationalism and sovereignty politics are easy to find in other parts of the EU. For instance, following a crushing victory in the Hungarian parliamentary election of April 2010, a new conservative nationalist government led by Prime Minister Viktor Orbán, whose Fidesz party won a constitutional supermajority of seats in Parliament (while a right-wing extremist and

3 Constitutional Court of Spain, *Sentencia* STC 031/2010, de 28 de junio de 2010 (BOE núm. 172, de 16 de julio de 2010), para. 7.

4 For a more general overview, Scott L. Greer, *Nationalism and Self-Government: Politics of Autonomy in Scotland and Catalonia* (Albany, NY: SUNY Press, 2008); for more specific information on the Spanish economic crisis and political mobilization in Catalonia, see Guillem Rico, 'The 2010 Regional Election in Catalonia: A Multilevel Account in an Age of Economic Crisis', *South European Society and Politics* 17(2) (2012): 217.

openly anti-Semitic and anti-Roma party Jobbik managed to attract 17 per cent of the national vote), announced a constitutional revolution and immediately enacted two laws. Surprisingly, these laws did not deal with the colossal economic problems of the country. One act was aimed at strengthening bonds with ethnic Hungarians living abroad by giving them a chance to acquire Hungarian citizenship. The other act declared June 4 – the day in 1920 when the post-war Treaty of Trianon, which ended Hungarian political domination in many parts of the former Habsburg monarchy and decreed that millions of ethnic Hungarians would henceforth live outside the post-1918 Hungarian state, was signed – a 'day of national remembrance'.

More significantly, this nationalist imagination was a driving force behind the constitution-making project of the Orbán government, resulting in the new constitution of Hungary which was enacted by Parliament in April 2011 and went into force on 1 January 2012 despite fundamental protests by the Hungarian political opposition parties and European political representations and expert bodies.[5] The new Hungarian constitution has effectively dismantled republican and liberal achievements of the post-1989 democratic constitutionalism and replaced them with nationalist intuitions and settlement promoting the clientelist authoritarian state.[6] Nevertheless, this settlement was approved by the electorate in the 2014 parliamentary election in which Prime Minister Orbán, following the election law change and Parliament's reconstruction, managed to secure the constitutional majority while the extremist Jobbik party emerged even stronger with 21 per cent of the national.

Sovereignty as Part of European Political and Constitutional Semantics

These national identity politics, old and new, show the paradox of both the inadequacy and persistence of national statehood and sovereignty. Traditional control and the solidarity of a state's inhabitants are being questioned in the globalized world of which Europeanization is just one of many segmented manifestations. State loyalties, political identities and communal bonds are becoming ever more multiple, loose and fragmented. However, one does not need examples of stateless forms of ethnic nationalisms in the EU, the rhetorical and legal excesses of contemporary Hungarian nationalists, corrupt Greek élites, the German media and angry crowds on European streets and squares to see that political propaganda and economic or legal reasoning based on the notion of state and national sovereignty are strong. Despite the ongoing transformation of

5 See especially 'Opinion on the New Constitution of Hungary: European Commission for Democracy Through Law (Venice Commission)', in *Constitution for a Disunited Nation: on Hungary's 2011 Fundamental Law*, ed., Gábor Attila Tóth (Budapest: CEU Press, 2012), 491.

6 See especially János Kis, 'From the 1989 Constitution to the 2011 Fundamental Law', in Gábor Attila Tóth, ed., supra n. 5, 1.

international law and statehood in European and global society,[7] the semantics of sovereignty persists in both political and legal communication[8] and even thrives within the discourse of emerging European post-sovereign constitutionalism.[9]

Observing the European Court of Justice's (hereinafter ECJ) historical drive towards the constitutionalization of European law and increasingly diverse national responses to it, one can see emerging patterns of post-sovereign supranational constitutional structures and semantics which, nevertheless, keep drawing on the concept of state sovereignty. Political and legal conflicts and debates in the EU, especially those following post-Maastricht Treaty and post-Amsterdam Treaty integration and enlargement,[10] the process of constitution-making and eventually the ratification of the Lisbon Treaty,[11] show that the concept of state and constitutional sovereignty remains highly popular[12] among citizens, peoples, politicians, civil servants and judges living and working in the European post-national and post-sovereign constellation.[13] Political leaders and senior judges also increasingly speak out against the idea of a supranational EU limiting its Member States in some kind of federal or other state-like constitutional settlement.[14]

The tirelessly discussed democratic deficit[15] of the Union and potential risks attached to the erosion of the democratic legitimacy of Member States cannot

7 Martti Koskenniemi, 'The Future of Statehood', *Harvard International Law Journal* 32 (1991): 397.

8 Jean L. Cohen, *Globalization and Sovereignty. Rethinking Legality, Legitimacy and Constitutionalism* (Cambridge: Cambridge University Press 2012).

9 Christoph Schreuer, 'The Waning of the Sovereign State: Towards a New Paradigm of International Law?', *European Journal of International Law* 4 (1993): 447.

10 Ingolf Pernice, 'Multilevel Constitutionalism and the Treaty of Amsterdam, European Constitution Making Revisited', *Common Market Law Review* 36 (1999): 703.

11 Andrea Biondi, Piet Eeckhout and Stephanie Ripley, eds, *EU Law after Lisbon* (Oxford: Oxford University Press, 2012).

12 Jack Hayward and Rüdiger Wurzel, eds, *European Disunion: Between Sovereignty and Solidarity* (London: Palgrave, 2012).

13 Jürgen Habermas, *Postnational Constellation: Political Essays* (Cambridge: Polity, 2001); William Wallace, 'Europe after the Cold War: interstate order or postsovereign regional system?', *Review of International Studies* 25(5) (1999): 217–218.

14 See, for instance, Roman Herzog, Germany's former federal President, and Lüder Gerken, *Stop the European Court of Justice* manifesto, EU Observer, 10 September 2008. For further comments, see Gerard Conway, *The Limits of Legal Reasoning and the European Court of Justice* (Cambridge: Cambridge University Press, 2012), 83.

15 For academic views regarding the EU's democratic deficit, see, for instance, Andrew Moravcsik, 'In Defence of the "Democratic Deficit": Reassessing Legitimacy in the European Union', *Journal of Common Market Studies* 40 (2002): 603; Giandomenico Majone, 'Europe's "Democratic Deficit": The Question of Standards', *European Law Journal* 4 (1998) 5; Andreas Follesdal and Simon Hix, 'Why There is a Democratic Deficit in the EU: A Response to Majone and Moravcsik', *Journal of Common Market Studies* 44 (2006): 533; and finally Andrew Moravcsik, 'The Myth of Europe's Democratic Deficit', *Intereconomics: Review of European Economic Policy* 43 (2008): 331.

easily be countered by ideas of the governance-based post-sovereign and post-constituent supranational European polity. As regards the EU's Member States and their state sovereignty, in the United Kingdom, for instance, it is not only the tabloids blaming Brussels for all the ills of the British Isles that invoke the special need to defend state sovereignty against the supranational power of the EU. Parliamentary sovereignty, its exercise and democratic constitution are major issues of electoral campaigns, often internally dividing both government and opposition. In parliamentary debates, the issue of sovereignty is increasingly raised whenever it comes to matters of European integration, foreign policy, immigration, defence, judicial independence and other topics associated with the territorial nation state.[16]

In German constitutional debates reflecting on the process of European integration, the Bundesverfassungsgericht (German Federal Constitutional Court, hereinafter BVerfG) has famously and repeatedly ruled that constitutional sovereignty and the rights of German citizens take precedence over European law and thus established the divided sovereignty doctrine. In its classic and endlessly discussed *Maastricht* judgment,[17] the Court controversially stated:

> If the peoples of the individual States (as is true at present) convey democratic legitimation via the national parliaments, then limits are imposed, by the principle of democracy, on an extension of the functions and powers of the European Communities. State power in each of the States emanates from the people of that State. The States require sufficient areas of significant responsibility of their own, areas in which the people of the State concerned may develop and express itself within a process of forming political will which it legitimates and controls, in order to give legal expression to those matters which concern that people on a relatively homogenous basis spiritually, socially, and politically.[18]

Using the 'no demos thesis', the BVerfG argued in favour of the complainants, four members of the European Parliament from the Green Party and a high-ranking civil servant of the European Commission, that the ECJ, due to its ultimate lack of democratic legitimacy, cannot possess the jurisdictional authority to limit national judicial and constitutional authority.[19] Because of the non-existence of a European

---

16 Mark Elliott, 'United Kingdom: Parliamentary Sovereignty under Pressure', *International Journal of Constitutional Law* 2(3) (2004): 545.

17 See, for instance, Matthias Herdegen, 'Maastricht and the German Constitutional Court: Constitutional Restraints for an "Ever Closer Union"', *Common Market Law Review* 31(1994): 235; Trevor C. Hartley, *European Union Law in a Global Context: Text, Cases and Materials* (Cambridge: Cambridge University Press, 2004), 159–160.

18 German Federal Constitutional Court's judgment of 12th October 1993, BVerfGE 89, 155; Brunner v European Union Treaty CMLR [1994] 57. Section C/I/2/b2.

19 Karen J. Alter, *Establishing the Supremacy of European Law: The Making of an International Rule of Law in Europe* (Oxford: Oxford University Press, 2001), 105.

demos, constitutional sovereignty of Germany as the EU Member State must be protected by its system of constitutional justice.[20]

Despite the fact that the judgment echoed Hermann Heller's idea of constitutional democracy and popular sovereignty emanating from social homogeneity,[21] the Court was criticized for promoting the pre-political notion of a nation.[22] However, the BVerfG did not treat the sovereign nation state as an absolute organization and an existential reservoir of political values and principles. It, rather, considered it an organization and instrument and guarantee of the democratic selfhood, self-rule, welfare generated by social solidarity and popular government[23] – something the Court summarized in its recent *Lisbon Judgment* in the following words:

> Within the order of the Basic Law, the structural principles of the state laid down in Article 20 of the Basic Law, i.e. democracy, the rule of law, the principle of the social state, the republic, the federal state, as well as the substance of elementary fundamental rights indispensable for the respect of human dignity are, in any case, not amenable to any amendment because of their fundamental quality.[24]

In the German context, the constitutional sovereignty argument was a response to the progressive political and legal integration of the EU in the 1990s.[25] The *Lisbon Judgment* of the BVerfG refers to the state as a democratic primary space and, in the classical dualist view of international law applied to the EU,[26] states that 'the Member States are the constituted primary political area of their respective polities, the European Union has secondary, i.e. delegated, responsibility for the tasks conferred on it'.[27]

Reflecting on the growing tension between the democratically legitimate and representative bodies of Member States and the primarily technocratic and expert-

20 Jiří Přibáň, *Legal Symbolism: On Law, Time and European Identity* (Aldershot: Ashgate, 2007), 106, 132–134.

21 The Court's reference was: Hermann Heller, 'Politische Demokratie und soziale Homogenität' [1928] in *Gesammelte Schriften, vol. 2*, ed. Christoph Müller (Leiden: Sijthoff, 1971), 421.

22 Joseph H.H. Weiler, 'Does Europe Need a Constitution? Demos, Telos and the German Maastricht Decision', *European Law Journal* 1(3) (1995): 219.

23 For recent theory of the constitutional subject and its identity, see Michel Rosenfeld, *The Identity of the Constitutional Subject: Selfhood, Citizenship, Culture, and Community* (London: Routledge 2009).

24 The German Federal Constitutional Court's judgment of 30 June 2009, BVerfG, 2 BvE 2/08, para. 217. Available at: http://www.bverfg.de/entscheidungen/es20090630_2bve000208en.html [last accessed on 24 January 2014].

25 Donald P. Kommers and Russell A. Miller, *The Constitutional Jurisprudence of the Federal Republic of Germany. 3rd edition, revised and expanded* (Durham, NC: Duke University Press, 2012): 331–342.

26 Ibid., 345.

27 Supra n. 24, para. 301.

driven legitimacy of the administration and justice of the EU,[28] the drafters of the Lisbon Treaty explicitly recognized different forms of constitutional settlement, national identities and state sovereignty in Article 4(2) which reads:

> The Union shall respect the equality of Member States before the Treaties as well as their national identities, inherent in their fundamental structures, political and constitutional, inclusive of regional and local self-government. It shall respect their essential State functions, including ensuring the territorial integrity of the State, maintaining law and order and safeguarding national security. In particular, national security remains the sole responsibility of each Member State.[29]

The article protects the constitutional identity of Member States and thus legally confirms what legal theorists have been describing as a state of constitutional, legal and political pluralism and the end of the EU law's absolute primacy doctrine.[30] Furthermore, it potentially offers an argumentative tool to protect and even reclaim sovereign operations of Member States of the post-sovereign supranational EU.

A Brief History of Sovereignty in New Member States of the Enlarged EU

Since the communist regime's fall in 1989, constitutional developments in post-communist countries may be summarized as a gradual shift from simple interpretations to more complex doctrines and jurisprudence of constitutional sovereignty and statehood in the post-sovereign EU constellations.[31]

Early constitutional and political transformations were typical of regaining, rebuilding and legitimizing the sovereign constitutional and democratic state, yet the same process was instrumental for one of the most fundamental goals, namely accession to the EU.[32] These parallel processes of constitution-making

28 See, for instance, James A. Caparaso, 'The European Union and the Forms of State: Westphalian, Regulatory or Post-modern', *Journal of Common Market Studies* 34 (1996): 29.

29 Consolidated Version of the Treaty on European Union, *Official Journal of the European Union*, 9th May 2008, C115/17.

30 Armin von Bogdandy and Stephan Schill, 'Overcoming Absolute Primacy: Respect for National Identity under the Lisbon Treaty', *Common Market Law Review* 48 (2011): 1432.

31 See especially Anneli Albi, *EU Enlargement and the Constitutions of Central and Eastern Europe* (Cambridge: Cambridge University Press, 2005), 9–13. For more general comments on the EU enlargement process, see Marise Cremona, ed., *The Enlargement of the European Union* (Oxford: Oxford University Press, 2003) and Christophe Hillion, ed., *EU Enlargement: A Legal Approach* (Oxford: Hart Publishing 2004).

32 Alexander H.E. Morawa and Kyriaki Topidi, eds, *Constitutional Evolution in Central and Eastern Europe: Expansion and Integration into the EU* (Aldershot: Ashgate 2011).

reconstituting state sovereignty and EU integration limiting exactly this reconstituted sovereignty and using it as a primary vehicle of entering the exclusive club of EU Member States have been extensively analysed by legal and political scholars in the past two decades.[33]

Similarly, early constitutional arguments and deliberations on the supremacy of EU law and their effect on pre-accession candidate states of Central and Eastern Europe were the subject of numerous studies in constitutional theory and EU law.[34] Technical uses of constitutional sovereignty generally facilitated the accession of post-communist states to the EU, yet they also highlighted a more general problem of democratic legitimacy and accountability vis-à-vis these supranational integration processes. Constitutional bodies of different countries, especially constitutional courts, thus gradually adopted the post-accession doctrine of divided sovereignty and *Kompetenz der Kompetenz* reflecting on the supremacy of democratically legitimized national legal systems.[35]

A good example of the early semantics of sovereignty in the post-sovereign EU legal and political structures are the Polish Trybunał Konstytucyjny's (Constitutional Tribunal, hereinafter TK) *Accession Treaty* judgment of 2005[36] and the Czech Ústavní soud's (Constitutional Court of the Czech Republic, hereinafter ÚS) *Sugar Quota III* judgment[37] from March 2006. In the Czech *Sugar Quota III* case, the conservative opposition MPs argued that the EU regulation of the sugar market amounted to the violation of the right to free commerce activities. The Court declared the national regulation void on procedural grounds and basically reiterated the BVerfG's position regarding the delegation of powers and the relationship between Member State constitutions and EU law in the following words:

> … the conditional nature of the delegation of these powers is manifested on two planes: the formal and the substantive plane. The first of these planes concerns the power attributes of state sovereignty itself, the second plane concerns the

33 Adam Czarnota, Martin Krygier and Wojciech Sadurski, eds, *Spreading Democracy and the Rule of Law: The Impact of EU Enlargement on the Rule of Law, Democracy, and Constitutionalism in Post-communist Legal Orders* (Dordrecht: Springer 2006); Alfred E. Kellerman et al., eds, *The Impact of EU Accession on the Legal Orders of New Member States and (Pre-) Candidate Countries* (Dordrecht: Springer 2006).

34 See especially Wojciech Sadurski, *Constitutionalism and the Enlargement of Europe* (Oxford: Oxford University Press, 2012), 66–79.

35 Wojciech Sadurski, '"Solange, chapter 3": Constitutional Courts in Central Europe – Democracy – European Union', *European Law Journal* 14(1) (2008): 6–23.

36 See the Polish Constitutional Tribunal's Accession Treaty Case, K 18/04, Judgment on Poland's Membership in the European Union of 11 May 2005; see also the Tribunal's Procedural Decision no. 176/11/A/2006 on the Excise Duty Tax, 19 December 2006.

37 The Czech Constitutional Court's Judgment of 8 March 2006, Pl. ÚS 50/04 (the Sugar Quota III Case). Available at: http://www.usoud.cz/en/ [last accessed on 24 January 2014].

> substantive component of the exercise of state power. In other words, the delegation of a part of the powers of national organs may persist only so long as these powers are exercised in a manner that is compatible with the preservation of the foundations of state sovereignty of the Czech Republic, and in a manner which does not threaten the very essence of the substantive law-based state.[38]

The Court also acknowledged 'a definite principle of constitutional self-restraint'[39] regarding economic measures flowing from the EU policies and the case law of the ECJ. Due to this self-restraint in economic matters, the Court refused to review the EU law-based sugar quota regulations.[40] Repeating the BVerfG's *so long as (Solange)* formula in the Czech context,[41] the Court, nevertheless, specifically recalled Article 9(2) of the Czech Constitution protecting the substantive core of the democratic state which is considered unchangeable by any constitutional amendments and laws.

Another example of dealing with EU law challenges to the national constitutions is the Polish TK's judgment in the *European Arrest Warrant* case related to internal sovereignty of the state and its obligation to protect the state's citizens.[42] The Tribunal was asked to decide upon the surrender of a Polish citizen to the Netherlands for the purpose of prosecution using Article 607t of the Code of Criminal Procedure incorporating the Arrest Warrant to the Polish legal system. The Tribunal ruled that 'surrender' is of the same substance like 'extradition' and, because extradition of Polish nationals was prohibited by the constitution (Article 55 of the Constitution), the Article was declared unconstitutional. The general obligation to interpret national law in conformity with EU law did not apply in this case where it could determine the introduction or aggravation of criminal liability.[43] Nevertheless, on the basis of Poland's commitment to the EU, the article's annulment was postponed by the Tribunal for the period of 18 months during which the Polish constitution was amended to accommodate the European

---

38 Ibid., part VI. B.

39 Ibid., part VI.A-3.

40 This position was criticized by some scholars, such as Aneli Albi, as weakening the protection of constitutional rights of citizens in the new Member States of the EU after its enlargement in 2004. See Anneli Albi, 'Ironies in Human Rights Protection in the EU: Pre-Accession Conditionality and Post-Accession Conundrums', *European Law Journal* 15(1) (2009): 46.

41 Sadurski, supra n. 35, 6–9.

42 Judgment of the Polish Constitutional Tribunal P 1/05, on the European Arrest Warrant, Official Collection of the Constitutional Tribunal Jurisdiction, OTK ZU, No. 4/A/2005.

43 Massimo Fichera, 'The European Arrest Warrant and the Sovereign State: A Marriage of Convenience?', *European Law Journal* 15(1) (2009): 82.

Arrest Warrant in the national system of positive law. It is noteworthy that the amendment was proposed by the TK itself.[44]

The adopted doctrine of divided sovereignty was further elaborated by the ÚS in its Lisbon Treaty judgments. In the *Lisbon I* Judgment, the judges stated that 'today sovereignty can no longer be understood absolutely; sovereignty is more a practical matter'.[45] Sovereignty, therefore, is not an existential matter of the *either, or* choice. Instead of theorizing sovereignty as a rigid legal or political concept, the Court considers sovereignty a practical concept opening the possibility for states to be active players and negotiators at international and global level of political and legal interdependence and networking.[46] This is a profound shift from political and constitutional essentialism to the pragmatist concept of sovereignty as a technique enhancing operative power of states in global legal and political settings and making them more flexible and adaptable to the emergence of supranational and transnational legal and political networks.[47]

The Court also makes a lengthy comment on state sovereignty and globalization in its judgments when it states:

> The global scene can no longer be seen only as a world of isolated states. It is generally accepted that the state and its sovereignty are undergoing change, and that no state is such a unitary, separate organization as classical theories assumed in the past. An international political system is being created in the global scale that lacks institutionalized rules of its own self-government, such as the international system created by sovereign states had until now. It is an existential interest of the integrating European civilization to appear in global competition as an important and respected force. These processes quite clearly demonstrate that the sovereign legitimate state power must necessarily observe the ongoing developmental trends and attempt to approach them, understand them, and gradually subject this spontaneous globalization process, lacking hierarchical organization, to the order of democratic legitimacy.[48]

---

44 Angelika Nussberger, 'The Poland: the Constitutional Tribunal on the implementation of the European Arrest Warrant', *International Journal of Constitutional Law* 6(1) (2008): 162–170.

45 The ÚS's judgment of 26 November 2008, Pl ÚS 19/08 (The Treaty of Lisbon I Case) Available at: http://www.usoud.cz [last accessed on 24 January 2014], para. 4 of the introductory reasoning summary.

46 Ibid., para. 107; the Court quotes from David P. Calleo, *Rethinking Europe's Future* (Oxford: Oxford University Press, 2001), 141.

47 Jean L. Cohen, 'Sovereignty in the Context of Globalisation: A Constitutional Pluralist Perspective', in *The Philosophy of International Law*, eds Samantha Besson and John Tasioulas (Oxford: Oxford University Press, 2010), 261.

48 Supra n. 45, para. 105.

This conclusion and emphasis on efficient and principled governance beyond the nation state in global society[49] is different from, for instance, the BVerfG's *Lisbon* Judgment which mainly highlights the precondition of sovereign statehood[50] and reiterates the old task of the EU to keep peace in Europe and to strengthen the possibilities of policy-making by joint coordinated action.[51] Indeed, the BVerfG referred to the *Lisbon I* Judgment of the ÚS[52] and its reserved power to review whether legal instruments of the EU institutions remain within the limits of the sovereign powers conferred on them. However, the BVerfG actually has recursively referred to its *so long as (Solange)* doctrine formulated several decades ago. Invoking 'the obligation under European law to respect the constituent power of the Member States as the masters of the Treaties',[53] the BVerfG effectively reiterated the impossibility of the ECJ to claim the *Kompetenz der Kompetenz* to unilaterally determine whether the principle of enumerated powers has been respected.

Unlike the BVerfG's *Lisbon* Judgment,[54] the ÚS engaged in more profound consideration of European and national legal and political developments as coeval and mutually intertwined processes. Where the German Court separates European integration and national democracy,[55] the Czech Court highlights the legitimation issues and deficits of both national democracies and EU regulatory and governance networks and practices. In this respect, it is significant that the ÚS re-enters the problem of legitimation by the fundamental democratic and rule of law values to the EU level by stating that these are commonly shared and constitute the legitimation foundation of both European integration and constitutional democracy of the EU Member States. Instead of simply contrasting national representative democracy to the supranational organization of the EU, it calls for scrutinizing all forms and techniques of governing, whether local, national or supranational, in terms of their consistency with the democratic values which obviously cannot be limited

49 Martti Koskenniemi and Päivi Leino, 'Fragmentation of International Law? Postmodern Anxieties', *Leiden Journal of International Law* 15 (2002): 553.

50 Daniel Thym, 'In the Name of Sovereign Statehood: A Critical Introduction to the Lisbon Judgment of the German Constitutional Court', *Common Market Law Review* 46 (2009): 1795; see also Dieter Grimm, 'Defending Sovereign Statehood Against Transforming the European Union into a State', *European Constitutional Law Review* 5 (2009): 353.

51 Supra n. 24, paras 220 and 222.

52 Supra n. 24, para. 338.

53 Ibid., para. 235.

54 See, for instance, Damian Chalmers, 'European Restatements of Sovereignty', in *Sovereignty and the Law: Domestic, European and International Perspectives*, eds Richard Rawlings, Peter Leyland and Alison Young (Oxford: Oxford University Press, 2013), 205–206.

55 Daniel Halberstam and Christoph Möllers, 'The German Constitutional Court says "Ja zu Deutschland"', *German Law Journal* 10 (2009): 1241.

by forms and techniques of political representation exclusively facilitated at the nation state level.[56]

Beyond Kelsen and Schmitt? Legal Semantics of the EU's Divided Sovereignty

All these cases from the EU's Member States – old and new – show that European constitutionalism is best addressed as a form of social and epistemological constructivism,[57] part of which is the concept of divided sovereignty. The structures of legal integration and the semantics of the self-description of the European legal system have been developing in parallel in the process of European unification.

The history of European constitutionalism originally was the social history of a legal utopia pursued from the earliest stages of European integration by a very specific group of lawyers, most notably judges and advocate-generals of the ECJ, legal experts in the European Commission and the Council of Ministers, legal advisers to national governments and EU law theorists. The strategy of depoliticizing European integration by legalizing and constitutionalizing it led to the emergence of a controversial European jurisprudence legitimizing 'constitutionalism without a constitution'.[58] Different concepts and metaphors have been constructed to cope with the divisions, fractures and complexities of the pluralistic and polycentric body of European law and its constitutional context.

The EU legal semantics adopted the fiction of the Treaty of Rome having the nature of a constitution as early as in the mid-1960s. At the same time, European constitutionalism in practice mainly signifies the absence of a real constitution and the process of constitution-making by other means.[59] Horizontal and heterarchical rather than vertical and hierarchical communication emerges between the Member States and the EU's legal systems.[60] Within the legal system, the principle of the

56 For further details regarding the difference between the Czech and German Constitutional Courts' Lisbon judgments, see especially Mattias Wendel, 'Comparative reasoning and the making of a common constitutional law: EU-related decisions of national constitutional courts in a transnational perspective', *International Journal of Constitutional Law* 11(4) (2013): 987–990.

57 Thomas Christiansen, Knud E. Joergensen and Antje Wiener, eds, *The Social Construction of Europe* (London: Sage, 2001); Jo Shaw and Antje Wiener, eds, *Evolving Norms of Constitutionalism: Special Issue of European Law Journal* (Oxford: Blackwell, 2003); Gunther Teubner, 'How the Law Thinks: Toward a Constructivist Epistemology of Law', *Law & Society Review* 23 (1989): 727.

58 Antonin Cohen, 'Constitutionalism Without Constitution: Transnational Élites Between Political Mobilization and Legal Expertise in the Making of a Constitution for Europe (1940s–1960s)', *Law & Social Inquiry* 32 (2007): 113.

59 Ibid., 112.

60 Neil Walker, 'The Idea of Constitutional Pluralism', *Modern Law Review* 65 (2002): 337.

supremacy of European law turns out to be inseparable from the principles of proportionality, subsidiarity and self-containment.[61] European constitutionalism involves both 'a state-building dynamic' questioning the existing supranational and transnational regulatory practices of the EU[62] and the principle of mutual 'constitutional tolerance'[63] between EU law and national constitutional and legal systems and cultures. Similarly, legal principles can become an instrument of the EU's differentiation, such as the subsidiarity principle which

> … can, on the one hand, suggest a desire to reduce EU-level intervention into national policy, or, on the other hand, the normatively more attractive and positive desire to enhance self-government and to involve those most directly affected by decision-making as fully as possible in the process.[64]

The European constitutional debate definitely 'poses the most pressing paradigm-challenging test to what we might call constitutional monism'.[65] As Joseph Weiler notes, neither Kelsen nor Schmitt are of any use in the context of EU law because European constitutionalism cannot be modelled on state-centred constitution-making. It is simply unique, original and hard to grasp in the language of conventional constitutional theory – it is *Sonderweg*.[66]

The above listed 'semantic soup' of EU and Member States' legal and constitutional concepts, fictions and argumentative frameworks persuasively illustrates how unique and unorthodox the path of European constitutionalism can be and how, at the same time, it seeks to preserve the semantic value of the general concept of *sovereignty* which consists of *translating the contingency of the social multitude into the conceptual unity of the collective will operating in the political system or the legal authority operating in the legal system.*

The EU's specific structural problem is that there is no detectable single collective will operating in its political system and authority operating in its legal system. Member States are no longer the ultimate centres of constitutional authority and the European integration process has always been developing beyond the traditional limits of international law. Constitutional aspirations

---

61 Antonio Estella, *The EU Principle of Subsidiarity and its Critique* (Oxford: Oxford University Press, 2002); Takis Tridimas, *The General Principles of EU Law* (Oxford: Oxford University Press, 2006).

62 Neil Walker, 'Europe's Constitutional Engagement', *Ratio Juris* 18 (2005): 394.

63 Joseph H.H. Weiler, 'In defence of the status quo: Europe's constitutional *Sonderweg*', in *European Constitutionalism Beyond the State*, eds Joseph H.H. Weiler and Marlene Wind (Cambridge: Cambridge University Press, 2003), 15.

64 Gráinne de Búrca, 'Legal Principles as an Instrument of Differentiation? The Principles of Proportionality and Subsidiarity', in *The Many Faces of Differentiation in EU Law*, eds Bruno De Witte, Dominik Hanf and Ellen Vos (Antwerpen: Intersentia, 2001), 133.

65 Neil Walker, supra n. 60, 337.

66 Joseph H.H. Weiler, supra n. 63.

and imagination of the EU have been coeval with the continuing constitutional regulations, aspirations, imaginations and transformations of its Member States. While the Member States are significantly limited as sovereign entities, the same states also continue to dominate and pursue their interests both inside and outside the EU institutions.

Calls for building European statehood[67] and constitutionalizing the principle of the supremacy of the jurisdiction of the ECJ over national constitutional courts[68] can hardly result in the establishment of a monistic European constitutional system because the principle of respect for national constitutional systems is guaranteed by the body of European law. The EU's specific sovereignty paradox may be formulated as 'sovereignty manifesting itself by its limitations'.[69] The concept of divided sovereignty, therefore, has become both a major point of reference and tool concerning further European political and legal integration.[70] It replaces the Kelsenian monistic theory of legal validity and norm formation with an epistemology and semantics built on the notion of social difference, cleavages, fractures and the multiplicity of social communication. It introduces plurality and divisions into the concept of sovereignty which, according to its common definition, cannot be divided without being destroyed.

However, the EU jurisprudence of divided constitutional sovereignty does not result in the paralysis of political or legal institutions and the arbitrariness of their decision-making but reasserts itself as an internal part of EU legal communication. It establishes the very meaning of the EU legal system which distinguishes it from its both national and international environment and thereby constitutes it as a self-referential system. Its legal meaning is not to modify national sovereignty of EU Member States into a quasi-federal or confederate system of EU politics but to develop semantic guidelines for specific programmes of the self-constituted EU legal system. In other words, on the basis of these systemic programme specifications, judges, attorneys, corporate lawyers or bureaucrats can communicate, especially dispute what counts as legal/illegal in the system of EU law.

Constitutional Pluralism in the EU

In the EU, the concepts of divided sovereignty and legal pluralism are immediately associated with constitutional pluralism and conflicts arising between European

---

67 Federico G. Mancini, *Democracy and Constitutionalism in the European Union* (Oxford: Hart Publishing, 2000), 51–66.

68 Monica Claes, *The National Courts' Mandate in the European Constitution* (Oxford: Hart Publishing, 2006), 723–724, 730–733.

69 Margreth H.M. de Bonth, 'Sovereignty Revisited', in *Flexibility in Constitutions: Forms of Closer Cooperation in Federal and Non-Federal Settings; Post Nice Edition*, ed. Annette Schrauwen (Groningen: Europa Law Publishing, 2002), 101.

70 Jan Zielonka, *Europe as Empire* (Oxford: Oxford University Press, 2006), 65–91.

and Member State political and legal institutions. The autonomy of the system of European law and its principles of supremacy and direct effect adjudicated on by the ECJ historically contributed to the strong belief in the basic norm of EU law that would be superior to the basic norms of the respective constitutional systems of Member States.

For instance, the concept of a 'transnational constitution' was paradoxically born out of the supranational federalist vision of European statehood and drew on European legal monism and the supremacy of the European basic norm. It was coined by Eric Stein to signify the increasing juridification of the EU and its hierarchical 'federal-type' political structure.[71] The idea that Europe 'needs a constitution'[72] originated from a belief in the political and legal supremacy of the structures, decision-making processes and operations of European institutions. The constitution and its authority were to enhance the legitimacy of European integration[73] but also to open further space for this 'ever closer' Union.[74]

Nevertheless, the supremacy of the EU's basic norm has been challenged by Member State constitutional courts claiming that each state's basic norm remained unaffected by European legal integration. The European Union thus evolved into a hybrid pluralistic model contradicting the monistic conception of one exclusive basic norm but equally stretching far beyond the framework of dualistic theories of international law.[75]

As Neil MacCormick commented before the EU's failed constitution-making:

> Where there is a plurality of institutional normative orders, each with a functioning constitution (at least in the sense of a body of higher-order norms establishing and conditioning relevant governmental powers), it is possible that each acknowledge the legitimacy of every other within its own sphere, while none asserts or acknowledges constitutional superiority over another.[76]

---

71 Eric Stein, 'Lawyers, Judges, and the Making of a Transnational Constitution', *American Journal of International Law* 75 (1981): 1.

72 Jürgen Habermas, 'Does Europe Need a Constitution?', in Jürgen Habermas, *Time of Transitions* (Cambridge: Polity Press, 2006), 89.

73 Miguel Maduro, 'The Importance of Being Called a Constitution: Constitutional authority and the authority of constitutionalism', *International Journal of Constitutional Law* 3 (2005): 332.

74 Federico G. Mancini, 'The Making of a Constitution for Europe', *Common Market Law Review* 26 (1989): 595.

75 See, for instance, Martin Borowski, 'Legal Pluralism in the European Union', in *Law and Democracy in Neil MacCormick's Legal and Political Theory: The Post-Sovereign Constellation*, eds Agustín J. Menendez and John E. Fossum (Dordrecht: Springer, 2011), 189.

76 Neil MacCormick, *Questioning Sovereignty: Law, State and Nation in the European Commonwealth* (Oxford: Oxford University Press, 1999), 104.

Instead of depending on the will of one constitutional sovereign, transnational and supranational systems, such as the EU, constitute their stability through a multiple network of legal and constitutional institutions and practices of cooperation and conflict resolution.[77]

Though the concept of constitutional pluralism originally evolved as a specific theoretical reflection and positive assessment of the process of European constitution-making, it also turned out to be a useful model explaining the failure of the Union's constitution-making. It is able to critically reassess the major principles and operations of EU law and its relationship with the legal systems of Member States, a relationship full of structural and semantic collisions and contestations.

The theoretical idea of constitutional pluralism has been elaborated, in particular, by Neil Walker who responded to the challenges and risks of permanent contestations, conflicts, frictions and fragmentation related to the communication between national legal systems and European law. Walker is aware of the complexities raised by the recent popularity of the constitutionalism discourse and its post-Westphalian transnational context. For him, as for a number of other scholars, constitutional pluralism liberates the discourse from the limitations of state-centred images and institutional frameworks of constitutionalism. Among other remarks, he criticizes the current discourse of constitutionalism especially for its 'state-centredness', the 'constitutional fetishism' permeating the political imagination, its 'normative bias' and 'ideological exploitation'.[78] Walker subsequently argues in favour of a plurality of different constitutional sites and heterarchical structures in transnational law. As regards European law, he states that

> [C]onstitutional monism merely grants a label to the defining assumption of constitutionalism in the Westphalian age ... that the sole centres or units of constitutional authorities are states. Constitutional pluralism, by contrast, recognizes that the European order inaugurated by the Treaty of Rome has developed beyond the traditional confines of inter-*national* law and now makes its own independent constitutional claims, and that these claims exist alongside the continuing claims of states. The relationship between the orders, that is to say, is now horizontal rather than vertical – heterarchical rather than hierarchical.[79]

Nevertheless, the reader should not be distracted by Walker's deployment of the language of social theory to describe the heterarchy of functionally differentiated social systems because Walker's project of 'developing constitutional pluralism'[80] involves a number of the prescriptive thoughts and ideas of political constitutionalism.

77 Ibid., 119.
78 Neil Walker, supra n. 60, 319.
79 Ibid., 337.
80 Ibid., 339.

There is more continuity than discontinuity with the modern constitutional discourse in Walker's constitutional pluralism theory. Though recognizing constitutional phenomena that are not polity-bound, especially governance and societal criteria and processes of constitutionalism, Walker asks a critical question:

> If polities within a multi-dimensional order can be sectorally or functionally delimited, how far can such limitation be permitted without undermining the very idea of a constitutional *polity*?[81]

Facing subnational, supranational and transnational pressures, state law's superior and official status is increasingly relativized and contextualized as part of both EU and global legal regulation. This social development, nevertheless, cannot avoid the persisting question of which communities are represented by these supranational and transnational legal networks and constitutional systems.

In his response, Walker draws on the normative political problem of the constitution of a polity and the limits to the process of constitutionalization without a polity. For him, constitutionalism gets dissociated from statehood and state sovereignty but equally continues to reflect on the first political condition – the condition of commonality. The pursuit of the common in pluralistic politics and law in Europe and beyond finds its expression in respective notions of citizenship, polity and constitutionalism which, according to Walker, 'pre-date the modern state'[82] but also set normative limits to the functional differentiation of constitutional non-polity sites and their particular authority. The idea of constitutional pluralism as a plurality of unities subsequently translates to the idea of 'metaconstitutionalism',[83] without a fixed meta-constitution but with a new framework of open-ended negotiating processes between different constitutional authorities, mutual learning, dialogue and cross-experimentation.[84]

Walker's theory of constitutional pluralism continues to be a primarily normative political project searching for post-national and global forms of political deliberation, conflict resolution, negotiation and imagination. It is open to processes of depoliticized governance and societal self-reflections beyond the state and polity. Nevertheless, it perceives all these processes as part of an open-ended constitutional dynamic which has a political dimension of regulating and steering our post-Westphalian and post-state polity in Europe and elsewhere.

81 Ibid., 347.
82 Ibid., 350.
83 Ibid., 357.
84 Ibid., 359.

European Constitutionalism of Post-Sovereign *Juristenrecht*

There is a close relationship between the EU's supranational constitutionalism and governance established by EU institutions.[85] The legislatures of 'hard law' are often accompanied by the effective networks of 'soft law' usually defined as a set of rules of conduct without directly binding legal force but with potentially strong force of persuasion and practical effects.[86] Apart from 'hard' laws of the Union's official *acquis communautaire*, 'soft' laws of informal practices, administrative techniques and uses of expert knowledge in decision-making processes have always played a formative role in European integration, including constitution-making.[87] These 'soft' laws are even described as faithfully reflecting the heterogeneic character of European integration and governance.[88] They reveal one of the most typical features of the EU law but also any other form of supranational and transnational law – the fact that its operative capacity depends on *epistemic communities* of legal and other experts.

The heterarchy of European law, its self-referential communication and heavy reliance on 'soft' legal methods have always been significantly enhanced through the differentiated multiple channels of European 'lawyers' law' or *Juristenrecht*.[89] The sociological concept of *Juristenrecht* introduced to legal science by one of the founding fathers of sociology of law, Eugen Ehrlich,[90] grasps the complexity of European constitutionalism, especially its reliance on specific professional knowledge groups, their decision-making techniques and capacity to operate beyond the body of legislated laws and to create their own 'soft' practices and informal rules of decision-making.

---

85 Neil Walker, 'EU Constitutionalism and New Governance', in *Law and New Governance in the EU and the US*, eds Gráinne de Búrca and Joanne Scott (Oxford: Hart Publishing, 2006), 15.

86 Francis Snyder, 'Soft Law and Institutional Practice in the European Community', in *The Construction of Europe: Essays in Honour of Mile Noel*, ed. Stephen Martin (Dordrecht: Kluwer, 1994), 198.

87 Karel C. Wellens and Gustaaf M. Borchart, 'Soft Law in EC Law', *European Law Review* 14 (1989): 267; David Trubek and Louise Trubek, 'Hard and Soft Law in the Construction of Social Europe: the Role of the Open Method of Co-ordination', *European Law Journal* 11 (2005): 352–362; David Trubek, Patrick Cottrell and Mark Nance, '"Soft Law", "Hard Law" and EU Integration', in Graínne de Búrca and Joanne Scott, eds, supra n. 85, 65.

88 Linda Senden, *Soft Law in European Community Law* (Oxford: Hart Publishing, 2004), 111–117.

89 Miriam Aziz, *The Impact of European Rights on National Legal Cultures* (Oxford: Hart Publishing, 2004), 17.

90 Eugen Ehrlich, *Fundamental Principles of the Sociology of Law* (New York: Arno Press, 1975) [Originally published in 1936], 121.

The impossibility of achieving a European constitution in the 1950s[91] led to the gradual constitutionalization of European law by the ECJ. The political act of constitution-making and building a federal Europe was replaced by the transformation of constitutionalization politics into technical legal matters, self-referential arguments and self-constitutive semantics of European legal integration. Since the landmark decision *Costa v. ENEL* and the Court's view that the Treaty of Rome has 'the nature of a real constitution', EU jurisprudence built upon the legal fiction of considering the treaty 'as if it were a constitution'.[92]

The ECJ's enforcement of the principles of supremacy and the direct effect of European law should not be perceived 'only as the translation of a political mobilization into the language of law, but also as the legal expression of the social autonomization of a specialized body of lawyers'[93] and as the self-referential organization of the functionally differentiated and socially self-limiting system of European law. This differentiation of European politics and law and the evolving self-reference of the body of European law subsequently requires shifting the analytical focus from the ultimate (economic, political, cultural, moral and so on) foundations of an emerging European polity toward social understanding, knowledge and practices adopted in different sectors of the EU.[94] It means shifting the focus from official legal documents to the multitude of professional customs, practices and unofficial rules.

The 'cooperation relationship'[95] and the practice of 'judicial dialogue'[96] between European and national judges have been beneficial for both groups because they empower them in the political and legal systems of both the EU and Member States.[97] However, the very concept of dialogue also shows the conflictual dynamic and often contradictory nature of the relationship. As Miriam Aziz comments: 'The jurisdictional tug of war which has prevailed between the ECJ and the constitutional courts of the Member States serves to illustrate the lengths to which jurists will go to have the last word as regards the locus of

---

91 Richard T. Griffiths, *Europe's First Constitution: The European Political Community, 1952–1954* (London: Federal Trust, 2000).

92 Eric, Stein, 'Toward Supremacy of Treaty-Constitution by Judicial Fiat: On the Margin of the Costa Case', *Michigan Law Review* 63 (1965): 513; Antonin Cohen, supra n. 58, 126–127.

93 Antonin Cohen, supra n. 58, 128.

94 Antje Wiener, 'Editorial: Evolving Norms of Constitutionalism', *European Law Journal* 9 (2003): 3.

95 Christian Joerges, 'The Law in the Process of Constitutionalizing Europe', in *Constitution-Making and Democratic Legitimacy, Arena Report 5/2002*, eds Erik O. Eriksen, John E. Fossum and Agustín J. Menendez (Oslo: Arena, 2002), 13.

96 Anne-Marie Slaughter, Alec Stone Sweet and Joseph H.H. Weiler, eds, *The European Court and National Courts: Doctrine and Jurisprudence. Legal Change in its Social Context* (Oxford: Hart Publishing, 1998).

97 Karen J. Alter, supra n. 19, 209–232.

the ultimate authority'.[98] Nevertheless, national and European legal élites have common political and professional interests and their tug-of-war enhances the process of the self-constitutionalization of the European legal system – the process giving them more power and influence.

In the EU, there may be a number of authorities claiming constitutional supremacy and demanding to have the final decision-making power.[99] However, the conflict-driven jurisdictional dynamic and the need to introduce European 'soft' lawyers' laws actually derive from the impossibility of determining authoritatively who has the final sovereign authority and the competence to decide on the applicability of EU law. This apparent crisis in fact reveals how the European legal system produces its internal operations and self-regulations. National and European top judges and legal élites happily struggle to answer the question of who is the ultimate arbiter without any clear legal solution but with the clear knowledge that their conflict is, in fact, an intrinsic part of operations of the EU's self-constitutionalized legal system.

Multiple Sovereignty and Functional Differentiation in the EU

EU Member States have lost much of their former sovereign power over territory and citizens. This power has been transferred to EU supranational institutions operating independently of Member State political systems and irreversibly transforming the modern notion of national territorial statehood.[100] At the same time, the EU has never transformed into a federal or confederate state despite the Eurofederalist imagination strongly influencing European integration since its early stages in the 1950s. The EU does not have operative capacity to channel information exchange between law and politics in the manner of the constitutional democratic state.

The failed Constitutional Treaty replacing all previous European treaties was expected to legislate for EU constitutional, economic, political, civic, educational and all other imaginable social foundations. It was to recreate a nineteenth-century constitutional organization to facilitate legal legitimacy of the EU.[101] In this sense, it represented a unique example of *retro-politics* driven by calls for quasi-state democratic settlement as the legitimation basis of further European integration.

---

98 Miriam Aziz, supra n. 89, 45.

99 Miriam Aziz, 'Sovereignty Lost, Sovereignty Regained? Some Reflections on the Bundesverfassungsgericht's Banana Judgment', *Columbia Journal of European Law* 9 (2002): 109.

100 Sonja P. Riekmann, Monika Mokre and Michael Latzer, eds, *The State of Europe: Transformations of Statehood from a European Perspective* (Cambridge: Cambridge University Press, 2005).

101 Jürgen Habermas, *Divided West* (Cambridge: Polity, 2006), 139–142.

However, this recent constitutional and political history of the EU also shows that popular sovereignty hardly can be substituted for by judicial sovereignty[102] of the ECJ shared with other top judges in Member States through channels of 'constitutional cooperation' or 'judicial dialogue'.[103] The existing framework rather leads to uniquely polycentric, differentiated and fragmented forms of political and constitutional integration.[104] Instead of common forms of international cooperation of sovereign states, the EU is perceived as a multilevel governance system which recursively enhances the EU's multilevel polity formation.[105] Instead of the settlement of European sovereignty backed by the jurisprudence of constitutional monism, the EU's constitutional system consists of 'bits and pieces'.[106]

The body of European law has been shaped as a legal technical project of the epistemological community of lawyers which made very effective use of the internal paradoxes and external aspirations of European integration. Sovereignty, by definition undividable, has been divided to make the sense of changes in multiple legal and political structures of European society. The paradoxical concept of divided sovereignty has been operating in the self-referential and very productive mode within the context of the polycentric and pluralistic EU legal system. It is part of the EU's legal communication responsible for further evolution and creative possibilities of EU law.

From the legal point of view, the EU divided sovereignty debate has never been a matter of constructing one overarching sovereign authority and delimiting all other 'minor' sovereignties, but a problem of internal explanation of the EU legal system's functioning. The concept of divided sovereignty relates a legal plurality to a semantic unity which is part of the EU law's self-referential communication and translates social experiences into legal meanings.[107] In other words, the concept is part of the semantics managing the structural differences and complexities of EU's constitutional pluralism.

The EU is not just another international organization, an expansion of the nation state or a geographically enlarged form of the civil society. It is rather typical of the very different tendencies of specific functional systems which are impossible to integrate into an overarching constitutional unity. The social system

102 For the concept of judicial sovereignty, its general jurisprudential meaning and contextualisation in other countries, such as India, see Pratap B Mehta, 'The Rise of Judicial Sovereignty', *Journal of Democracy* 18(2) (2007): 70.

103 Francis Jacobs, 'Judicial Dialogue and the Cross-Fertilization of Legal Systems: The European Court of Justice', *Texas International Law Journal* 38 (2003): 550.

104 Marlene Wind, 'The European Union as a polycentric polity', in Joseph H.H. Weiler and Marlene Wind, eds, supra n. 63, 103.

105 Liesbet Hooghe and Gary Marks, *Multi-Level Governance and European Integration* (Oxford: Rowman & Littlefield, 2001).

106 Deirdre Curtin, 'The Constitutional Structure of the Union: A Europe of Bits and Pieces', *Common Market Law Review* 30 (1993): 17.

107 Niklas Luhmann, *Social Systems* (Stanford, CA: Stanford University Press, 1995), 92–96.

of the EU organization does not have any (economic, political, legal, ethical and so on) foundation and consists of a plurality of subsystems that are both universal and particular.[108] While using the universal media of money, truth, power, legality and so on, the functionally differentiated systems of European economy, science, politics and law also can communicate particular regional, cultural, religious and other differences.

European constitutionalism, therefore, 'is a self-referential concept – not a reflection of something that contains or embodies something else (like values) but the reflection of the very thing itself'.[109] The current legal imagination and theories of EU constitutional pluralism and divided sovereignty subsequently need to address the multiple and heterarchical processes of functional differentiation rather than indulging in theoretical projects to shape new hierarchies and foundations for the politics and law. This approach assumes treating the EU legal system as just one of many functionally differentiated systems of European society.

108 Niklas Luhmann, *Theory of Society. Volume 2* (Stanford, CA: Stanford University Press, 2013), 208–209.

109 Joseph H.H. Weiler and Marlene Wind, 'Introduction: European constitutionalism beyond the state', in Joseph H.H. Weiler and Marlene Wind, eds, supra n. 63, 3.

Chapter 2
Sovereignty, or Post-Sovereignty?: A Social Systems Theoretical Perspective

Contemporary globalized society in Europe and worldwide demonstrates the impossibility of conceptualizing power exclusively in terms of the institutional hierarchy of the nation state, its indivisibility and the ultimate decision-making power and enforcement of supreme will within a political community. Changes in the meaning and uses of control of both territory and inhabitants – these two definitional signs of sovereignty – significantly question state sovereignty and its functions. Power formerly associated with political sovereignty has become much more dispersed in society and stretches beyond the framework of a nation as the ultimate subject of sovereignty and the democratic nation state.

However, legal and political fragmentations and the emergence of different sectors of transnational law should not be considered as either democratically illegitimate structures resembling pre-modern autocratic political settlements, or the most recent example of what Jeremy Bentham described as 'anarchical fallacies'[1] of law that is not commanded by the political sovereign and draws on hasty generalizations and abstract propositions susceptible to the moral and political abuse.

In this chapter, I therefore initially address the proliferation and critique of the sovereignty discourse and the normative expectations of some major and typical theories of sovereign and post-sovereign politics and law. I subsequently engage in a historical and conceptual analysis of sovereignty and highlight its persistence in the systems of positive law and politics. In the second half of the chapter, I draw on the autopoietic systems theory's distinction of social structures and semantics and consider sovereignty as part of the self-referential semantics of both the legal and political systems. However, sovereignty cannot be perceived as a concept signifying the unity of society integrated by fundamental values and ultimately governed and controlled by one power centre and its laws. I argue that theories and images of sovereignty as unity need to be replaced by the autopoietic social systems theoretical view in which the self-limiting and self-referential concept of sovereignty concurrently operates through the functionally differentiated systems of politics and law at national, supranational and transnational global level.

1 Jeremy Bentham, 'Anarchical Fallacies', in *The Works of Jeremy Bentham*, Vol. II, ed. John Bowring (Edinburgh: Tait, 1843), 491.

Theories of Post-Sovereignty and Globalization

Some major streams seeking to either completely replace or radically reformulate the concept of sovereignty in current global politics and law have emerged in legal, social and political theory. These streams can be classified as studies in globalized: a) *social* networks and/or systems of *governance*; b) *ethics* of cosmopolitan values and human rights; c) power *politics*.

The first stream is represented, for instance, by political, social and normative theories of Manuel Castells, Immanuel Wallerstein and many other scholars working in the field of networks and systems of global governance. According to these theories, 'a governance model of sovereignty' has been emerging in which sovereignty is 'fragmented and distributed across a range of institutions'.[2] They claim that the historical role of the state as a central social and political organization is over and believe that hierarchical political structures are gradually being replaced by horizontal networks of political communication and decision-making increasingly facilitated by non-governmental institutions and global 'world systems'.[3] These theories commonly build on the specifically modern contrast between state, government or sovereign politics and administrative governance or depoliticized social engineering. It is a contrast between the state and civil society in which the 'soft' power of civil society eventually prevails over the 'hard' power of the modern state. Political governments are allegedly being replaced by depoliticized forms of global governance. Different forms of societal management and constitutionalism[4] assume the state's authority. Global social engineering gradually marginalizes the importance of national sovereign politics.

The second stream is equally critical of the concept of state and national sovereignty and often has the same political ethos like theories of global and transnational governance. However, it is less interested in the spontaneity of evolution and self-constitution of global society. It rather builds on the prescriptive concept of social and political transformation of global society[5] and is typical of the discourse of global human rights, cosmopolitan ethics and democracy[6] which methodologically represents an eclectic mixture of universalist ethical normativism

---

2 Kanishka Jayasuriya, Globalization, Sovereignty, and the Rule of Law: From Political to Economic Constitutionalism?', *Constellations* 8 (2001): 445.

3 Immanuel Wallerstein, *World-Systems Analysis: An Introduction* (Durham NC: Duke University Press, 2004).

4 David Sciulli, *Theory of Societal Constitutionalism: Foundations of a Non-Marxist Critical Theory* (Cambridge: Cambridge University Press, 1992).

5 Jackie Smith, Charles Chatfield and Ron Pagnucco, eds, *Transnational Social Movements and global Politics: A Solidarity Beyond the State* (Syracuse NY: Syracuse University Press, 1997).

6 See, for instance, Thomas W. Pogge, 'Cosmopolitanism and Sovereignty', *Ethics* 103 (1992): 48.

and sociological constructivism.[7] According to these theories, globalization allegedly leads to the global civil society[8] and a global sociology of human rights.[9] Adherents of a cosmopolitan legal system of human rights and universal civic virtues, such as Ulrich Beck, David Held, Mary Kaldor, Daniel Levy, Thomas Pogge and others, insist that the decoupling of society and the nation state has significantly transformed the notion of sovereignty and that it is time to transform humanitarian ideals into a regime of global protection of human rights that 'can be considered as a Leviathan writ large'.[10]

The existing international frameworks, including the body of international law, allegedly need to be redesigned and used as the foundation of the global political power necessary to tackle contemporary planetary challenges, especially the strategies, risks and disasters of global capital.[11] Global 'foundations have developed in the lifeworld for a *cosmopolitan republicanism* centred on freedom of the individual'[12] which will politically challenge the dominance of the global market and the epistemological rule of economics. This dominance needs to be countered by a sovereign cosmopolitan legal order enhancing the protection of human rights instead of imperial interests[13] and the emerging global political order based on the sovereignty of cosmopolitan values and governance.[14] According to this view, human rights are social institutions unlimited by state borders and national cultures.[15]

Contrary to these views and calls for global post-sovereign governance, cosmopolitanism and globally sovereign human rights ethics, the third stream of political and legal thinking claims that power politics associated with state sovereignty has not disappeared but acquired new forms and modes of social communication and supranational or transnational organizations. In the spirit of Hegelian philosophy, these theories, therefore, analyse sovereignty's transformation rather than its disappearance. Scholars, such as Anthony Carty, Jean Cohen, James Rosenau and others, examine how the sovereign nation states have been swamped by the totalizing tendencies of new power configurations operating at global

7 See, for instance, Ulrich Beck, *The Cosmopolitan Vision* (Cambridge: Polity Press, 2006), 18–19.

8 Mary Kaldor, *Global Civil Society: An Answer to War* (London: Polity Press, 2003).

9 Daniel Levy and Natan Sznaider, 'Sovereignty Transformed: a sociology of human rights', *The British Journal of Sociology* 57(4) (2006): 657.

10 Ibid., at 665.

11 Ulrich Beck, *Power in the Global Age: A New Global Political Economy* (Cambridge: Polity Press 2005).

12 Ulrich Beck, *What Is Globalization?* (London: Polity, 2000), 9.

13 Gerard Delanty, *Citizenship in a Global Age* (Buckingham: Open University Press, 2000).

14 David Held, *Democracy and the Global Order: From the Modern State to Cosmopolitan Governance* (Cambridge: Polity, 1995).

15 For a sociological theory of human rights, see, for instance, Bryan S. Turner, 'Outline of a Theory of Human rights', *Sociology* 27(3) (1993): 489.

level. They subsequently urge to rethink state sovereignty in this period of crisis in international law and politics and to reinforce the democratic legitimacy of the international order by reinforcing and reinventing democratic legitimacy and decision-making procedures at nation state government level.[16]

According to these theoretical views, the sovereignty of the nation state and international politics have been significantly weakened by much more powerful global networks, institutions and agencies.[17] The democratic political form of the sovereign nation state, therefore, needs to be used to construct democratically legitimate political institutions at supranational and global levels. Popular sovereignty and democratic legitimacy existing at the nation state level thus have to be preserved and used as a tool for strengthening the democratic legitimation of the international and global political order. In other words, supranational and global democratic transformation is impossible without the democratic procedures and tools successfully used by the nation state.[18]

Responding to the legal and political challenges of contemporary global world society and reflecting on the notion of sovereignty and power in international relations, Jean Cohen, for instance, critically asks: 'What is to be the new "nomos" of the earth and how should we understand globalized law?'[19] In her answer, she admits that the sovereignty-based model of international law gives way to an Empire-based world order which sidelines the project of cosmopolitan justice and universal human rights. Nevertheless, Cohen insists on the usefulness of the discourse of state sovereignty in international politics and law and calls for the revitalization of the sovereignty-based paradigm of international public law to confront the Empire's power and domination in international affairs.[20] In this concept of international law, sovereignty is treated as 'a concept of eternal return'[21] and mutually equal sovereign states can be bound even against their will by an authorized international agency.

16 See, for instance, Anthony Giddens, *Runaway World: How Globalization is Reshaping Our Lives* (London: Routledge, 2003).

17 See, for instance, James Rosenau, *Along the Domestic-Foreign Frontier: Exploring Governance in a Turbulent World* (Cambridge: Cambridge University Press, 1997).

18 For the relation between the nation state and sovereignty, see Anthony Giddens, *The Nation-State and Violence: Volume Two of A Contemporary Critique of Historical Materialism* (Berkeley, CA: University of California Press, 1985).

19 Jean L. Cohen, *Globalization and Sovereignty. Rethinking Legality, Legitimacy and Constitutionalism* (Cambridge: Cambridge University Press 2012); Jean L. Cohen, 'Whose Sovereignty? Empire Versus International Law', *Ethics & International Affairs* 18 (2004): 1.

20 For a similar account of international law, see Martti Koskenniemi, *The Gentle Civilizer of Nations: The Rise and Fall of International Law 1870–1960* (Cambridge: Cambridge University Press, 2004).

21 Anthony Carty, 'Sovereignty in International Law: A Concept of Eternal Return', in *Reclaiming Sovereignty,* eds Laura Brace and John Hoffman (London: Pinter, 1997), 101–116.

Between the Empire, International Public Law and the State of Exception

Critics would say that the emancipation of global society from the nation state favoured by social scientists leads to the loss of the political in the constant struggle of dominant economic and social interests. Political conflicts are neutralized by the normative ideal of governmentality. The modern state is in danger of being reduced to the economic state (*Wirtschaftsstaat*) of an unceasing struggle between particular interests. The neutralization of the political by legal norms and economic welfare paralyses the possibility of performative politics and the genuine articulation of common goals.

Contemporary globalized political societies continue to be challenged by the question whether law – national, international, supranational and transnational – is just an empty machine, an administration technology trapped by the logic of repetition and the illusion of normality that masks real political life full of sovereign power and unlimited decisions imposed by a sovereign on the rest of a political community. Is international law just a rationalization of excessive and abusive state power? Is every sovereign state virtually a rogue state able to transgress law and having ultimate recourse to terror and fear justified by the need to protect its citizens? Is it possible to separate the classical tradition of freedom and political self-determination from the institutional framework of political sovereignty as suggested by cosmopolitan thinkers? And is governance as the politics of globalization just another obfuscation of the conflictual character of democracy replacing democratic representation by technocratic administration?

As Jacques Derrida points out: '[O]ne cannot combat, *head-on, all* sovereignty, sovereignty *in general*, without threatening at the same time, beyond the nation state figure of sovereignty, the classical principles of freedom and self-determination'.[22] Sovereignty is inseparable from the rationalism of the state and the principle of unconditionality. However, the modern state's sovereign power to decide on the exception and the right to suspend all legislated rights and freedoms is inseparable from the very existence of civil rights, political freedoms and the democratic character of statehood.

According to this view, sovereignty transgresses the technology of political power and its discriminations and injustices within liberal constitutional settlements. The administrative violence of sovereign power goes hand in hand with political self-determination and force, transforming the constitutional settlement. Sovereignty thus opens the possibility of constitutional and political change.

This position has been advocated, in particular, by Giorgio Agamben who, along the same lines of argument as Carl Schmitt almost a century ago, states that legal sovereignty may be defined by the ability to suspend itself. The central characteristic of sovereignty is its extra-legal surplus that can be used to

22 For these claims, see Jacques Derrida, *Rogues: Two Essays on Reason* (Stanford, CA: Stanford University Press, 2005), 158.

introduce extra-constitutional political change.[23] Agamben paints a dark picture of contemporary Western civilization and its liberal democratic regimes in which citizens are always at risk of becoming '*homo sacer*' – a person that can be detained and even killed without legal reason.[24] The political existence of human beings cannot be separated from their everyday lives, and the exception becomes the rule and 'a paradigm of government'.[25] The state of exception as normality, instead of Schmitt's extra-juridical power and Kelsen's supreme rule of the juridical system, is the originary structure of sovereignty and its basic law.[26]

Writers such as Agamben, Derrida or Hardt and Negri attempt to destabilize current national and global political settlements and explore different agencies and strategies for the transformation of politics, law, identity and ethics. Their primary goal is dictated by fear that the constituent power of a political collectivity may be contained and fatally rationalized by formal legality and constitutional democratic institutions. They seek to escape the trap of 'constituting the constituent power' by various suggestions of activism, resistance, openness, ethical exposure to the otherness, reflexivity, critique and so on.

As Agamben comments, constituent power is never constituted, and calls upon the constituted power to act. The problem of constituent power becomes the problem of 'the constitution of potentiality'.[27] However, it would be superficial and wrong to treat these highly aestheticized and speculative philosophical treatises as just another addition to the typically modern discourse on constitutionalism, especially the relationship between the constituent power of the people, as one indivisible collective agency, and the constituted power of formal legal rules, procedures and state institutions. The argument is not about the fact that constituted power depends on its constituent founder whose composition, ethical and political characteristics may always be questioned and challenged. It, rather, attacks the self-referential capacity of constituted power to generally and exclusively constitute political power.

Sovereignty and the Seductive Ethics of Critical Theory

While theories favouring emerging horizontal forms of global societal management and constitutions involve a typically modern social theoretical and political belief

23 See Giorgio Agamben, *Potentialities: Collected Essays in Philosophy* (Stanford, CA: Stanford University Press, 1999).

24 Giorgio Agamben, *Homo Sacer: Sovereign Power and Bare Life* (Stanford, CA: Stanford University Press, 1998), 71–80.

25 Giorgio Agamben, *State of Exception* (Chicago, IL: The University of Chicago Press, 2005), 1–31.

26 Giorgio Agamben, supra n. 24, 28.

27 Ibid., at 43–45. In this chapter, Agamben draws on Antonio Negri's concept and book *Il potere costituente: Saggio sulle alternative del moderno* (Milan: SugarCo, 1992).

in the diminishing role of the state and the growing role of spontaneous societal processes, theories warning against the political risks of globalization either seek to strengthen the democratic legitimacy of the politics of global governance, or reinvent the democratic sovereign state as a first pillar of the legitimate global political order. In other words, some theories favour new variations on the theme of the withering away of the state and the growing role of soft laws and depoliticized administration while others either design global ethics of human rights and cosmopolitan values, or continue to believe in the hard laws of power and sovereignty politics and mainly seek to reinvent and transfer the principles and values of modern democratic politics from the nation state to the global level.[28]

Modern political and legal philosophies and theories often combine theoretical, practical and evaluative ambitions and controversially employ key concepts in both descriptive and normative terms. Abstract concepts such as sovereignty, nation, legitimacy, justice, fairness and polity invite critical judgments and substantive considerations beyond the analytical framework of social sciences. The fact that the concepts of sovereignty and post-sovereignty are highly generalized, vague and susceptible to metaphorical use also means that these concepts are *ethically seductive*.[29] They are an intrinsic part of the popular 'life-as-philosophy' belief according to which it is possible to change the world if you know how to describe it and find the most persuasive conceptual tools.

Recent theoretical calls to abandon the concept of sovereignty and replace it by a more suitable conceptual framing of politics and law, which would better respond to the profound structural changes of political 'sovereignty in transition',[30] often do not deny their primarily political purposes. They subject a descriptive scientific enterprise to a superior prescriptive politics and ethics. They construct normative and semantic alternatives to the existing legal, political and international practices and language canons and often coincide with the political zeal and ethics of late humanist projects.[31] Legal and political theorists and philosophers call for humanity to be rescued from economic exploitation, environmental disasters and so on through global political and legal organization and engagement beyond the limits of the sovereign state.

---

28 For the distinction of hard and soft law, see, for instance, Kenneth Abbott and Duncan Snidal, 'Hard and Soft Law in International Governance', *International Organization* 54 (2000): 434.

29 However, adherents of critical theory equally accuse other theories of their specific 'seducements'. See especially a challenging study by Thomas McCarthy who accuses Luhmann's systems theory of 'conceptual imperialism'. Thomas McCarthy, *Ideals and Illusions: On Reconstruction and Deconstruction in Contemporary Critical Theory* (Cambridge, MA: The MIT Press, 1993), 173.

30 Neil Walker, ed., *Sovereignty in Transition* (Oxford: Hart Publishing, 2003).

31 Among many examples, see, for instance, Rafael Domingo, *The New Global Law* (Cambridge: Cambridge University Press, 2010).

However, these calls fall into a particularly dangerous trap, that of critical theory aimed at constructing correct theoretical hypotheses and concepts to open a route for correct political practices.[32] According to these streams within critical theory, correct practice will circularly feed the process of ever more correct theory. The absolute distinction of the world as it is and the world as it ought to be – this counterfactual imperative of any prescriptive critical theory – thus continues to build on early modern semantics of social science as a form of the social world's foundation and/or transcendence and theoretical observation as a necessary precondition for correcting the failures and manifold forms of 'alienation' of this world.[33]

This 'dialectic' effort to transform society by a critical and prescriptive theory draws on the idea of a historical progression and the deviant state of existing social and political condition. State sovereignty and national governments must be replaced by global post-sovereign politics, cosmopolitan ethics and human rights, multinational democracy and post-national governance which are treated as both analytical concepts and counterfactual projects yet to be achieved by political and legal agents with a little help from their theorizing friends. For instance, the recently popular critical thoughts of Hardt and Negri have been driven by the ideal of the self-organization of the globalized multitude against the malign sovereign power of the Empire. Their apocalyptic visions are informed by a moralistic distinction between the natural goodness of the multitude and the evil nature of the Empire and the ultimate victory of good over evil.[34]

In modernity, sovereignty was addressed in many different ways by many of the finest political and legal scholars and philosophers, from Bodin and Hobbes to Habermas and Foucault. Its numerous definitions and conceptualizations continue to circulate in the body of legal and political knowledge and thinking. Understanding the extent and meaning of current critical approaches to sovereignty, therefore, requires analysing and contextualizing the history and evolution of the concept of sovereignty and its theories.[35] In the next section, I, therefore, briefly summarize this evolution and historical reconceptualizations of sovereignty.

---

32 For these expectations of critical theory and philosophy, see, for instance, David Couzens Hoy and Thomas McCarthy, *Critical Theory* (Oxford: Blackwell, 1994).

33 For a critique of critical theory's foundationalism and a call for its pluralistic critical reflection, see James Tully, 'Wittgenstein and Political Philosophy: Understanding Practices of Critical Reflection', *Political Theory* 17(2) (1989): 183.

34 For a very insightful and radical critique of Hardt and Negri's moralistic fallacy, see William Rasch, *Sovereignty and its Discontents* (London: Birkbeck Law Press, 2005), 110–116.

35 See, for instance, Michael Fowler and Julie Marie Bunck, *Law, Power and The Sovereign State: The Evolution and Application of the Concept of Sovereignty* (University Park, PA: The Pennsylvania State University Press, 1995).

The Evolution of Sovereignty in Modern Politics and Law: a Brief Historical Reconceptualization

> Our constitution is called a democracy because power is in the hands not of a minority but of the whole people ... We are free and tolerant in our private lives; but in public affairs we keep to the law. This is because it commands our deep respect.[36]

These famous sentences, noted in Thucydides's *History of the Peloponnesian War*, are from Pericles's funeral oration over Athenian soldiers who died during the first year of the Peloponnesian War. They describe the overall settlement of the Athenian *polis* including the rule of law and the distinction between private morals and public interests which directly contradicts the modern misconception of 'the liberty of the Ancients'[37] falling short of private autonomy. Constitution is a matter of political power, the law's ultimate command of public affairs and the general social condition of life in *polis*. It stretches from power politics to the authority of law and mores conducting both private and public affairs of the Athenian society. In other words, it describes issues and problems commonly associated in modern political and legal theory and philosophy with the concept of sovereignty as power of a command, its juridical form and the overall life form of political society.

The question of sovereignty is relatively recent and modern, yet its structural and semantic preconditions are ancient.[38] It seems inexhaustible because of the mutual interdependence and relationships between politics and law and their reflections on the overall life form and social settlement of different polities. The law rules, yet its foundations are not legal as Hobbes summarized in one of the most quoted statements of modern political philosophy – *auctoritas, non veritas facit legem*. However, without the laws, political authority and its power would descend into the tyranny of arbitrary force. These general and intrinsic tensions and conflicts were equally well summarized by Pascal: 'Justice without force is impotent; force without justice is tyrannical. Justice without force is contradicted, because there are always bad people; force without justice stands accused. ... Justice is subject to dispute; force is easy to recognize and indisputable'.[39]

---

36 Thucydides, *History of the Peloponnesian War*, Book II, 37. This translation from John Burrow, *A History of Histories* (London: Allen Lane, 2007), 29.

37 Benjamin Constant, 'The Liberty of the Ancients and the Moderns', in *French Liberalism in the 19th Century: An Anthology*, eds Robert Leroux and David M. Hart (Oxon: Routledge, 2012), 68.

38 Jens Bartelson, *A Genealogy of Sovereignty* (Cambridge: Cambridge University Press, 1995).

39 Blaise Pascal, *Pensée* (New York: Dutton, 1958), 85; for this translation, see, however, Jacques Derrida, *The Beast and the Sovereign. Volume I* (Chicago, IL: The University of Chicago Press, 2009), 8.

Long before Pascal, in the fourteenth century, Bartolus of Saxoferrato already argued that sovereignty is a matter of legal form and thus further emphasized the inseparability of political authority from legal normativity. Power exercised without the legal title is illegitimate. In the same historical period, when Marsilius of Padua defended the claim of Ludwig of Bavaria, the elected candidate for Holy Roman Emperor, that the Holy Roman Empire is independent from the Papacy and identified 'the supreme legislator of the human race' with 'the totality of mankind, to whom the sanctions of Law fall to be applied',[40] he effectively supplanted the principle of divine sovereignty with popular sovereignty. According to Marsilius, the sovereign power of kings and princes derived from the affected secular polity and was not to be subordinated to the Church and papal interference.[41]

Defining the question of sovereignty in terms of human laws and polity and removing it from the realm of divine authority, Marsilius, nevertheless, only shifted the legitimacy foundations of political power while keeping the sovereignty as 'a transcendent principle behind the power'.[42] The very notion of sovereignty is part of the historical growth of political power, its monopolization and centralization in the Middle Ages and final transformation from the monarchical to the democratic notion of sovereignty as the popular self-rule legally defined and limited by the constitution.

The medieval and early modern concept of sovereignty signified superior power in the complex system of political hierarchy. Sovereignty used to be absolute in the sense of *legibus solutus* – being exempt from the laws. At the same time, political power in medieval times was commonly limited by other autonomous authorities, such as the Church, and shared in the feudal assemblies. However, sovereignty as a principle of political organization and legal fiction emerges only after the collapse of this medieval world of imperial and clerical hierarchies.

Modern political philosophy and theory considered sovereignty central to the institutional architecture of political life. Historically, it was introduced into the theory of the state by Jean Bodin in response to a particular political struggle for the independence of the French king from the Pope and the Holy Roman Emperor.[43] From the very beginning, its central issue was the supremacy of political power over other powers exercised on the territory of what became the French state. Bodin's concept of sovereignty already incorporated the duality of political authority and law.[44] Bodin's theory also presented the first

40 Quoted from Bertrand de Jouvenel, *On Power: Its Nature and the History of Its Growth* (Boston, MA: Beacon Press, 1962), 30.

41 Francesco Maiolo, *Medieval Sovereignty: Marsilius of Padua and Bartolus of Saxoferrato* (Delft: Eburon Publishers 2007).

42 Bertrand de Jouvenel, supra n. 40, 42.

43 J.H.M. Salmon, 'The Legacy of Jean Bodin: absolutism, populism, or constitutionalism?', *History of Political Thought* 17(4) (1996): 507.

44 Sofia Nasstrom, 'What Globalization Overshadows', *Political Theory* 31 (2003): 815–816.

elaboration of an idea of public law as a special type of political law based on practical political reason.[45] The subject of the study of sovereignty was the art of governing, including skills and practices related to the newly established domain of public law.[46]

Spinoza subsequently formulated the difference between power and sovereignty as the difference between *potentia* and *potestas* which is still commonly accepted as the definition of the difference between the capacity and authorization of the use of force.[47] In the *Tractatus Theologico-Politicus*, Spinoza acknowledges that the (fear of the) power (*potentia*) of the multitude is the limit of sovereign power (*potestas*): 'Every ruler has more to fear from his own citizens … than from any foreign enemy' and this fear is 'the principal brake on the power of the sovereign or state'. In other words, the fear of the power of those subjects of the sovereign power is its most effective check.

However, it was a much more intricate and complex view elaborated by Thomas Hobbes which first formulated the concept of the political sovereign as a supreme authority capable of restoring political order to European societies plagued by the civil wars of the seventeenth century.[48] The political duality of security/obedience and the origin of political unity guaranteed by the rule of law – these hallmarks of political modernity – both originate in Hobbes's concept of political sovereignty.[49] Legality became a medium of the social contract between the sovereign who guaranteed civil order and his obedient governed subjects.[50] The unity of sovereign power guaranteed the unity of society, its survival and persistence. The exercise of such power by the modern state both reaffirmed the society's existence and differentiated it from other political societies by demarcating the state's territorial borders.[51]

The problem of political supremacy was accompanied by the question whether the sovereign can be limited in exercising power over his subjects. While some constitutional theories assume that the very nature of constitutional sovereignty is based on a system of checks and balances and limited power, other theoretical streams see untameable power and political will as an intrinsic part and a

45 John Rawls, *The Law of Peoples* (Cambridge, MA: Harvard University Press, (1999), 4.

46 Martin Loughlin, *The Idea of Public Law* (Oxford: Oxford University Press, 2003), 76.

47 See, for instance, Gilles Deleuze, *Spinoza, Practical Philosophy* (San Francisco, CA: City Lights Books, 1988), 97.

48 Preston King, *The Ideology of Order: A Comparative Analysis of Jean Bodin and Thomas Hobbes* (London: Allen and Unwin, 1974), 237–239.

49 Brian Tamanaha, *On the Rule of Law: History, Politics, Theory* (Cambridge: Cambridge University Press, 2004), 57.

50 Michael Edwards, *Civil Society* (Cambridge: Polity Press, 2009), 6–7.

51 Alan James, 'The Practice of Sovereign Statehood in Contemporary International Society', *Political Studies* 47(3) (1999): 457.

definitional mark of sovereignty.[52] Understanding the concept of sovereignty subsequently requires one to reflect upon both the unconstrained character of the sovereign's political will and the normative architecture of a constitution. This political and legal semantics of sovereignty thus contributes to self-reflections and self-images of political society and its self-constitutionalization as a self-governing constitutional polity.[53]

The Self-Reference of Sovereignty: Rethinking Foucault, Rereading *Leviathan*

Early modern political and juridical theories of sovereignty commonly distinguished between the political power of a sovereign and the plurality of social power exercised within the sovereign state, such as family power, spiritual power, economic and commercial power and so on. The relationship between a sovereign and the rest of society was that of the transcendental order of the state and the immanent order of society. Submission to sovereignty was the ultimate end of sovereignty. The common good and welfare – the very purpose of sovereignty – were defined as obedience to the laws and, therefore, as nothing but submission to sovereignty.

Modern politics and the state as its particular organization, therefore, have their specific rationality. As Michel Foucault put it:

> … [t]he end of sovereignty is the exercise of sovereignty. The good is obedience to the law, hence the good for sovereignty is that people should obey it. This is an essential circularity; whatever its theoretical structure, moral justification, or practical effects, it comes very close to what Machiavelli said when he stated that the primary aim of the prince was to retain his principality. We always come back to this self-referring circularity of sovereignty or principality.[54]

It is paradoxical that Foucault was so insightful as to identify this circularity and self-reference as intrinsic to the political and legal rationality of sovereignty, yet insisted that modernity was typical of the end of political sovereignty and the rule

52 For further comments, especially regarding the revolutionary power see, for instance, Ulrich Preuss, 'Constitutional Powermaking for the New Polity: Some Deliberations on the Relations between Constituent Power and the Constitution', *Cardozo Law Review* 14 (1992–1993): 643.

53 Andrew Arato, 'Constitutionalism and the Founding of Constitutions: Carl Schmitt and the Revival of the Doctrine of the Constituent Power in the United States', *Cardozo Law Review* 21 (2000): 1739.

54 Michel Foucault, 'Governmentality', in *Power. Essential works of Foucault 1954–1984, volume 3*. ed. James D. Faubion (London: Penguin, 2000), 210.

of law. For him, modernity is defined, rather, by disciplinization and the increasing power of social norms and not by legal rules.[55]

Foucault's conclusion that modernity leads to the decline of political sovereignty and the rule of law is even more paradoxical because it ignores the whole sovereignty discourse of modern politics and the genealogy of conflicting and subversive political strategies of popular and national sovereignty. Social and political struggles and inclusion/exclusion techniques related to the concept of a sovereign nation and political sovereignty are not examined as a specific discursive formation producing truth and knowledge about modern political and social life. It is therefore necessary to ask why Foucault acknowledged the self-reference of sovereignty and its laws while ignoring the self-formative and self-policing power of the discourse of the people as a political sovereign in full control of its social and cultural condition and destiny. In the following parts of this book, Foucault's neglect of the self-description of modern populations as a people, therefore, will be addressed as well as the productive discursive power of the concept of sovereignty which marked the birth of modern democracy and continues to inform our political and legal reality.

Contrary to Foucault's claims, the self-referential circularity and specific systemic rationality makes sovereignty one of constitutive concepts of political modernity. Because of sovereignty's self-reference, it is possible to consider modern politics as institutionally autonomous. Because of sovereignty, power is established as a medium of political communication and politics becomes differentiated from other social domains, such as religion, commerce and family. Individuals are subject to the laws of a sovereign only in the sense of political submission and not through the pervasive control of religious faith and morality.[56]

Furthermore, a genealogical view of sovereignty[57] reveals its continuing persuasive force and the different political strategies associated with it, but especially the fact that the concept of sovereignty continues to produce political conflicts and legal arguments and thus represents a specific form of autonomy and self-policing in modern populations that use the term 'nation' as their mode of self-description and self-reference. Foucault is right when he explores the importance of the army, justice and the administration for the emergence of modern nations, yet ignores the political and social mobilization associated with the juridical notion of the self-governed political nation and popular sovereignty which will be analysed in the fifth chapter of this book.

---

55 For one of the most insightful assessments of Foucault's complicated interpretation of modern law, see François Ewald, 'Norms, Discipline, and the Law', in *Law and the Order of Culture*, ed. Robert Post (Berkeley, CA: University of California Press, 1991), 138.

56 For a typical social theoretical view, see Talcott Parsons, 'On the Concept of Political Power', *Proceedings of the American Philosophical Society* 107(3) (1963): 235.

57 For Foucault's concept of genealogy as an 'anti-method', see Larry Shiner, 'Reading Foucault: Anti-Method and the Genealogy of Power-Knowledge', *History and Theory* 21(3) (1982): 386–392.

The self-reference of sovereignty and the differentiation of politics from other systems of modern society had already found a powerful and very clear voice in the sceptical nominalist philosophy of Thomas Hobbes. Unlike Bodin's sovereign prince whose absolute power consists of 'the right to impose laws generally on the subjects regardless of their consent'[58] and who cannot be subject to his own laws, Hobbes's concept of sovereign authority draws on an agreement between those individual wills – the social contract – as the founding internal mechanism of political society.[59]

According to Hobbes, the rational abilities of men are in the service of passions dictating the ends of human actions. However, in the state of nature, passions cannot be coordinated and individuals may pursue their interests in an unlimited way. The purposive rationality of individuals thus leads to a permanent fight for survival, security and scarce resources. This instability in the state of nature, resulting in an individualistic utilitarian chaos and a war of all against all, necessarily requires a self-regulatory mechanism for creating collective stability and security at the expense of purely individual ends. Hobbes therefore had to expand the concept of purposive rationality by the contractual act of forming a rational will with one another.[60]

The practical rationality of the social contract means an artificial coordination and regulation of human conduct which is the very essence of politics and political sovereignty. In this framework of contractual rationality, sovereignty is considered as the acquisition of generalized influence on the rest of society – the influence originally exercised by everyone on everyone else. Instead of using deception and force, the social contract causes political society to function on the basis of rational persuasion and consensus formation by means of debate, stretching the original rationalism of utilitarian individuals to the level of autonomous and self-regulatory political rationality through mutual recognition and consensus.[61]

The social contract constitutes an artificial, self-referential and self-regulatory political order of *civitas* governed by the sovereign.[62] This political order is a unity generated by many individual wills. Instead of divine law, the nature of man and his capacity of reasoning and agreement constitute the political order of the sovereign who acts as a law-maker and not an arbitrary power. The sovereign's rule is the rule of law, and sovereignty becomes a central pillar of the historically new concept of politics without theological arguments, which completely abandons the

58 Jean Bodin, *Six Books of the Commonwealth* (Oxford: Blackwell, 1955), 32.

59 Preston King, supra n. 48, 180–183.

60 David Gauthier, 'Hobbes's Social Contract', in *The Social Contract Theories: Critical Essays on Hobbes, Locke, and Rousseau*, ed. Christopher Morris (Oxford: Rowman & Littlefield, 1999), 59.

61 Rex Martin, 'Hobbes and the Doctrine of Natural Rights: The Place of Consent in His Political Philosophy', *Western Political Quarterly* 33 (1980): 380.

62 Michael Oakeshott, *Rationalism in Politics and Other Essays* (Indianapolis, IN: Liberty Fund, 1991), 260.

perspective of legitimacy through invoking eternity, and draws on the reality of command structures and the exercise of political power previously consented to by its subjects. Because of the notion of sovereignty, politics can be viewed as a self-referential system of rules permanently seeking its internal coherence.

The 'Hobbesian Problem' in Social Systems Theory – Value Integration, or the Systemic Self-Reference?

The philosophy of Thomas Hobbes profoundly inspired modern social, political and legal thinking. For instance, Talcott Parsons famously considered the problem of constituting a legitimate political order 'the Hobbesian problem', and critically addressed Hobbes's concept of men as solitary subjects with the ability to act in a purposive way and pursue their own interests rationally.[63]

A whole sociological tradition thus builds on critical reflections on the particular and contestable interpretation of Hobbes's notion of the sovereign as ultimate political authority which is external to the rest of political society, imposes sanctions and enforces the observance of legal norms. According to these sociological criticisms, the sovereign's externality and distance from the rest of society actually weaken the political and social order. The sovereign's power cannot be based merely on the collective instrumentalism of an order protecting individuals against each other's interests and potentially destructive purposive actions.

In his theory of modernization, Durkheim, for instance, considered the sovereign state a body representing collective consciousness which cannot be exclusively constructed by the social contract as an agreement of individuals driven by their private goals and self-interest. In other words, the purposive rationality and utilitarian nature of the social contract does not have the binding force of the pre-modern sacred mechanic solidarity and 'the State is a special organ whose responsibility it is to work out certain representations which hold good for the collectivity'.[64]

Obedience of political and legal subjects thus must have a moral foundation and legitimacy as a reflection of totality of a polity. Political foundations of the modern state are not contractual and require a universal foundation capable to replace the older semantics of the sacred nature of social and political order. The modern state can be legitimate if it represents organic solidarity of a political society's universalized concepts of morality.

Durkheim, Parsons and many other sociologists and social theorists believed that Leviathan's commonwealth of self-interested individuals suffered from

63 Thomas Burger, 'Talcott Parsons: The Problem of Order in Society', *American Journal of Sociology* 83 (1978): 320.

64 Emile Durkheim, *Professional Ethics and Civic Morals* (London: Routledge, 1957), 50.

profound instability. The social contract-based artificial political order securing the observance of norms through external sanctions could not last and needed to be guaranteed and legitimized by a common orientation to values and their internalization by the members of a political society.

Nevertheless, this concept of political legitimacy by the internalizing of cultural values drew criticism itself for reducing the complex problem of legitimacy to conformity to substantive ethics that Hobbes originally and uncompromisingly eliminated from the public realm of politics. The idea of legitimizing a political order through values integrating the whole of society always bears a risk of substantiating politics and law and making the legal and political procedures of decision-making part of the problem of conformity to values. This risk can be partly reduced by further proceduralization of ethics, such as Habermas's project of discourse ethics, but can never be fully eliminated from politics and law.[65]

Social theories critical of Hobbes's instrumental reason and political utilitarianism thus run into the opposite problem of substantiating political and legal processes through cultural and moral values. They draw on the notion of Leviathan representing the ultimate cultural integration of a political community. Nevertheless, Hobbes's sovereignty is irreducible to the notion of Leviathan transcending and constituting the whole society. Hobbes was not just the first thinker who brought together now familiar concepts of the social contract, human nature, sovereignty, political unity, the rule of law, civil society and liberty, thus creating the language of political modernity. His contribution to the legal and political theory of sovereignty was much more profound because he treated sovereignty as a vehicle for the functional differentiation of politics and religion and as a form of systemic closure of the specific functionally differentiated systems of law and politics.[66]

In the modern system of positive law, sovereignty means the self-reference of legal communication. In the modern system of politics, sovereignty equally signifies the limits of any political decision-making and a point of reference for bureaucratic administration, party politics and public opinion communicated via the mass media. Instead of referring to the totality of society, the concept of sovereignty, whenever used in political and legal communication, thus exclusively refers to the systems of politics and/or law while semantically excluding other social domains, such as science, technology, economy, religion and so on.[67]

---

65 See especially Jürgen Habermas, *Moral Consciousness and Communicative Action* (Cambridge, MA: The MIT Press, 1990), 43.

66 For an interesting remark on Hobbes, functional differentiation, and systems theory, see Thomas Vesting, 'The Network Economy as a Challenge to Create New Public Law', in *Public Governance in the Age of Globalization*, ed. Karl-Heinz Ladeur (Aldershot: Ashgate, 2004), 256.

67 For the self-reference in politics, see, for instance, Niklas Luhmann, *Political Theory in the Welfare State* (Berlin: Walter de Gruyter, 1990), 41.

Sovereignty, therefore, needs to be reassessed in light of the process of functional differentiation in modern society and its current global setting. Hobbes's greatest contribution to contemporary social theory of politics and law is precisely the description of politics as a closed, self-referential system with power as the medium of political communication. The arbitrary power of the state of nature was replaced by the sovereign's law-making power that was legitimized by the general capacity of human beings to reason and come to agreement. The sovereign's rule of law leads to the functional differentiation of the system of positive law and makes legality its medium. Law cannot operate without the sovereign power and its 'sword of justice'.[68] However, this power equally cannot operate without laws. Power and legality are certainly not identical. At the same time, power is not hierarchically superior to the rules of law because its operative capacity depends on legal communication. Instead, power and legality coexist and are structurally independent of each other.

At this point in the functional differentiation of politics and law, society loses its structural simplicity and evolves towards much more complex structures of social modernity.[69] The constitutional constraints of political power certainly give sovereignty its legal form as the rule of law but they also help any government to achieve its goals by legal means. The legalization of politics and the political instrumentalization of law are merely two aspects of the same modern process of functional differentiation. Spinoza's early differentiation of the rightful power of rule (*potestas*) and the actual power of government to achieve its goals (*potentia*) is thus fully realized in the differentiation between the constitutional rule of law and political government. Furthermore, this government in modern democracy always takes the form of the self-rule of the people and its self-constitutionalization.

The semantics of sovereignty is thus part of the complex political semantics. However, it is equally part of the semantics of legal authorization intrinsic to legal reasoning and communication. It, therefore, needs to be treated as a concept indicating the social self-limitation of the constitutional democratic state and the rule of law rather than a metaphor for social and cultural unity, integration and homogeneity.

From (Post)-Sovereignty Studies to the Autopoietic Social Systems Theory of Sovereignty

The emphasis on sovereignty as part of modern political and legal semantics, as opposed to the common picture of Leviathan as a sovereign ruler integrating

68 Norberto Bobbio, *Thomas Hobbes and the Natural Law Tradition* (Chicago, IL: University of Chicago Press, 1993), 62.

69 Ross Harrison, *Hobbes, Locke and Confusion's Masterpiece: An Examination of Seventeenth-Century Political Philosophy* (Cambridge: Cambridge University Press, 2003), 78.

the totality of society by the external power of his sword, calls for further conceptualizations and explanations.

Leviathan was the first myth of civil society based on sovereignty as its political structure.[70] More complex social theoretical approaches to the study of society, which abandoned the centrality of state organization, understandably started questioning the concept of sovereignty and Leviathan as a metaphor of society integrated by the political sovereign's power. Social systems theories, for instance, describe society as a heterarchical and functionally differentiated system consisting of different social systems, such as politics, morality, law and economy, which are self-regulated and operate concurrently without any hierarchical ordering. According to these theories, society consists of a multitude of communication networks and a plurality of subsystems functioning according to their internal operations, and not on the basis of some ultimate value integration, stability, cohesion or moral fabric.[71]

Following the autopoietic systems theoretical perspective, the political and legal semantics of sovereignty can be reformulated as a specific mode of the political and legal systems' self-reference and self-description. The self-description of the political system through the historical introduction of the concept of political sovereignty, and the coeval self-description of the legal system, introducing the concept of constitutional sovereignty or legal authorization, therefore, signifies the difference between system and environment and not the political and cultural integration of modern society and the state as its central organization. This signification already belongs to the system and contributes to its self-regulation.[72]

As long as it continues to be used by politicians, activists, judges, lawyers and the public, sovereignty scarcely can be treated as just a redundant metaphor, a concept unrelated to the operations of the globalized politics and law. It continues to be a distinct self-referential conceptualization of specific legal and political problems of global, international, supranational (especially European) and constitutional law and politics and, therefore, remains part of the observation of, information about, and symbolic explanations of political and legal operations.

The concept of sovereignty is part of both legal and political autopoiesis because, as demonstrated in the previous chapter, it contributes to and regulates

70 David Van Mill, *Liberty, Rationality, and Agency in Hobbes's Leviathan* (Albany, NY: SUNY Press, 2001), 154.

71 The most prominent is the autopoietic social systems theory elaborated by Niklas Luhmann. See especially Niklas Luhmann, *Social Systems* (Stanford, CA: Stanford University Press, 1995) and Niklas Luhmann, *Observations on Modernity* (Stanford, CA: Stanford University Press, 1998); for the legal and political context, see especially Gunther Teubner, *Law as an Autopoietic System* (Oxford: Blackwell, 1993); Michael King and Chris Thornhill, *Niklas Luhmann's Theory of Politics and Law* (Houndmills: Palgrave Macmillan, 2006); Jiří Přibáň and David Nelken, eds, *Law's New Boundaries: The Consequences of Legal Autopoiesis* (Aldershot: Ashgate, 2001).

72 Niklas Luhmann, *Social Systems*, supra n. 71, 437–439.

the system's self-reference, self-production and self-maintenance even in the Europeanized and globalized world.[73] The functional differentiation of modern politics and law and its original description by Hobbes's metaphor of Leviathan show that the concept of sovereignty, rather, signifies a process of generating autonomous political reality and knowledge and concurrent legal reality and knowledge. Hobbes's philosophy is thus instrumental to our current understanding that modern society evolves by the self-regulation of different social systems and not by one centralized form of political regulation imposed on the totality of society.[74]

In this context, critical voices calling for the end of sovereignty and prescriptively announcing the era of post-sovereignty appear to be premature if not ill-informed and drawing on the belief that a 'good' theory and its concepts can lead to a 'better' society and politics, this time politics of transnationalism, cosmopolitanism, globalism and any other 'isms'. They need to be taken as just fragmentary reflections of the complexity of global society and its political and legal systems.[75]

Instead of prescriptive reflections, conceptual innovations and normative speculations, the concepts of self-reference, self-reproduction and self-organization which all describe social autopoiesis need to be employed to describe the level of interference and interdependence between the structures and semantics of globalized law and politics as well as their systemic closure and autopoiesis, part of which is the self-referential semantics of sovereignty.[76] The current systems of Europeanized and globalized politics and law operate through making productive use of the paradox of the coexisting plurality of power structures and their persistent conceptualizations in the language of political and constitutional sovereignty. The theoretical semantic difference between sovereignty and post-sovereignty, respectively (democratic) government and (administrative) governance, draw on this paradox. Current uses and radical criticisms rather show that the concept of sovereignty retains its strong nominal value, essentially contested character and a capacity for semantically transforming the social multitude and its contingency into the fictional unity of the will operating in the political system, or legal authority operating in the legal system of global society.

Because of its continuing discursive force and political symbolism, the concept of sovereignty can mobilize the public for or against particular political programmes and decisions. One must also ask why clearly post-sovereign supranational structures and integrative processes, such as those typical of the EU or the WTO,

73 Gunther Teubner, supra n. 71, 23–24.

74 Ibid., 65.

75 See Andreas Philippopoulos-Mihalopoulos, *Niklas Luhmann: Law, Justice, Society* (London: Routledge-GlassHouse, 2010), 16.

76 Samantha Ashenden, 'The Problem of Power in Luhmann's Systems Theory', in *Luhmann on Law and Politics: Critical Appraisals and Applications*, eds Michael King and Chris Thornhill (Oxford: Hart Publishing, 2006), 128–130.

still persistently communicate through the code of sovereignty. Contrary to the traditional and commonly held views of influential streams of jurisprudence and political theory,[77] sovereignty studies thus require the methodology and perspectives of the social theory of law and politics, facilitating study of the evolution and structural changes in modern law and politics and parallel semantic changes in their conceptualization in the field of legal and political theory. The interplay of social structures and semantics needs to become a central focus of examining the political and legal evolution of sovereignty and its theoretical reflections and normative expectations invested in them. Self-descriptions of law and politics continue by using the concept of sovereignty and thus coincide with structural self-reproductions of the legal and political systems and contribute to both legal and political autopoiesis.

A sociological reconceptualization of sovereignty as part of modern political and legal semantics and one of many power structures opens up the possibility of reformulating sovereignty as a dynamic concept with its specific political and legal genealogy and history. Secondly, a social-systems theoretical approach critically deals with the semantics of sovereignty as a symbol of ultimate social unity and normative integration. Finally, sovereignty can be sociologically analysed within the context of productive rather than limiting power functions.

In the following parts of this book, I, therefore, pursue the goal of reconceptualizing sovereignty within the context of the autopoietic social systems theory to understand its historical and theoretical diversity and comprehend its recent semantic changes and pragmatic uses in the systems of positive law and politics.

77 The sociology of law and its methodology used to be heavily criticised by normativist legal theorists, such as Hans Kelsen. See especially Hans Kelsen, 'Eine Grundlegung des Rechtssoziologie', in Hans Kelsen and Eugen Ehrlich, *Rechtssoziologie und Rechtswissenschaft. Eine Kontroverse (1915–1917)* (Baden Baden: Nomos, 2003), 3–54.

PART II
Concepts and Theories

Chapter 3

Sovereignty and the Constitutional State: On the Systemic Self-Referencing and Differentiation in the Kelsen-Schmitt Debate

Many books and articles have been published recently about the Kelsen-Schmitt debate and other scholars' work and ideas related to these close-to-a-century-old controversies regarding the methodology of legal science and its relationship to other social sciences and disciplines of philosophy.[1] Why do current legal theorists concern themselves with this archaeology of jurisprudential knowledge and engage in various reinterpretations of scholars such as Kelsen, Schmitt, Ehrlich, Heller and others and the application of their theoretical concepts to our systems of globalized law and politics?

Adherents of international and global legal normativism recall Kelsen's pure theory of law and apply its monism to the juridification of international, supranational and global politics.[2] Critics of this juridification often employ Schmitt's decisionist theory to preserve the agonistic, open and deliberative character of politics. Surprisingly, Schmitt has thus inspired many radical critics of political and legal globalization and the emergence of a global liberalism of human rights.[3] In this time of profound structural changes and crises in Europeanized and globalized law and politics, legal and political theorists continue to look for their conceptual framework and inspiration in grand theoretical concepts and disputes that inform theoretical debates reflecting on the evolution of modern legality and both national and international politics.

---

1 See, for instance, David Dyzenhaus, *Legality and Legitimacy: Carl Schmitt, Hans Kelsen and Hermann Heller in Weimar* (Oxford: Oxford University Press, 1997); Martti Koskenniemi, *From Apology to Utopia: The Structure of International Legal Argument* (Cambridge: Cambridge University Press, 2006), 226–255; Cesare Pinneli, 'The Kelsen/Schmitt Controversy and the Evolving Relations between Constitutional and International Law', *Ratio Juris* 23(4) (2010): 493; Hidemi Suganami, 'Understanding Sovereignty Through Kelsen/Schmitt', *Review of International Studies* 33 (2007): 511; Lars Vinx, *Hans Kelsen's Pure Theory of Law: Legality and Legitimacy* (Oxford: Oxford University Press, 2007).

2 Jörg Kammerhofer, *Uncertainty in International Law: A Kelsenian Perspective* (Oxon: Routledge, 2011).

3 John P. McCormick, *Carl Schmitt's Critique of Liberalism: Against Politics as Technology* (Cambridge: Cambridge University Press, 1998).

Introduction: a Systems Theory Interpretation of the Kelsen-Schmitt Debate

The aim of this chapter is to reinterpret the classic Kelsen-Schmitt debate in the context of current social systems theory and retrospectively rethink its major concepts and arguments as early reflections on modern legal and political self-reference and functional differentiation. The early functional differentiation of politics and religion, which had been already captured by the concept of sovereignty in Hobbes's philosophy, was reformulated in modern political and legal theory as the differentiation of law and politics, and the famous theoretical and methodological controversy between Kelsen and Schmitt is one of its finest examples.

Kelsen and Schmitt's theories obviously were constrained by modern semantics of the constitutional state, sovereignty and international law and cannot be treated as early examples of theory of self-referential and functionally differentiated autopoietic social systems. Nevertheless, specific forms and conceptualizations of legal and political self-reference of the state and the functional differentiation of law and politics elaborated by both scholars are applicable to the current autopoietic systems of globalized law and politics unlimited by the state's organization.

In Kelsen's case, it is the exclusion of sovereignty from juridical logic that opens a way to the self-reference of positive law as a normatively closed and socially autonomous subsystem operating at national, European and global level. Similarly, Schmitt's contribution to current political and constitutional theory consists of addressing the problem of the social differentiation of politics and economy, law, administration and religion and identifying the friend/enemy distinction as the binary code of politics. Schmitt constructed his concept of the political as a self-referential system of political operations protected from the social environment by the medium of power. Unlike many other constitutional and international law scholars looking for sovereignty's territory and political location, he identified sovereignty with a system of general power operations. This system, therefore, is not limited by the nation state's framework and can be adopted by current theories of supranational and transnational law and politics.

Drawing on these reflections and retrospective interpretations of Kelsen and Schmitt's theories as specific examples of legal and political self-reference, functional differentiation and the self-limitation of law and politics, I critically argue that the process of legal and political Europeanization and globalization effectively rules out the possibility of formulating substantive theories of the sovereign state associating this particular social organization with metaphysical values and an ultimately self-validating collective identity and pre-political existence. Despite elements of political existentialism in Schmitt's theory of constituent power, Kelsen and Schmitt both continue to be influential and inspirational figures of current non-metaphysical theories of globalized law and politics. However, the constitutional state and sovereignty need to be reformulated as a meeting point of functionally differentiated and globalized legal and political communications and not as their ultimate end or substance.

Yet Another Lesson from the Kelsen-Schmitt Debate?

The close-on-a-century-old polemic between the Pure Theory of Hans Kelsen and the decisionist legal theory of Carl Schmitt has become the centre of gravity of many discussions of sovereignty, constitutionalism and the popular will, including recent debates on European constitutionalism and Euro crisis. In one of the most important studies of the concept of sovereignty to appear in the last century, Carl Schmitt remarked: 'A jurisprudence concerned with ordinary day-to-day questions has practically no interest in the concept of sovereignty'.[4] According to this view, the routinization of jurisprudential issues obfuscates the true nature of politics as the realm where a sovereign decides. Schmitt's notorious and much-quoted definition of a sovereign as 'he who decides on the exception'[5] provides a picture of sovereignty as the indivisible and unlimited authority to suspend the entire existing order of positive law. In this state of exception, the rule of law and legal mechanisms based on repetition and predictability give way to the power of real life, and the decision in its absolute purity becomes the supreme juristic element governing the immanent validity of legal norms.

Schmitt's concept of sovereignty is complex and inspirational for radical thinkers of both the political Left and Right. However, political science and philosophical interpretations often neglect its normative jurisprudential aspect. Schmitt's study was a critical response to the legal normativist thinking of Hans Kelsen who claimed that 'the concept of sovereignty must be radically repressed'[6] and transferred the problems of both state sovereignty (constituted power) and popular sovereignty (constituent power) to the sovereignty of laws.

Kelsen's Pure Theory of law disposes of the state and its sovereignty as a theoretical problem. Identifying the state with legal order, it represented the liberal positivist and normative project, a primary target of Schmitt's critique. Kelsen, indeed, did not deny the existence of political power and accepted the truism that the law cannot exist without power. However, he insisted that any legal state required all acts of political power to be expressed exclusively through the medium of law. Political acts are legally mediated and, therefore, must observe the criteria of legal validity. The essence of the modern state is the rule and authority of laws. The fact that a legal order is sovereign is merely a logical consequence

4 Carl Schmitt, *Political Theology: Four Chapters on the Concept of Sovereignty* (Chicago, IL: The University of Chicago Press, 1985), 12.

5 Ibid., 5.

6 'Die Souveränitätsvorstellung freilich muss radikal verdrängt werden', in *Das Problem der Souveranität und die Theorie des Völkerrechts: Beitrag zu einer reinen Rechtslehre* [*The Problem of Sovereignty and the Theory of International Law: A Contribution towards a Pure Theory of Law*], Hans Kelsen (Tübingen: Mohr, 1920), 320; furthermore, see Hans Kelsen, 'Sovereignty', in *Normativity and Norms: Critical Perspectives on Kelsenian Themes*, ed. Stanley L. Paulson (Oxford: Oxford University Press, 1999; the essay originally published in 1962) and Carl Schmitt, supra n. 4, 21.

of the system having its basic norm. The state's only function is to make law and thus to establish the legal priority and importance of different political interests. If a political act violates the basic norm, society faces the problem of revolution which, if successful, results in the constitution of a new legal system with its own basic norm.[7]

For Kelsen, the state is the *agency* that exercises political power in conformity with the laws. It is an acting subject represented by the acts of its legally qualified officials, which are authorized by a higher-level norm. Legal authorization is thus regressive and the final normative authorization can be traced back to a 'first constitution' enacted by a self-empowered agency, either an individual lawgiver, or a collective legislative assembly. Kelsen's basic norm is consequently nothing but a self-referential act of original legislation that is not empowered by the system of positive law.[8] However, the self-creation of a legislative body and its self-authorization are contradictory terms because each act by a state official requires legal authorization. The historical first lawgiver, therefore, is authorized retrospectively by the pure basic norm. The possibility of the sovereign exercise by the people of their constituent power becomes nothing more than a self-empowered act of self-constituted power of an assembly or an individual lawgiver.[9]

The juristic perception of the systemic unity of law, labelled a 'monistic view' by Kelsen,[10] ignores the connection between actual power and supreme legal authority. For Kelsen, 'the people' is a juristic fiction.[11] The unity of the people and its representative leaders as the first presupposition of democracy may only be established in a purely normative sense and at the level of the unity of the state's legal order which governs the behaviour of all its inhabitants.[12]

Schmitt was fundamentally critical of the concept of law as a dynamic self-regulatory and self-creating system reducing political sovereignty to the problems of legal authorization and validity. According to him, constitutional developments within the modern liberal state seek to eliminate sovereign power. However, the valid system of positive law, although informing the operation of the constitution, does not have the power to decide whether the constitution in its entirety can be suspended.

7 Hans Kelsen, *Introduction to the Problems of Legal Theory: A Translation of the First Edition of the Reine Rechtslehre or Pure Theory of Law* (Oxford: Oxford University Press, 1992), 59–60.

8 Hans Kelsen, *The Pure Theory of Law* (2nd edition, Berkeley, CA: University of California Press, 1970, orig. 1960), 291.

9 For this analysis of the basic norm, see especially Bert van Roermund, *Law, Narrative and Reality: An Essay in Intercepting Politics* (Dordrecht: Kluwer, 1997).

10 Hans Kelsen, supra n. 8 at 328–329; see also Joseph G. Starke, 'Monism and Dualism in the Theory of International Law', in *Normativity and Norms: Critical Perspectives on Kelsenian Themes*, ed. Stanley L. Paulson (Oxford: Oxford University Press, 1999; the essay originally published in 1938).

11 David Dyzenhaus, supra n. 1, 141.

12 Hans Kelsen, supra n. 8, 292.

According to Schmitt, 'whether the extreme exception can be banished from the world is not a juristic question'[13] and Kelsen's Pure Theory is 'the ideology of the lawyer-bureaucrat practising in changing political circumstances, who, under the most diverse forms of authority and with a relativistic superiority over the momentary political authority, seeks to order systematically the positive decrees and regulations that are handed down to him'.[14] Schmitt's critique of Kelsen's neo-Kantianism, therefore, was a critique of the legal form based on the notion of the self-referential basic norm governing the formation of a system of positive law as well as the application of a positive legal norm by the judiciary or administration.

However, these preliminary descriptions and comparisons need to be substantially expanded and further qualified and contextualized to critically assess and appreciate the importance of both theories to the current debates regarding the supranational and transnational European and global legal and political systems and the persistence of the semantics of sovereignty in these profoundly post-sovereign settings.

Value Integration Replaced by the Sovereign's Self-Reference

In his study *Politische Demokratie und soziale Homogenität* (Political Democracy and Social Homogeneity), Schmitt's intellectual and political opponent Hermann Heller defined sovereignty in terms of territoriality, exclusive nature, power hierarchy (the highest power on the state's territory), independence and irresistibility.[15] Though Heller famously criticized Schmitt's pre-political existential concept of constituent power, he held the view that shared political values were a precondition of democracy's success and resilience. He argued that a minimum level of social homogeneity was necessary for democratic unity.

In opposition to Schmitt, Heller claimed that:

> … the intellectual basis of parliamentarism is not the belief in public discussion as such, but belief in the existence of a common ground for discussion and in fair play for the opponent, with whom one wants to reach agreement under conditions that exclude naked force.[16]

---

13 Carl Schmitt, supra n. 4, 7.

14 Ibid., 45.

15 'Die Staatsgewalt ist souverän, das heisst sie ist auf ihrem Gebiete oberste, ausschliessliche, unwiderstehliche und eigentständige Macht', in *Staatslehre, 6th edition*, Hermann Heller (original print Leiden: Sijthoff, 1934; Tubingen: JCB Mohr, 1983), 246, respectively 278.

16 Hermann Heller, 'Politische Demokratie und soziale Homogenität' [1928], in *Gesammelte Schriften, vol. 2*, ed. Christoph Müller (Leiden: Sijthoff, 1971), 427.

Heller's treatment of the social plurality of modernity was thus based on a conventional view of parliamentarism and the public sphere as the foundations of civilized discussion and deliberation resulting in reasonable political compromise and the elimination of violence. However, it is the social fact of shared values guaranteeing social homogeneity and cultural value integration that is the precondition of such discussion. Factual social homogeneity is indispensable for normative constitutional and political legitimacy. The recognition of social values precedes the validity of legal norms and the acceptance of political decisions.[17]

Indeed, Schmitt's political and legal philosophy has often been interpreted as a kind of return to political metaphysics and a critique of modern legal and social scientific positivism which takes the social and existential unity of the sovereign people as substance and the normative unity of law as its form. This misreading is based on a common mistake, seeing the constitutional state as just a form of the substantive constitution of society.

However, Schmitt actually denied the possibility of substantive unity in modern political society and emphasized the impossibility of identifying the constitution of the state with the constitution of society. He recognized social plurality full of political and moral ruptures, normative and value conflicts and differences impossible to reconcile by some form of political negotiations and rational consensus or morality. In this sense, Schmitt's theory is a lot more radical than Heller's democratic search for common ground and political integration through shared values.

Schmitt's notion of the social unity and homogeneity of the constituent power of the people, therefore, is not to be taken as the substantive precondition for democratic or any other politics and the constitutional state. His ontological premise that a concrete, living order of a sovereign people precedes the normative order of law does not mean that the political order could restore a substantive natural order to society and its politics.[18] His constitutional theory is based on the supremacy of the existing constituent power over constituted power and, therefore, the supremacy of the political sphere and its sovereign decisions over the legal sphere and its hierarchy of authorized legal norms or the moral sphere of generally shared values.[19]

Schmitt insisted that the political self-constitution of the actually existing people precedes any legal normative interpretation and conceptualization of the

17 Ellen Kennedy, *Constitutional Failure: Carl Schmitt in Weimar* (Durham, NC: Duke University Press, 2004), 129.

18 Heinrich Meier, *The Lesson of Carl Schmitt: Four Chapters on the Distinction Between Political Theology and Political Philosophy* (Chicago, IL: The University of Chicago Press, 1998), 5.

19 Hans Lindahl, 'Constituent Power and Reflexive Identity: Towards an Ontology of Collective Selfhood', in *The Paradox of Constitutionalism: Constituent Power and Constitutional Form*, eds Martin Loughlin and Neil Walker (Oxford: Oxford University Press, 2007), 22.

constitution and constitutionalism.[20] According to him, the state does not have a constitution because 'the state is constitution' and 'an actually present condition, a *status* of unity and order'.[21] It is self-legitimized by its existential status and not recursively validated by a set of constitutional norms or moral values. Unlike Hobbes, who could not ask the question of constituent power as political agency in his times,[22] Schmitt constantly questioned the existential process of transforming the social multitude into political unity and considered it the self-reference and self-legitimation of the sovereign's decision.[23]

Social Totality and the Functional Differentiation of Politics

As regards the functional differentiation of modern society, especially economy, politics and law, Schmitt's political theory obviously cannot be treated as intrinsic part of the functionalist social science paradigm. Nevertheless, Schmitt was aware of the process of functional differentiation of modern society. Schmitt's theory is deeply ambivalent about this differentiation and both represents its radical critique and adopts it as a necessary precondition of the concept of the political and sovereignty.[24] Schmitt's view that the state is 'defined and understood from the political'[25] and ultimately converts the political pluriverse to its universe is an example of the functional differentiation of politics.

This differentiation needs to be analysed in the context of Schmitt's belief that the political sphere is to be protected from various social contaminations such as ethics, economy, religion, administration and so on. Schmitt refused to consider the state as a socially totalizing organization because the absorption and total state control of society leads to the destruction of politics. He criticized the concept of the total state politically controlling and administering the totality of social life but equally dismissed all theories contrasting state and society, and the liberal notion of the neutral state operating side by side with the depoliticized spheres of economy and law.[26]

---

20 Massimo La Torre, *Law as Institution: Normative Language Between Power and Values* (Dordrecht: Springer, 2010), 26–42.

21 Carl Schmitt, *Constitutional Theory* (Durham, NC: Duke University Press, 2008), 60.

22 David Dyzenhaus, 'Hobbes and the Legitimacy of Law', *Law and Philosophy* 20 (2001): 491.

23 David Dyzenhaus, 'The Politics and the Question of Constituent Power', in eds Martin Loughlin and Neil Walker, supra n. 19, 136–137.

24 This view was quite typical of the radical Left political and legal critique as well. For details, see William E. Scheuerman, *Between the Norm and the Exception: The Frankfurt School and the Rule of Law* (Cambridge, MA: The MIT Press, 1994), 157–188.

25 Carl Schmitt, *Politische Theologie II* (Berlin: Duncker und Humblot, 1969), 21.

26 William E. Scheuerman, *Carl Schmitt: the End of Law* (Oxford: Rowman & Littlefield, 1999), 86.

Schmitt considered the total state and the Western liberal concept of the state as just two different forms of the same general modern view of the state as a functioning machine based on the notion of social administration and the technical neutralization of politics.[27] According to him, modern society tends to establish total states penetrating all social spheres. The total state is, by its nature, the administrative state, drawing on instrumental legality and the technical powers of bureaucracy. As early as 1931, Schmitt analysed two alternative forms of this tendency – the weak 'quantitative' welfare state and the strong 'qualitative' total state, such as Mussolini's fascist state.[28]

Schmitt thus considered functional differentiation as an intrinsic part of his political theory of sovereignty. The highest risk for politics is its colonization by other codes of social communication, such as profit, the moral good and worthiness, efficiency and so on. In *The Concept of the Political*, Schmitt states:

> The equation state = politics becomes erroneous and deceptive at exactly the moment when state and society penetrate each other … Heretofore ostensibly neutral domains – religion, culture, education, the economy – then cease to be neutral in the sense that they do not pertain to state and to politics. As a polemical concept against such neutralizations and depoliticalizations of important domains appears the total state, which potentially embraces every domain. This results in the identity of state and society. In such a state, therefore, everything is at least potentially political, and in referring to the state it is no longer possible to assert for it a specifically political characteristic.[29]

These statements indicate Schmitt's awareness of the self-constitution of different codes of communication and the functional rationality of specific social systems which is further emphasized by the following conclusions:

> Let us assume that in the realm of morality the final distinctions are between good and evil, in aesthetics beautiful and ugly, in economics profitable and unprofitable. The question then is whether there is also a special distinction which can serve as a simple criterion of the political and of what it consists. The nature of such a political distinction is surely different from that of those others. It is independent of them and as such can speak clearly for itself.

27 Carl Schmitt, *The Leviathan in the State Theory of Thomas Hobbes: Meaning and Failure of a Political Symbol* (Chicago, IL: The University of Chicago Press, 2008), 42.

28 Carl Schmitt, 'Die Wendung zum totalen Staat' (1931), in *Positionen und Begriffe im Kampf mit Weimar-Genf-Versailles: 1923–1939* (Hamburg: Hanseatische Verlagsanstalt, 1940), 146.

29 Carl Schmitt, *The Concept of the Political. Expanded Edition* (Chicago, IL: .The University of Chicago Press, 2007), 22.

> The specific political distinction to which political actions and motives can be reduced is that between friend and enemy ... Insofar as it is not derived from other criteria, the antithesis of friend and enemy corresponds to the relatively independent criteria of other antitheses: good and evil in the moral sphere, beautiful and ugly in the aesthetic sphere, and so on. In any event it is independent, not in the sense of a distinct new domain, but in that it can neither be based on any one antithesis or any combination of other antitheses, not can it be traced to these.[30]

Schmitt thus aims at dissociating the political from the moral, aesthetic and other social spheres. The political does not have moral, economic or any other social foundations. It is reproduced through the irreducible distinction of 'friend' and 'enemy'.

The Suppression of Sovereignty by Legal Self-Reference: on Kelsen's Pure Legal Normativity

Despite many principal theoretical and political differences, Schmitt's critique of political integration by social values is surprisingly close to Kelsen's view of the social multitude and plurality which also goes beyond conventional views of the political morality and value integration of modern representative democracy.

Kelsen uses the sociological argument to claim that a democratic polity is typical of social (national, economic, religious and so on) conflicts and frictions.[31] He is highly critical of Schmitt's political theory and claims that democratic sovereignty as collective self-rule does not derive from the pre-existent unity of a political collectivity and its self-constitution in the existential sense. The alleged unity of a democratic collective subject is impossible to formulate through the pre-political and pre-constitutional self-reference of this constituent power of a democratic community.[32]

Kelsen admits that constitutional principles can be interpreted sociologically and that, for instance, majority rule appears to be informed by the sheer power of social integration. The application of these constitutional principles may be limited

---

30 Ibid., 26. It is noteworthy that Schmitt uses the 'good/evil' distinction when discussing the moral sphere rather than the 'good/bad' distinction which would be more reflexive of the secular character of modern morality. His terminology is thus closer to the terminology of theology. In this chapter, I shall keep the good/evil distinction whenever discussing Schmitt's theory and use the good/bad distinction only when generally discussing semantics and coding of the moral system.

31 Hans Kelsen, 'On the Essence and Value of Democracy' [1927] in *Weimar: A Jurisprudence of Crisis*, eds Arthur Jacobson and Bernhard Schlink (Berkeley, CA: University of California Press, 2000), 89.

32 See especially David Dyzenhaus, supra n. 1, 157.

by natural social barriers, such as culture and language.[33] Nevertheless, cultural divisions need to be left to the constitutional principle of political autonomy to avoid the abuses of majority rule and state centralization.

Kelsen thus firmly insists that the only deparadoxification of the substantive concept of the political community empowered by the legal force of a legal constitution is by converting the social multitude into the self-reference, self-constitution and pure self-grounding of the positive system of legal norms. Political concepts of democratic self-empowerment and constitutional representation become part of legal semantics regulated by the fictions of the basic norm and the first lawgiver. Democratic collective agency can be approached only regressively as the end point of legal attribution. The problem of the social multitude, which may be turned into constituent power and act politically, is eliminated, and discussions of the political will and acts of constituent power are replaced by the normative problem of the legal authorization of constituted power.[34]

Kelsen was absolutely clear about the links between the social multitude, the political unity of the people, and its legal representation in the democratic state when he stated:

> [I]t seems to be a basic condition of democracy that a *multitude of human beings* becomes a *unity* in it. For democracy, the "people" as a unity is even more essential, as it is not only, or not so much the *object* as the ruling *subject* – or should be, according to the idea ... Split by national, religious, and economic conflicts, that unity is – according to sociological findings – more a bundle of groups than a coherent mass of one and the same aggregate state. Only in a *normative* sense can one speak of a unity. For the unity of the people as a concord of thought, feeling, and desire, as a solidarity of interests, is an ethical political *postulate* declared to be real by the national or state ideology by means of a fiction that is generally used and therefore no longer thought about.[35]

According to Kelsen, the legal system can accommodate the political agency of constituent power only in terms of power exercised in conformity with the law, that is, as constitutionally self-referential constituted power. The general will of the political community and its political formation as the state's will are just conceptualizations of the normative order of the community. The state's will is an anthropomorphic expression of the community's order that normatively predetermines the behaviour of a multitude of individuals belonging to it.[36]

---

33 Hans Kelsen supra n. 31, 102–103.

34 For further comments on Kelsen's formalism and its European contextualisation, see John P. McCormick, *Weber, Habermas, and Transformation of the European State: Constitutional, Social, and Supranational Democracy* (Cambridge: Cambridge University Press, 2007), 132–133.

35 Hans Kelsen, supra n. 31, 89–90.

36 Ibid., 99.

The law can think of power and authority only as legal power and authorization and not some form of sovereign decision preceding and founding the law's normativity.[37]

Kelsen was always prominent among critics of the concept of sovereignty, and his call for its radical suppression in the name of pure theory of law is still considered one of the most complex and methodologically persuasive theoretical criticisms of sovereignty.[38] According to his theory, normative logic was expected to spare legal and political scholars the voluntarist extravagancies associated with political sovereignty. The political reality of conflicts, clashes and particular interests was to be eliminated from the realm of pure legal normativity and science.[39]

Kelsen's doctrine of the basic norm reformulated the self-referential paradoxes of constituted and constituent power – as the juridical self-reference of legal normativity. This conceptualization of sovereignty as a process of legal self-reference permanently communicated through the medium of legality was possible only by theoretically excluding all social and political facts and translating them into legal norms and exclusive legal concepts. Sovereignty was reduced to 'a quality of a normative order'[40] devoid of any political meaning, especially the meaning of popular sovereignty as politically constituent power preceding all legally normative qualification of the democratic state.

The constitutive function of the basic norm, therefore, consists of a retrospective normative interpretation of the empowering sovereign act of constituent power as an empowered act.[41] This reinterpretation of the exercise of constituent power as an already legally constituted exercise is the only way to bring legal order to its existence.[42] Kelsen argued that, from the perspective of legal logic, the political concept of self-empowerment was a contradiction in terms and that:

> [F]undamentally, only a *legal* element can be conceived more or less precisely as the unity of the people: the *unity* of the *state's legal order*, which rules the behaviour of the human beings subject to its norms. In this unity and through the content of its norms, the unity of the variety of human action is constituted, which the 'people' as an element of the state, as a specific social order, represents.[43]

37 Bert van Roermund, 'Authority and Authorisation', *Law and Philosophy* 19 (2000): 201.

38 Panu Minkkinen, 'Why is Law a Normative Discipline? On Hans Kelsen's "Normology"', *Res Publica* 11(3) (2005): 235.

39 James W. Harris, 'Kelsen's Concept of Authority', *The Cambridge Law Journal* 36 (1977): 353–363.

40 Hans Kelsen, *General Theory of Law and State* (Cambridge, MA: Harvard University Press, 1945), 383.

41 For this function, see Hans Lindahl, 'Dialectic and Revolution: Confronting Kelsen and Gadamer on Legal Interpretation', *Cardozo Law Review* 24 (2003): 798.

42 Stanley J. Paulson, 'The Weak Reading of Authority in Hans Kelsen's Pure Theory of Law', *Law and Philosophy* 19 (2000): 152–153.

43 Hans Kelsen, supra n. 31, 90.

In Kelsen's pure theory of law, the paradox of the normativity of the factual thus takes the form of the recursive self-reference of the legal system and gets reformulated as the facticity of the normative authorization of constituent power. The state is identified with the system of positive laws. Exclusivity, supremacy, independence and other aspects of sovereignty become operations of the legal system.

Self-Limiting Sovereignty and International Legal Monism

The concept of sovereignty as self-limitation of the state's power can already be found in Georg Jellinek's theory of public law and the state in which he proclaimed that sovereignty was 'the quality of a state in virtue of which it alone can be linked legally with its own will'.[44] Unlike the concept of sovereignty as exclusivity and political externality, Jellinek's notion of sovereignty drew on the self-obligation and limitation of power of the modern state emerging through the medium of constitutional law.

According to this view, exclusive sovereign power coincides with power to constitute legal obligations on exercising this power. However, Kelsen stretched Jellinek's concept of sovereignty as legal self-limitation further when he replaced it by the concept of legal authorization and defined in terms of international law.[45] Emphasizing legal normativity and connecting it to the universality and objectivity of the international legal domain, Kelsen sought to eliminate the nation state's institutional and territorial constraints dictated by sovereignty and make it part of a general theory of international legal monism.[46]

Following his earlier refutation of the concept of sovereignty, and in an effort to rebuild international law and politics after the Second World War, Kelsen, as early as in 1944, proposed that:

> [S]overeignty of the States, as subjects of international law, is the legal authority of the States under the authority of international law ... the State's sovereignty under international law is its legal independence from other States.[47]

---

44 Georg Jellinek, *Die Lehre von den Staatenverbindungen* (Vienna: Alfred Holder, 1882), 34. The translation quoted from Rafael Domingo, *The New Global Law* (Cambridge: Cambridge University Press, 2010), 69.

45 Jochen von Bernstorff, *The Public International Law Theory of Hans Kelsen: Believing in Universal Law* (Cambridge: Cambridge University Press, 2010), 44–56.

46 For very insightful comments on Kelsen's concept of international law, see Norberto Bobbio and Danilo Zolo, 'Hans Kelsen, The Theory of Law, and the International Legal System: A Talk', *European Journal of International Law* 9 (1998): 355.

47 Hans Kelsen, 'The Principle of Sovereign Equality of States as a Basis for International Organisation', *Yale Law Journal* 53 (1944): 208.

This view radically reformulates the international legal notion of sovereignty because the international legal order is not constituted by sovereign states. Rather, this order constitutes sovereignty as the specific rights and duties of particular states as subjects of international law. In this sense, sovereignty is the dynamic legal status of a state as defined by international law and therefore is part of the evolution of international law and its changes. Instead of representing the unrestricted will of the state, sovereignty is treated as the conceptualization of legal constraints on the freedom of state actions in the domain of international law.[48]

Kelsen's early conclusions actually coincided with the post-war shift from the principle of 'sovereignty' to the 'equality' of states in international law.[49] *The Charter of the United Nations* famously does not refer to 'sovereignty' but incorporates the principle of 'the sovereign equality' of all Member States of the United Nations in its Article 2(1). This sovereign equality of states clearly does not mean that all states are equal in terms of their power and international influence. Rather, it means the equality of all states as subjects of international law, equally constrained in their freedom of action and required to fulfil their legal obligations.

The historical process of juridifying international politics, indeed, was theoretically inspired by the Kelsenian concept of legal monism, the normative supremacy of international law and its instrumentalization as a tool of world 'peace through law'.[50] The result of this paradigm shift is the ever growing constitutionalization of international law. In this international legal and political order,

> Sovereign equality is the legal authority and autonomy of a state as defined and guaranteed by the constitution of the international community. It denotes the entitlement of a state, and the people constituting it, to autonomous development and self-responsibility within the limits set by international law.[51]

Despite regular and heavily loaded criticisms of Kelsen's normative formalism, many scholars acknowledge that the project of international legal monism was the first complex response to the social processes of globalization. According to these voices, Kelsen was the first scholar to ask seriously: 'What juridical source, what fundamental norm, and what command can support a new order

48 Hans Kelsen, *Principles of International Law* (New York: Rinehart & Comp, 1952), 438–443.

49 For further insights and comments, see Bardo Fassbender, 'Sovereignty and Constitutionalism in International Law', in *Sovereignty in Transition*, ed. Neil Walker (Oxford: Hart Publishing, 2003), 128–129.

50 Hans Kelsen, *Peace Through Law* (Chapel Hill, NC: The University of North Carolina Press, 1944).

51 Bardo Fassbender, supra n. 49, 131.

and avoid the impending descent into global disorder?'[52] Traditional views of international law as a domain of coexistence for modern territorial states, with their central governments exercising internal sovereignty over their territory and citizens and external sovereignty in international law (commonly described as state independence), were shaken by Kelsen's doctrine of sovereignty as legal authority.

A Political *Pluriverse* as a Critique of Normativism

Criticisms of Kelsen's pure legal normativism are often inspired by the decisionist theory of Carl Schmitt had already become the most prominent critic of Kelsen in the 1920s.[53] Schmitt's definition of sovereignty had profound consequences for both political and legal theory as it was intended, in equal measure, to define the political sphere's code of communication based on the friend/enemy distinction and also to challenge normativist views of the constitutional state and international law entirely regulated by legal norms, thus neutralizing the sovereign manifestations of political will.[54]

According to Schmitt, the fiction of the sovereignty of the constitution and its norms obscures the fact that sovereignty lies in the domain of genuinely political decisions eluding normative classifications. Arguing against modern positivism and legal normativism, Schmitt claimed that:

> [A] constitution is not based on a norm, whose justness would be the foundation of its validity. It is based on a political decision concerning the type and form of its own being, which stems from its political being. In contrast to any dependence on a normative or abstract justice, the word 'will' denotes the essentially existential character of this ground of validity.[55]

The idea of the absolute normative quality and the sovereign binding force of the constitution merely blurs a fundamental question regarding sovereignty which is always existentially superior to the norm, and precedes it.

Schmitt was very critical of Kelsen's normativism but his critique was different from that of classical liberal positivism and its doctrine of constitutional

52 Michael Hardt and Antonio Negri, *Empire* (Cambridge, MA: Harvard University Press, 2000), 8.

53 For original comparisons of Kelsen and Schmitt's theories of international law, see Anthony Carty, 'Interwar German Theories of International Law: The Psychoanalytical and Phenomenological Perspectives of Hans Kelsen and Carl Schmitt', *Cardozo Law Review* 16(3&4) (1994–1995): 1235.

54 Sylvie Delacroix, 'Schmitt's Critique of Kelsenian Normativism', *Ratio Juris* 18(1) (2005): 34.

55 Carl Schmitt, supra n. 21, 154.

sovereignty and the supremacy of value-neutral legality. According to Schmitt, Kelsen no longer believed in the liberal sovereignty of reason, and elaborated on a rather contradictory normativist theory which completely eliminated political conceptualizations of sovereignty and continued to build on the concept of the sovereign constitution. It treated the sovereign constitution merely as a set of more or less general constitutional norms alterable by a constitutional process. The absolute sovereign constitution was thus legally imaginable only as the relative constitution of individual sets of norms and processes.[56]

Kelsen radically changed legal positivist thinking because he rejected the common view of law as a system of rules issued by a political sovereign; instead, he considered it a hierarchically self-referential system of norms authorizing officials to make decisions and held together by the fiction of the pure basic norm. To this theory, Schmitt critically responded that Kelsen wanted politics to disappear completely from law, so that the machine of a legal order could run itself as a closed and normatively self-constituted system.[57]

According to Schmitt, sovereignty is the state's *will to decide*. The constitutional order does not reside in the normative structure of legality but organically grows out of the concrete life and actual existence of a particular collectivity. The state's unity and order are manifested in the power and energy of a political unit. The state as constitution, therefore, coincides with the principle of the dynamic emergence of political unity, its internal contestations and constantly renewed formation. The constitution as a 'form of forms' (*forma formarum*) is not static and corresponds to the intrinsic dynamic of collective political life, with its permanent conflicts, ruptures, self-constitution and self-reflection of its unity 'always arising anew'.[58]

Schmitt's radical critique of normativism from the perspective of political existentialism and life philosophy subsequently raises several important methodological and ontological problems, especially the problem of will as an intrinsic part of the internal structure of a norm, and the problem of the modern state's sovereignty and its ontological status. This problem becomes even more acute vis-à-vis Schmitt's remark that the 'political world is a *pluriverse*, not a universe',[59] indicating that state sovereignty needs to be considered part of political plurality and its exceptional status tested against the general political distinction of friend and enemy and its many manifestations in political life. It is therefore important to establish Schmitt's view as regards the position of state sovereignty within the plurality of political structures.

56 Ibid., 106.
57 Carl Schmitt, supra n. 4, 48.
58 Carl Schmitt, supra n. 21, 60–61.
59 Carl Schmitt, supra n. 29, 53. Emphasis added.

Legal Legitimacy and the State's Self-Constitution

Schmitt obviously was a stern critic of the structural and organizational plurality of modern politics and dismissed political and legal theories of pluralism. He famously treated pluralist theories of state as a theory of 'the dissolution or rebuttal of the state'.[60] At the same time, he nevertheless acknowledged the pluriversalistic structure of the political sphere. Though falling short of any general sociological outline and systematic methodology, and despite regular criticisms of the sociological positivism and methodology of institutional and organizational pluralism, Schmitt's decisionist theory effectively accommodates Weber's sociological concepts and theoretical views of the state, power and law.

Schmitt particularly relied on Weber's theory of secularization in his critique of 'political theology' in which he critically claimed that major concepts of modern theory of the state including sovereignty and its representation were merely secularized theological concepts.[61] Furthermore, Schmitt's political philosophy was profoundly informed by Weber's theory of modernization as the permanent growth of expert knowledge, instrumental rationality and technicalization.[62] Schmitt even agreed with Weber's view of the growing bureaucratization of society and argued that the increasing role of expert knowledge and legality enhances the legitimacy of presidential decrees which turn out to be more stable than parliamentary acts.[63] However, he strongly rejected Weber's plain formula of legitimacy by legality and pursued the goal of legitimizing political domination by recourse to the Hobbesian idea of political consent and the possibility of political resistance to an illegitimate political system.

Schmitt's ambivalent use of Weber's sociological views is detectable in his analysis of *Leviathan*, considering it simultaneously a 'great man' and a 'machine'.[64] Schmitt elaborated on these Cartesian motives in Hobbes and critically perceived political modernization as a tendency towards the instrumentalization and technical bureaucratization of the political sphere.[65] The state is a product of the technical age that is both 'body and soul, a *homo artificialis*, and, as such, a machine'.[66] The state machinery and its engineer-creator are the same, namely, men, and legality is established as the factual mode of operation of the state machinery.

---

60 Ibid., 44.

61 Luc J. Wintgens, 'Sovereignty and Representation', *Ratio Juris* 14(3) (2001): 273.

62 For comparisons of Schmitt and Weber, see Catherine Colliot-Thelene, 'Carl Schmitt versus Max Weber: Juridical Rationality and Economic Rationality', in *The Challenge of Carl Schmitt*, ed. Chantal Mouffe (London: Verso, 1999), 139–140.

63 See, for instance, Carl Schmitt, *Legality and Legitimacy* (Durham, Duke University Press, 2004), 89.

64 John P. McCormick, supra n. 3, 271.

65 Chris Thornhill, *Political Theory in Modern Germany: An Introduction* (Cambridge: Polity, 2000), 78.

66 Carl Schmitt, supra n. 27, 98.

According to Schmitt, '... [t]he state itself changes into a positivist system of legality. The *legislator humanus* became a *machina legislatoria*'.[67] Modern legitimacy through legality is possible only when the sovereign legislator is transformed into the legislative machinery. Modern legal positivism and normativist theory are merely theoretical reflections and justifications of this drive towards legality as the state technique.[68] Leviathan as the godlike sovereign of the state was historically destroyed from within by the process of political modernization which led to the increasing technicalization of state organization. Legality became a property of bureaucracy.[69]

Nevertheless, despite all criticisms, Schmitt effectively used Weber's sociological categories and concepts when he sought to prove that state sovereignty is not reducible to a calculable system of legal rules and is defined by its power to exceed them. Schmitt was influenced by Weber's view that the most fundamental questions of politics were left unregulated by the modern system of positive law and had to be resolved through the medium of political conventions and internal rationality of the political system.[70] However, he exploited the theoretical contradictions of Weber's notion of legitimacy by legality and treated legitimacy as the very antithesis of legality.

According to Schmitt, *belief* in the legitimacy of political *will* precedes belief in its *reason* and 'the normative fiction of a closed system of legality emerges in a striking and undeniable opposition to the legitimacy of an instance of will that is actually present and in conformity with law'.[71] The internal tension between legality and legitimacy is thus finally reconciled in the sovereign, who 'is highest legislator, judge, and commander simultaneously. He is also the final source of legality and the ultimate foundation of legitimacy'.[72] In the sovereign's decision on exception, legality is suspended and political will is believed to be, and identified as, the legitimate expression of the unity of a polity.[73] The decision requires no legitimation by an ethical or legal norm and makes sense purely in terms of political existence.

This type of political unity cannot legitimize itself as a just order.[74] Its legitimacy is given by its very existence and its power dynamically to seek its permanent renewal and self-constitution. In other words, the legitimacy of a constitution of the

---

67 Ibid., 65.

68 Ibid., 45.

69 Carl Schmitt, *The Nomos of the Earth in the International Law of the Jus Publicum Europaeum* (New York: Telos Press, 2003), 71.

70 Max Weber, *Economy and Society 1* (Berkeley, CA: University of California Press, 1978), 330.

71 Carl Schmitt, supra n. 63, 6.

72 Ibid., 5–6.

73 John P. McCormick, 'The Dilemmas of Dictatorship: Carl Schmitt and Constitutional Emergency Powers', *The Canadian Journal of Law & Jurisprudence* 10 (1997): 163.

74 Carl Schmitt, supra n. 21, 136.

state is defined by its political self-reference and self-constitution, uncontaminated by legal and/or moral normativity.

The State, Power and Social Plurality

According to Weber, '[T]he assumption that a state "exists" only if the coercive means of the political community are superior to *all* other communities, is not sociological'.[75] The state is a political organization emerging in the process of functional differentiation of economy, politics and law which establishes political community by monopolizing and legitimizing violence over a particular territory and persons living on it either permanently, or temporarily. Reflecting on this differentiation, structural co-evolution and interdependence of modern economy, law and politics, Weber summarized that '... [a]n economic system, especially of the modern type, could certainly not exist without a legal order with very special features which could not develop except in the frame of a public legal order ...'[76] According to him, however, there are other agencies and institutions, such as churches with their legal orders and professional bodies with their codes of conduct, and the modern state regulated by legal rules is just one of many organizations of power in society.

Unlike Weber, Schmitt believed in the very special function of sovereign state power ultimately to delineate the political sphere,[77] and criticized legal and political doctrines which treat the state as just another organization of society and, as in Gierke's theory of association, 'as one association equal to other associations'.[78] Gierke and Preuss's association theories of law considered sovereignty a residue of the absolutist and authoritarian state and argued that the final source of law is the life of the people, and that the state is but the political organ of the people.[79] This democratically constituted community could manage without sovereignty, and its ultimate form was the legal consciousness of the people.

For Schmitt, these politically democratic and socially pluralistic views had the following consequences for the theory of state sovereignty: they led either to the totalization of the state penetrating all societal spheres,[80] or the pluralization of the state vis-à-vis the existing social plurality and the individual's freedom and

75 Max Weber, supra n. 70, 316.

76 Ibid., 336.

77 For similarities between Weber and Schmitt, see, for instance, Chris Thornhill, 'Carl Schmitt after the Deluge', *History of European Ideas* 26 (2001): 235.

78 Carl Schmitt, supra n. 29, 25.

79 For a critique, see Carl Schmitt, supra n. 4, 24–25.

80 Schmitt associates this theory of the total state with Rudolf Smend's integration theory. See Carl Schmitt, supra n. 29, 25.

association with a variety of social associations, such as church, nation, family and so on.[81]

Nevertheless, in *The Concept of the Political* published in 1932, Schmitt came much closer to Weber's sociological analysis of social power and the recognition of social plurality because he considered the state as a political organization of power with capacity ultimately to establish who is considered the enemy and to decide on the state of exception. Schmitt's criticisms of pluralist theories of the state, law and politics are thus accompanied by a much more favourable contextualization of state sovereignty as part of a self-constituted, self-reproductive and self-referential political pluriverse. This contextualization actually resembles Weber's view of politics as the struggle and power as being everywhere and defining all areas of social life.[82]

As early as 1922, in his treatise *Political Theology*, Schmitt treated sovereignty as a manifestation of real life when stating:

> [T]he exception is more interesting than the rule. The rule proves nothing; the exception proves everything: It confirms not only the rule but also its existence, which derives only from the exception. In the exception the power of real life breaks through the crust of a mechanism that has become torpid by repetition.[83]

According to Schmitt, state sovereignty feeds on the existential combat between friend and enemy. Its purpose is constantly to reproduce itself through deciding who is the enemy and what measures of political power need to be used against this enemy. Sovereignty, therefore, is one of many power operations making the friend/enemy distinction.

Schmitt's Existentialism and Cultural Critique of Modernity

Schmitt argues that theoretical differences ultimately circulate around the relationship between the state and society.[84] He associates anarchism with the political fallacy of believing in the natural goodness of man which leads to the radical denial of state authority and government. Furthermore, he alleges that the same moral classification of politics is typical of liberalism that similarly aims at making the state serve society. Schmitt even quotes Thomas Paine's saying that 'society is the result of our reasonably regulated needs, government is the result of our wickedness'[85] to

81 In this respect, Schmitt is particularly critical of G.D.H. Cole, J.N. Figgis and Harold Laski's theory of pluralism. See Ibid., 40–41.

82 Max Weber, 'The Nation State and Economic Policy', in *Political Writings*, Max Weber, (Cambridge: Cambridge University Press, 1994), 16.

83 Carl Schmitt, supra n. 4, 15.

84 Carl Schmitt, supra n. 29, 60.

85 Ibid., 61.

dismiss these theories of 'good' human nature and reason spontaneously organizing our society and operating against the wicked and corrupting power of politics.

Schmitt claimed that the general need of political domination was real and existential and stripped of all symbols and metaphors. The plurality of power operations makes the sovereign state an indispensable authority in political matters. However, this concept of the state also refers to the general human condition and thus ends up in the same normative claims which Schmitt so vigorously criticized in liberal theories of the state and politics.

It would be difficult to find a more outright admission that all those criticisms of modern secularization, political and administrative machinery, instrumental legality and bureaucratic order have strong undercurrents of a cultural normative critique than in the final sentences of Schmitt's essay, *The Age of Neutralisations and Depoliticisations*, which read:

> [W]e recognize the pluralism of spiritual life and know that the central domain of spiritual existence cannot be a neutral domain and that it is wrong to solve a political problem with the antithesis of organic and mechanistic, life and death. A life which has only death as its antithesis is no longer life but powerlessness and helplessness. Whoever knows no other enemy than death and recognizes in his enemy nothing more than an empty mechanism is nearer to death than life. The comfortable antithesis of the organic and the mechanistic is itself something crudely mechanistic. A grouping which sees on the one side only spirit and life and on the other only death and mechanism signifies nothing more than a renunciation of the struggle and amounts to nothing more than a romantic lament. For life struggles not with death, spirit not with spiritlessness; spirit struggles with spirit, life with life, and out of the power of an integral understanding of this arises the order of human things. *Ab integro nascitur ordo.*[86]

These sentences reveal a profound contradiction in Schmitt's treatment of the plurality of the spheres/systems of modern society. While criticizing the depoliticization strategies of morality and economy, Schmitt admits that these strategies themselves are a form of politicization transformable to the friend/enemy distinction. While the good/evil distinction cannot be considered political, the friend/enemy politicization can strategically adopt the language and antitheses of morality, economy, aesthetics and any other social sphere.

As Leo Strauss correctly observed,[87] Schmitt was critical of political modernity and sought to critique it thoroughly and replace it with another concept of culture

86 Carl Schmitt, 'The Age of Neutralisations and Depoliticisations' [1929], in Carl Schmitt, supra n. 29, 95–96.

87 For insightful comments on the relationship between Schmitt and Strauss, see Heinrich Meier, *Carl Schmitt and Leo Strauss: The Hidden Dialogue* (Chicago, IL: The University of Chicago Press, 1995), 33–35.

specifically based on the concept of the political.[88] Schmitt's claim that the conceptual distinction of friend and enemy is not metaphorical or symbolic and needs to be understood in its 'concrete and existential sense'[89] means in effect that the enemy should exclusively be treated as the other – the stranger, existentially different and alien to a political community. The word 'combat' joins these existential notions of friend and enemy to refer to the possibility of killing and war that 'follows from enmity'.[90]

Schmitt discusses the distinction of friend and enemy in a manner in which the enemy takes precedence over the friend and the existential context of political reality is defined by the potential for a fight.[91] This view was strengthened by the fact that Schmitt actually analysed the potential of other distinctions, most of all the moral distinction good and evil, to be used in the political contest and copy the 'existentiality' of the distinction of friend and enemy.[92]

This politicization of the non-political has overtones of a fundamental cultural critique which Strauss insightfully considers to be Schmitt's attempt to overturn Hobbes's original notion of a culture of civility as transgressing the original state of nature. Strauss thus comments that '[t]he political that Schmitt brings to bear as fundamental is the "state of nature" that underlies every culture; Schmitt restores the Hobbesian concept of the state of nature to a place of honor'[93] and concludes that '[w]hereas Hobbes in an unliberal world accomplishes the founding of liberalism, Schmitt in a liberal world undertakes the critique of liberalism'.[94]

Schmitt's analysis of the differentiation of the political from the social environment and its closure by the friend/enemy distinction thus represents a powerful example of political self-reference which subsequently becomes obscured by existential concepts of life philosophy.[95]

The Ontology of the Decline of Modern Society, or the Functional Self-Reference of Politics?

The quotation above from *The Age of Neutralisations and Depoliticisations*, in which Schmitt cites Virgil's '*Ab integro nascitur ordo*', summarizes his belief in a concrete order of political community that is permanently reborn and reconstituted

88 Leo Strauss, 'Notes on Carl Schmitt's Concept of the Political', in Carl Schmitt, supra n. 29, 87.

89 Carl Schmitt, supra n. 29, 27.

90 Ibid., 29.

91 Leo Strauss, supra n. 88, 88.

92 Heinrich Meier, supra n. 18, 29.

93 Leo Strauss, supra n. 88, 90.

94 Ibid., 92–93.

95 Richard Wolin, 'Carl Schmitt, Political Existentialism, and the Total State', *Theory and Society* 19(4) (1990): 389.

from its life struggles. These struggles are an intrinsic part of the polity's organic life, impossible to contain by a pre-existent legal constitution or a bureaucratic order of the modern 'state machine'.

Modernization as cultural decline and political danger is an ontological hypothesis in Schmitt's political and legal philosophy. Indeed, this philosophy was part of an intellectual milieu at the beginning of the twentieth century, depicting and warning against the cultural decline of modern European civilization, especially its mechanization, bureaucratization, technicalization, instrumentalization, enforced (political) conformity (*Gleichschaltung*), loss of spirituality, specialization and excessive division of labour and other processes leading to the disintegration of values. However, these criticisms do not have much in common with conventional political and cultural conservatism because they recognize the impossibility of a return to pre-modern political traditions.

Like Walter Benjamin, Hermann Broch, Sigmund Freud, Edmund Husserl, Martin Heidegger and many other European thinkers, novelists and artists of the time,[96] Carl Schmitt believed that 'the Modern Era is the bridge that leads from the reign of irrational faith to the reign of the irrational in a world without faith'.[97] According to this view, the role of the irrational is much greater than modern people would acknowledge in their individual lives and in the life of our polities in general. Modern rationality gradually eliminated most of pre-modern political traditions but this victorious march of human reason through European history was marked by a total victory of irrational forces, with violence and wars seizing the continent. Traditions and their political transcendence simply ceased to be respected by modern society in which it became ever more difficult to satisfy a human call for social solidarity, political loyalty and individual sacrifice.

The unity of humankind proclaimed by great revolutions of the eighteenth century and the Enlightenment's ultimate values of liberty, equality and fraternity did not lead to the peaceful coexistence of different countries and peoples. Instead, modern history has become inseparable from the machinery of wars administered by states, turning individual citizens into the indistinguishable whole of 'human resources'. The profound experience of the First World War was that an individual could not escape the war machine, and the unity of humankind became the unity of human masses marching towards industrially executed death. What Husserl called the life-world became obscured by the modern rationalistic reduction of the world to a mere object of scientific investigation, technical domination and industrial or military conquest. Furthermore, modern reality has become obscured by symbols and phantasmata different from traditional cultures, yet no less powerful and considered real by modern people. The system of modern political symbols

96 See, for instance, Richard Wolin, *Heidegger's Children: Hannah Arendt, Karl Lowith, Hans Jonas and Herbert Marcuse* (Princeton, NJ: Princeton University Press, 2001), 227.

97 Milan Kundera, *The Art of the Novel* (London: Faber and Faber, revised edition 2005), 54.

replaced old traditions and substituted for their old forms of loyalty new forms of identity and the submission of individuals, driving them to total ideological and cultural wars. The other side became seen as an absolute evil that needed to be eradicated from political life and exterminated from the political community's living space (*Lebensraum*).

Schmitt abhorred the weakness of the Weimar parliamentary republic and its inability to deal with political violence and eliminate the destructive force of totalitarian ideologies and phantasmata which made political opponents 'the enemy of the people' and/or 'the enemy of the nation'. He considered this tendency towards totalitarianism the very symptom of modernity's mechanistic nature, replacing the exceptionality of the state with the totality of society. According to him, the Italian fascist or Russian Bolshevik totalitarian states were just specific examples of the ultimate bureaucratization of modern politics and the instrumentalization of legality.

Leaving aside all personal motives, political criticisms and moral condemnations, Schmitt's association with the Nazi regime and politics was thus philosophically motivated by its promise of a *new order* rather than a *totalitarian state* embracing and administering the whole of social life.[98] Schmitt's complicated and controversial relationship with Nazi power explains why his philosophy continues to draw the attention of radical scholars of both the Left and the Right. His ontological premise that a concrete, living order of a sovereign people precedes the normative order of law remains a powerful tool for scholars critical of various forms of legal and political liberalism and its 'juridification' of politics in particular and human life in general. It continues to be inspiration for all kinds of speculative political and legal existentialism and normative theories of constitutional politics.

The Self-Reference, Differentiation and Closure of Globalized Law and Politics beyond the Value Integration

Schmitt's decisionist theory represents a contradictory, yet fascinating example of attributing functional unity and self-reference to the political system through the concept of sovereignty. While Kelsen correctly criticized the notion of the existential and real unity of constituent power as the basis of all legally and constitutionally authorized powers in the state, Schmitt was much more reflective of the political role of the social multitude and collective volitional acts as an intrinsic part of modern constitutionalism and the self-referential legal order.

Kelsen's view was based on neutralization of the political multitude and its constituent power by the principle of representation and constitutional authorization. His description of modern law as a normatively closed system conceptualized by the fictional construct of the basic norm is one of the most persuasive examples of

98 Heinrich Meier, supra n. 18, 5.

legal self-reference. Nevertheless, the originality of Kelsen's description of legal self-reference is matched by Schmitt's analysis of the concept of the political and sovereignty which attributes functional unity and self-reference to the political system in the same manner in which Kelsen's concept of the basic norm attributes functional unity and self-reference to the legal system.

Schmitt realized that power operations distinguishing between friend and enemy are too numerous in the political pluriverse and therefore do not provide for operative precision and the capacity to turn the political sphere into a closed system. The use of power is not politically limited and other social antitheses can be reformulated as the friend/enemy distinction. The system's unity therefore needs additional structural and semantic support that would lead to the self-reference and self-description of political communication. For Schmitt, it is exactly the concept of the state and state sovereignty that facilitates this additional support.[99]

Analysing theoretical and conceptual controversies and arguments historically arising from the debate between Kelsen and Schmitt, it is possible to achieve a better general understanding of the evolving semantics of the functional differentiation, closure and self-reference of modern law and politics and the different theoretical conceptualizations of social and political pluralism. The whole debate, its legacy and profound influence on political and legal theory can be reinterpreted as typical examples of the semantic differentiation and incompatibility of legal normativity and sovereign power.[100] While originally addressed by Kelsen and Schmitt within limits of the modern nation state and international law, this differentiation has become a prominent feature of the current systems of post-national globalized law and politics. This is the reason why both Kelsen and Schmitt continue to semantically inspire contemporary legal and political theories despite profound structural changes of globalized society and the nation state's transformation in global politics and law.

The Kelsen-Schmitt debate thus made three decisive contributions to current theories of globalized law and politics. Apart from the differentiation of law and politics and their semantics, Kelsen and Schmitt contributed to the theoretical construction of both law and politics as closed self-referential systems with their internal medium of communication and self-reproductive operations. Finally, both Kelsen and Schmitt showed persuasively that neither law nor politics could be fully integrated into, and operatively controlled by, an ultimately superior system of moral values.

Eliminating the concept of sovereignty from the legal system, Kelsen effectively states that *law is not politics*. In the same argumentative style, Schmitt uses his concept of sovereignty to argue that *politics is not law* and that juridification of the political represents one of the greatest, yet most characteristic risks of

99 For critical evaluation, see Chris Thornhill, 'Niklas Luhmann, Carl Schmitt and the Modern Form of the Political', *European Journal of Social Theory* 10(4) (2007): 499.

100 Pavlos Eleftheriadis, 'Law and Sovereignty', *Law and Philosophy* 29 (2010): 539.

modernity. Following these arguments, the modern systems of politics and law can subsequently be treated as functionally differentiated and the constitutional state as a social organization through which this differentiation operates in modern society. Earlier theories commonly using political concepts to define legal institutions and operations, such as Austin's definition of law as the sovereign's command, which inspired the whole tradition of analytical jurisprudence, have to be abandoned because they fail to grasp the structural complexities of modern law and politics. They are too simple and eclectic and need to be replaced by more elaborate theories reflecting on the systemic differences and autonomy of the systems of law and politics in globalized society.

As regards the assumption of both theorists that law and politics need to be conceptualized as semantically and operatively *closed systems*, it turns out that the social function of Kelsen's basic norm as a conceptual fiction is to protect legal communication from the social environment and to facilitate the self-reference and self-organization of the system of positive law. In the same manner, Schmitt's critique of Kelsen's legalism and Weber's concept of legitimacy by legality leads to the self-constitution and self-reference of the political system by means of the sovereign's operative capacity to decide on the state of exception. The supremacy of power over law, which defines the concept of sovereignty, closes the political system in the same way in which Kelsen's basic norm closes the legal system founded on the supremacy of law over power.[101]

Finally, the third profound contribution of the Kelsen-Schmitt debate to the current theory of constitutional sovereignty is the *elimination of* the concept of the ultimate *value integration* of society. The closure of political semantics by the sovereign's power to decide on the state of exception and the similar closure of legal semantics by the fiction of the basic norm effectively protect law and politics from becoming morally substantive systems embracing the totality of society – global, European or national.

The Emergence of a Social Theory of Sovereignty from the Kelsen/ Schmitt Debate

In the debate between Kelsen and Schmitt, the four primal concepts of contemporary post-metaphysical constitutional and legal theoretical debates and semantics – sovereignty, legality, governance and the social multitude – had already been present and informed the general communication and specific paradoxes of the systems of modern law and politics. Unfortunately, neither Kelsen, nor Schmitt fully elaborated the problem of the functional differentiation of modern law and politics, their operative closure, systemic autonomy, interdependence and structural coupling.

101 Norberto Bobbio, *The Future of Democracy* (Minneapolis, MN: The University of Minnesota Press, 1987), 138–156.

Kelsen believed that the basic norm can replace political will and social facts and the contingencies of politics through the purely normative architecture and hierarchy of positive law. Criticizing this strong belief in legal normativity and its capacity to neutralize political conflicts and frictions, Schmitt similarly concluded that the political precedes the legal and constituent power of a polity, dominates over its constitution and determines its legal force by means of the sovereign's decision. Both theories thus wrongly assumed that systemic and social differences and the risk of substantively moral foundations to law and politics can be mitigated by a superior semantics of either legal normativity, or political decision-making power.

Apart from this failure to recognize the loss of hierarchy and centrality in functionally differentiated society, the non-redundancy of specific systems and their growing interdependence, another of Kelsen and Schmitt's theoretical shortcomings was that they both considered the social multitude and plurality merely as a space to be contained by either legal or political systems and not as their coexisting social environment. For instance, the famous statement that 'law is law' loses its meaning if this mode of self-reference is not contextualized against the communicative interdependence of law and other social systems including politics and morality. The statement that 'sovereign is he who decides on the state of exception' also falls short of recognizing the systemic plurality of modern society and the non-hierarchical autonomy of the political system. For Kelsen, social plurality was merely evidence of the inability of the constituent power of the people to govern beyond the realm of legal rules or without the sovereign's unbound will. Similarly, Schmitt did not think that the process of depoliticization by law, morality and economy was just a specific example of the most general risk of social de-differentiation and the conflation of different social systems.

According to Schmitt, modern sociology has accommodated functions previously associated with theories of natural law and rejected sovereignty as a residue of the absolutist state. In modern society, demands for justice and theoretical constructions of legal ideals are commonly formulated in the positivistic language of sociology and particular interests of different social groups and classes. Schmitt, therefore, criticized sociological pluralist theories of the state and defended the autonomy and uniqueness of the political against other social domains, especially economy, law, religion and ethics.[102] The state with its sovereignty was not supposed to be just one of many social associations and the theory of sovereignty should not end up in the trap of pluralism itself.

Unlike Schmitt, Kelsen was primarily preoccupied with criticisms of the sociological method as regards its incompatibility with the method of normative legal science.[103] Nevertheless, he also highlighted close links between natural law and sociology because of their common attempt to identify objective laws of

102 Ibid., 44.

103 Hans Kelsen, *Society and Nature: A Sociological Inquiry* (London: Kegan, Trench, Trubner & Comp, 1946).

human life and to deduce the just order of political society from them. According to Kelsen, the methodological fallacy of the confusion of descriptive and normative statements about social reality is typical of sociology and its treatment of the laws of historical and social evolution as a means of political justification makes it close to the classical natural law doctrine.[104]

Both criticisms of the sociology of law and politics, indeed, are still relevant today and applicable to the variety of contemporary political and social theories of law. Nevertheless, this chapter shows that both Schmitt's definition of the sovereign and Kelsen's jurisprudential fictions of the basic norm and the first lawgiver had also been strongly influenced by Weber's sociological definition of political domination as the territorially constrained exercise of the monopoly of political violence that involves the supremacy of legal norms and the power of authorities to enforce their will in a polity. The methodological difference between general sociology and jurisprudence, therefore, is not as fundamental as claimed by both Kelsen and Schmitt.

Furthermore, EU and global contextualization of the constitutional state makes it impossible to exclusively apply either the Kelsenian paradigm of international legal monism, or the Schmittian concept of political sovereignty unless one pursues the speculative goal of constructing either a cosmopolitan legal utopia, or a dystopia implied by a permanent state of global political exception.

Political and legal sociology actually can avoid the epistemological traps, internal contradictions and conceptual shortcomings of juridical normativist reductionism and decisionist or institutionalist theories of sovereignty. Kelsen and Schmitt elaborate elegant conceptualizations and criticisms of the modern state, its sovereignty and law, which can be sociologically reconsidered and reconceptualized within the context of a functionally differentiated global political and legal pluriverse. The semantics of the political and legal systems subsequently needs to conceptualize the constitutional state and sovereignty not as the ultimate end of European and global politics and law but as one of the meeting points of their communication and structural coupling. In the Weberian manner, one can thus conclude that the constitutional state has become, and therefore needs to be studied as, just one of many organizations of European and global society.

104 Hans Kelsen, 'The Natural-Law Doctrine Before the Tribunal of Science', in *What is Justice? Justice, Law, and Politics in the Mirror of Science*, Hans Kelsen (Berkeley, CA: University of California Press, 1957), 159–166.

Chapter 4
No More Sovereignty?: On the Concepts of Legal Pluralism, Living Law and Societal Constitutionalism

Recent theories of global political order, the constitutional democratic state and cosmopolitan human rights commonly emphasize the plain fact of legal, political and ethical plurality. A collective subject, the people, is characterized as intrinsically pluralistic and its members as enjoying multiple identities often neglected or even suppressed by the existing constitutional form. Society becomes another name for the sovereign people and criticisms of constitutionalism consequently are a lot more informed, if not guided by, the sociological methodology so heavily criticized by both Schmitt and Kelsen. In this legal pluralistic approach, *the multitude of society replaces the unity of sovereignty*.

The concept of legal pluralism often signifies the absence of sovereignty. Theories of legal pluralism are commonly perceived as critical of the very concept of sovereignty because the plurality of legal orders and regimes indicates the absence of the ultimate rule of recognition, decision-making power or the basic norm. They are equally critical of state law as a supreme legal order backed by political deliberation and decision-making and emphasize the role of non-state legal orders, agents and organizations.

The recent popularity, great variety and conceptual innovations of legal and constitutional pluralism theories often lead to the academic ritualization and banalization of the very concept of pluralism. Theories of legal pluralism are thus currently typical of the differentiation between the 'weak' juristic concept of legal pluralism drawing on the state legal systems and the 'strong' concept of legal pluralism drawing on sociological and anthropological perspectives of law.[1] In this chapter, I, therefore, pursue the goal of analysing transformations of the concept of sovereignty by critically examining and reconceptualizing theories of global legal and constitutional pluralism. I argue that John Griffiths's original dichotomy of 'weak' and 'strong' pluralism has to be reassessed because even 'weak' jurisprudential theories contain extremely useful sociological analyses of the internal differentiation and operations of specific legal orders, their overlapping, parallel validity, structural irritations and collisions at subnational, national, supranational and transnational levels.

1 John Griffiths, 'What is Legal Pluralism?', *Journal of Legal Pluralism and Unofficial Law* 24 (1986): 5–8.

In the second half of the chapter, I focus on more radical theories of legal pluralism, criticizing the very concept of official state law and drawing on Ehrlich's sociological notion of living law and spontaneously evolving normative orders and regulatory regimes. I particularly assess Teubner's concepts of societal constitutionalism, global constitutional fragmentation and civil constitutions as socio-legal concepts radically reformulating the concepts of global law and politics. However, Teubner's emphasis on non-state civil processes of self-constitutionalization leads to the virtual ignorance of power as medium of global politics and the constitutional sovereign state as the persisting social organization of a structural coupling between globalized law and politics. The concept of civil constitutions and its assumption of post-sovereign global law and politics thus depoliticize the problems of constitutionalism. Responding to these theoretical challenges, I subsequently reformulate the question of sovereignty as a sociological problem of complex power operations communicated through the constitutional state's organization and reconfigured within the supranational and transnational legal and political frameworks and their legitimation strategies.

Globalization and Theories of Legal Pluralism

Despite many differences, some themes have been common to all theories of legal pluralism and the remark that '[L]egal pluralism concerns the idea that more than one legal system operate in a single political unit'[2] can be taken as the minimum common understanding of legal pluralism. Theories of legal pluralism generally criticize the concept of law as a normative order sanctioned by the state's monopoly on political violence. They are equally critical of a 'creeping monism'[3] in international law. While monistic views look for a clear specification of legal authority and rules of legal validity, pluralistic views claim that these specifications are impossible in the presence of more legal systems operating in the same social environment. Theories of legal pluralism are particularly critical of state legal centralism that considers the law of the state to be the only form of law generally applicable to all persons and administered by state institutions. They criticize methodological individualism, instrumentalism and the assumption of the state's normative monopoly as typical failures of theories of state legal centralism.[4]

2 Boaventura de Sousa Santos, *Towards a New Legal Common Sense. 2nd edition* (London: Butterworths, 2002), 89.

3 Melissa A. Waters, 'Creeping Monism: The Judicial Trend toward Interpretive Incorporation of Human Rights Treaties', *Columbia Law Review* 107 (2007): 628.

4 See, for instance, John Griffiths, 'Legal Pluralism and the Theory of Legislation: With Special Reference to the Regulation of Euthanasia', in *Legal Polycentricity: Consequences of Pluralism in Law*, eds Hanne Petersen and Henrik Zahle (Aldershot: Dartmouth, 1998), 206.

Reflecting on the paradoxes and contradictions of legal globalization, Roger Cotterrell, for instance, notes:

> Globalisation's gift to law, for the moment, is a high degree of juristic chaos and indeterminate foundations of regulatory authority in many transnational fields. Transnational law is a work in progress without a basic norm or rule of recognition, a Hartian system of rules or Kelsenian hierarchy of norms, or any other juristic model of unity and authority.[5]

Global society supports anything but Kelsen's monistic belief in one ultimate basic norm overcoming the duality of national legal systems and international law. Current legal structures and networks are characterized by contestations, fragmentations and differences. In this society, different legal systems coexist and make independent claims of legal validity and authority.[6] The ultimate validity of the basic norm is replaced by a multiplicity of simultaneously valid basic norms of different and mutually independent legal orders – something considered logically impossible by Kelsen.[7]

The constitutional state as a typically modern form of political and legal organization cannot withstand the social pressure of globalization, and modern structural co-evolution of the state and law is replaced by new forms of global social organization of 'global law without a state'.[8] The plurality of laws in global society, therefore, constitutes a highly contested legal reality, unlimited by the constitutional structures and symbolism typical of the modern nation state[9] and often driven by the specific regulatory demands of non-state legal sectors.[10]

While supranational organizations, such as the EU, tend to establish their specific hierarchies as monistic claims of normative supremacy and a single rule of recognition determining their relationship to other (Member State) legal orders operating within the same field, transnational legal settings recognize different legal orders and their specific criteria of validity without seeking logical hierarchies and general authority.[11] Unlike concepts of supranational law and politics, which still accommodate some hierarchies and asymmetrical relationships typical of national and international law, and stretch them further by limiting state sovereignty,

5 Roger Cotterrell, 'Transnational Communities and the Concept of Law', *Ratio Juris* 21 (2008): 9.

6 See, for instance, Sally E. Merry, 'Legal Pluralism', *Law and Society Review* 22(5) (1998): 869.

7 Hans Kelsen, *General Theory of Law and State* (New York: Russell&Russell, 1961), 363.

8 Gunther Teubner, ed., *Global Law Without a State* (Aldershot: Dartmouth, 1997).

9 David Nelken, 'An Email from Global Bukowina', *International Journal of Law in Context* 3(3) (2007): 189.

10 Mireille Delmas-Marty, *Ordering Pluralism. A Conceptual Framework for Understanding the Transnational Legal World* (Oxford: Hart Publishing, 2009).

11 Ibid.

transnational law conceptualizes the condition of legal pluralism in which nation states and their legal systems perform a specific rather than constitutive function.[12]

Theories of legal pluralism, therefore, challenge the law of the modern state as a dominant form of legal regulation[13] and contrast it to allegedly more effective parallel non-state legal orders and systems.[14] The evolution of European and global legal pluralism and constitutionalism without state sovereignty indicates the need to move beyond the images and symbolism of politically and culturally integrated national society using the semantics of constitutional and popular sovereignty as its self-description, and human rights as its moral foundations.

The legal pluralism of European and global society thus coincides with unorthodox conceptualizations, such as 'constitutionalisation without the state',[15] 'post-constituent constitutionalism',[16] 'a subaltern cosmopolitan legality'[17] and so on. Pre-modern and early modern concepts of consociationalism and the multitude of jurisdictions have been redesigned to address the complexity of our globalized post-modern and post-national societies and their legal systems.

A Pluralist Critique of Sovereignty: 'Weak' and 'Strong' Theoretical Views

Recent theories of legal and constitutional pluralism involve a great variety of conventional jurisprudential conceptualizations of the basic fact of the plurality of legal and political orders in the global condition.[18] Jurisprudential theories of legal pluralism acknowledge the existence of different legal orders and ultimate rules of recognition that do not communicate with each other in terms of hierarchy and supremacy established by a superior rule-based process.[19] Instead of the ideal rule of law limiting politics and containing power, the legal pluralist condition typifies

12 Peer Zumbansen, 'Transnational Legal Pluralism', *Transnational Legal Theory* 10(2) (2010): 141.

13 See, for instance, Gunther Teubner, 'The Two Faces of Janus: Rethinking Legal Pluralism', *Cardozo Law Review* 13 (1992): 1443.

14 Franz von Benda-Beckmann, 'Who Is Afraid of Legal Pluralism?', *Journal of Legal Pluralism and Unofficial Law* 47 (2002): 63–65.

15 Gunther Teubner, 'Societal Constitutionalism: Alternatives to State-Centred Constitutional Theory?', in *Transnational Governance and Constitutionalism*, eds Christian Joerges, Inger-Johanne Sand and Gunther Teubner (Oxford: Hart Publishing, 2004), 7.

16 Neil Walker, 'Post-Constituent Constitutionalism? The Case of the European Union', in *The Paradox of Constitutionalism: Constituent Power and Constitutional Form*, eds Martin Loughlin and Neil Walker (Oxford: Oxford University Press, 2007), 247.

17 Boa de Sousa Santos, supra n. 2, 458–471.

18 Nicholas K. Tsagourias, ed., *Transnational Constitutionalism: International and European Perspectives* (Cambridge: Cambridge University Press, 2007).

19 Matthias Kumm, 'Who is the Final Arbiter of Constitutionality in Europe?: Three Conceptions of the Relationship Between the German Federal Constitutional Court and the European Court of Justice', *Common Market Law Review* 36(2) (1999): 351.

the absence of juridical hierarchy and the presence of permanent contestations and confrontations between political forces promoting the currently most persuasive juridical arguments and interpretations.[20]

Jurisprudential conceptualizations of legal and/or constitutional pluralism build on the absence of ultimate legal authority and the impossibility of reconciling conflicting claims to it by different official legal orders operating within the same context.[21] The operations of these official legal orders need to be coordinated without any subordination because each of them carefully preserves and keeps self-referring to its basic norm or the rule of recognition.[22]

For legal pluralists drawing on a much more radical concept of pluralism, this, however, is a 'weak' pluralism. It is considered theoretically unremarkable because of its reliance on the concept of official state law and conventional models of adjudicative cooperation.[23] Confronting this alleged 'weakness', the 'strong' concept of legal pluralism is expected to draw on the sociological and anthropological methods and juxtapose the unity of socially limited (if not marginal) official laws with the plurality of actually recognized social normative orders.

The difference between 'weak' and 'strong' or 'radical' pluralism established by John Griffiths and other sociologists and anthropologists of law certainly contributed to highlighting methodological differences between the sociology and jurisprudence of legal pluralism. It strictly separated legal pluralism studies from analytical jurisprudence and sociological positivism, exploring unofficial and/or living law from legal positivism and legalism of officially sanctioned rules.[24] However, Griffiths's initial combative tone and radical critique of juristic pluralism also obscured the sociological value and inspiration of the jurisprudence of legal pluralism, especially its analysis of parallel legal structures and jurisprudential conflicts within the context of either more general constitutionalism containing and neutralizing social conflicts and collisions,[25] or social governance networks and structures.[26]

'Weak' jurisprudential and 'strong' anthropological or sociological pluralistic views of law are in fact both informed by the methodology of social sciences.[27]

20 Emmanuel Mellisaris, *Ubiquitous Law: Legal Theory and the Space for Legal Pluralism* (Aldershot: Ashgate, 2009), 27–43.

21 Koen Lenaerts, 'Interlocking Legal Orders in the European Union and Comparative Law', *International and Comparative Law Quarterly* 52(4) (2003): 873.

22 Paul S. Berman, *Global Legal Pluralism: A Jurisprudence of Law Beyond Borders* (Cambridge: Cambridge University Press, 2012).

23 For 'weak' and 'strong' pluralism, see John Griffiths, supra n. 1, 5–8.

24 Anne Griffiths, 'Legal Pluralism', in *An Introduction to Law and Social Theory*, eds Reza Banakar and Max Travers (Oxford: Hart Publishing 2002), 289.

25 Miguel Maduro, 'Contrapunctual Law: Europe's Constitutional Pluralism in Action', in *Sovereignty in Transition*, ed. Neil Walker (Oxford: Hart Publishing, 2003), 501.

26 Francis Snyder, 'Governing Economic Globalisation: Global Legal Pluralism and European Law', *European Law Journal* 5 (1999): 334.

27 For a critique, see Brian Tamanaha, 'The Folly of the "Social Scientific" Concept of Legal Pluralism', *Journal of Law and Society* 20 (1993): 192.

Jurisprudential encounters commonly include sociologically inspired insights into the internal operations of transnational and supranational pluralistic legal systems and different ways of preserving their semantic unity and institutional operability. They often represent fascinating reflections on recent transformations and, in particular, the functional differentiation of legal systems and their semantics from the structures and semantics of politics and political sovereignty.

Instead of emphasizing the logic of legal normativity and its priority over political will and social facts, jurisprudential theories of legal pluralism highlight the *contingency* of the interaction between different legal normative systems and the collisions between them, requiring a more or less radical version of legal pluralism.[28] In making these claims, contemporary jurisprudential views are often profoundly influenced by the 'radical' methodology of social sciences, such as MacCormick's thesis of law 'beyond the sovereign state'[29] and its later critical modification 'questioning post-sovereignty'.[30] No wonder MacCormick described his jurisprudential methodology as 'radical pluralism', too, despite its fundamental difference from legal pluralists' radical criticisms of the state and official law-oriented legal positivism.[31]

MacCormick and Weinberger's institutional theory of law[32] was profoundly influenced by a general sociological theory of institutions[33] and legal realist ideas of law as a means of social integration and change and as a normative reflection and institutionalization of human political and social imagination. According to the institutional view, law is 'institutional fact'[34] which is not exclusively determined by the state and is actually generated by non-state institutions, such as churches and international organizations, as well.

Abandoning the modernist notion of law as the command of a sovereign, which considers the question of sovereignty as primarily a political problem that subsequently acquires its specific legal and constitutional form, the institutional theory of law ceases to be theoretically limited by the modern state's organization,

28 Neil MacCormick, 'Risking Constitutional Collision in Europe?', *Oxford Journal of Legal Studies* 18 (1998): 528–532.

29 Neil MacCormick, 'Beyond the Sovereign State', *The Modern Law Review* 56(1) (1993): 1.

30 Neil MacCormick, 'Questioning Post-Sovereignty', *European Law Review* 29 (2004): 852.

31 Neil MacCormick, *Questioning Sovereignty: Law, State and Nation in the European Commonwealth* (Oxford: Oxford University Press, 1999), 121.

32 Neil MacCormick and Ota Weinberger, *An Institutional Theory of Law: New Approaches to Legal Positivism* (Dordrecht: D. Reidel, 1986).

33 See, for instance, Helmut Schelsky, *Recht und Institution* (Berlin: Duncker und Humblot, 1985); see also Schelsky's influence on Weinberger's institutionalist theory of law in Ota Weinberger, *Law, Institution and Legal Politics: Fundamental Problems of Legal Theory and Social Philosophy* (Dordrecht: Kluwer, 1991), 196–205.

34 See an early article by MacCormick. Neil MacCormick, 'Law as Institutional Fact', *Law Quarterly Review* 90 (1974): 102.

its politically exclusive power and monistic legal system. It adopts legal pluralism as a response to the increasingly diverse conditions of legal validity and the complexity of globalized law and politics.

Close to the sociological and legal realist view of 'law as fact',[35] the association of law with social institutions rather than just the nation state opens up the possibility of analysing subnational, supranational and transnational legal systems beyond sovereignty and without recourse to their ultimate source of validity and hierarchical normative ordering. It can address the problem of multiple sources of validity in supranational and transnational legal systems and explain their operative efficiency and stability through the general operations of social institutions rather than the political exclusive architecture and symbolic legitimation of the nation state.

A Radical Critique of the Society of Official Law and the Sovereign State: is Ehrlich Having the Last Laugh?

Radical critics are correct when they say that jurisprudential theories of legal pluralism typically prioritize official legal norms over non-state social norms.[36] For instance, MacCormick's treatment of European constitutional pluralism was based on a critique of legal monism as a theory informed by a single sovereign source of validity. Nevertheless, it was later moderated by MacCormick's strong argument in favour of law as an institutionalized alternative to spontaneous social orders and the regulative ideal ultimately synthesizing pluralistic legal viewpoints and sources of validity at the EU's supranational level.[37] A number of legal regulations may be independent of state authority and the state system of law is just one system that does not necessarily subordinate other non-state supranational and transnational legal systems. However, the rationality of constitutionalism establishes official limits and a framework of political deliberation and thus ultimately determines the extent and content of multilevel communication between different constitutional sites and polities.[38]

'Strong' sociological theories of legal pluralism go far beyond this 'weak' critique of sovereignty and the notion of a plurality of official legal orders enforced by different social agencies and institutions. They favour a radical version of the

35 Among many examples, see, for instance, Karl Olivecrona, *Law as Fact* (London: Stevens, 1971).

36 Simon A. Roberts, *Order and Dispute* (New York: St Martin's Press, 1979), 25.

37 See, for instance, Jorge-Ramon Bengoetxea, 'Legal System as a Regulative Ideal', *Archiv für Rechts- und SozialPhilosophie [ARSP]* 53 (1994): 65.

38 See also, Miguel Maduro, 'Courts and Pluralism: Essay on a Theory of Judicial Adjudication in the Context of Legal and Constitutional Pluralism', in *Ruling the World? Constitutionalism, International Law and Global Governance*, eds Jeffrey L. Dunoff and Joel P. Trachtman, (Cambridge: Cambridge University Press, 2009), 353–358.

pluralism of unofficial legal orders spontaneously recognized by communities and operating despite a state legal order rather than as its parallel supplement. These theories commonly emphasize the basic fact of the plurality of social reality and its relevance for the legal system, especially the limits of the system's self-regulation and its external dependence on spontaneously recognized non-state and non-legal normative orders of society. According to these views, formal rules of official law and their sanctioning by the sovereign state are just one of many different normative structures and orders of society.[39]

These radical theories are often driven by a critique of official state law and present themselves as critical theories of state power and sovereign authority enforced on the state's territory and its populations.[40] They also commonly perceive the state and its law as a form of hegemony that needs to be challenged by alternative politics emerging at subnational, national and transnational levels of global society.[41] Finally, and most importantly, radical theories of legal pluralism often contrast the concept of constitutional and political sovereignty to spontaneously evolving sectors of society which, instead of being constituted by political force, engage in the parallel processes of self-constitutionalization and constitutional fragmentation.[42]

Though Eugen Ehrlich never established a theory of legal pluralism and did not even use the concept at all,[43] the sociological concept of legal pluralism continues to be closely associated with Ehrlich's concept of living law because theories of legal pluralism, like the sociology of law, focus on the internal operations and different regulations of society as a whole.[44] By extending the concept of law to the realm of social customs and reformulating it as a blurred domain of genuinely binding and socially heterogeneous rules, Ehrlich certainly overcame the modern identification of law and sovereign political power and the methodological limits of normativist legal logic.

---

39 See, for instance, Gunther Teubner and Andreas Fischer-Lescano, 'Regime Collisions: The Vain Search for Legal Unity in the Fragmentation of Global Law', *Michigan Journal of International Law* 25(4) (2004): 999.

40 Marc Galanter, 'Justice in Many Rooms: Courts, Private Ordering and Indigenous Law', *Journal of Legal Pluralism and Unofficial Law* 19 (1981): 1.

41 See, for instance, Balakrishnan Rajagopal, 'The Role of Law in Counter-Hegemonic Globalization and Global Legal Pluralism: Lessons from the Narmada Valley Struggle in India', *Leiden Journal of International Law* 18 (2005): 345.

42 See especially Gunther Teubner, *Constitutional Fragments: Societal Constitutionalism and Globalization* (Oxford: Oxford University Press, 2012); see also Nico Krisch, 'Who Is Afraid of Radical Pluralism? Legal Order and Political Stability in the Postnational Space', *Ratio Juris* 24(4) (2011): 386.

43 See Klaus Ziegert, 'Introduction to the Transaction Edition', in *Fundamental Principles of the Sociology of Law*, Eugen Ehrlich (New Brunswick, NJ: Transaction, 2002), xli, xlv.

44 Sally E. Merry, supra n. 6, 873.

Following the then popular distinction between society and community and adopting it in the context of legal theory, Ehrlich actually redirected academic attention from the official rule of society by state law to the spontaneously enforced rules of communal life beyond statehood. His concept of living law was a non-state concept of law recognized by a particular community. The unity of society was to be secured by the variety of spontaneously ordered associations of which people are members mutually coordinating their actions and reactions.[45]

Against the mainstream legal theoretical canon of official law sanctioned by the state, Ehrlich argued that the effectiveness of legal norms depends on the inner order of associations and its internal forms of enforcement rather than the power and organization of the modern state. According to this view, threats of force and official sanctions have very little effect and may indeed be counterproductive,[46] and the normative order of society evolves without the state's sanctioning power.

Ehrlich was criticized by sociologists as much as by legal theorists and political philosophers. For instance, Max Rheinstein criticized Ehrlich's confusion of law with custom and his reduction of legal science to sociology, and prudence to popular sentiment.[47] More significantly, Ehrlich's sociological method as a basis of a general theory of law was ignored by Max Weber who established his sociology of law by using common jurisprudential concepts of law, legal norms and sanctions or the relationship of law, the modern state and legal legitimacy.

Furthermore, Kelsen dismissed Ehrlich's theoretical views giving precedence to society and its general rules of existence and evolution over the system of positive law as a methodologically regressive return to the concept of natural law. Kelsen severely criticized Ehrlich's sociology of law for confusing facts and norms and turning autonomous legal normativity into a mere function of the forces and ultimate laws operating in society. The identification of law and society in Ehrlich's concept of 'living law' allegedly leads to the loss of methodological clarity and the reintroduction of the old-style metaphysical difference between positive and supra-positive law. According to Kelsen, this kind of sociology of law treating social facts indiscriminately as 'living law' faces the impossible task of establishing itself as a separate discipline independent from both general sociology, which focuses on the social facts of human behaviour, and legal science, which studies the normative character of a legal order.[48]

Similarly, Ehrlich's peculiar form of the philosophy of life, translating into the concept of living law as law prevailing in the social struggle for recognition, was completely foreign to Schmitt's notion of political struggle and the enemy/friend

---

45 Eugen Ehrlich, supra n. 43, 27.

46 Ibid., 402.

47 Max Rheinstein, 'Sociology of law, apropos Moll's translation of Eugen Ehrlich's Grundlegung der soziologie des Rechts', *Journal of Ethics* 48 (1983): 232.

48 Hans Kelsen, 'Eine Grundlegung der Rechssoziologie', in *Rechtssoziologie und Rechtswissenschaft: Eine Kontroverse (1915/1917)*, Hans Kelsen and Eugen Ehrlich (Baden-Baden: Nomos Verlagsgesellschaft, 2003), 3.

distinction. Ehrlich's concept of society drawing on general forces constantly recreating the unity of pluralistic social life and spontaneously recognized as law was the opposite of Schmitt's world full of frictions, differences and conflicts. Indeed, Schmitt's vigorous criticisms of theories of political and legal pluralism because of their identification of legal and political reality with social totality applied to Ehrlich's sociological theory of law.

Nevertheless, it almost looks as if Eugen Ehrlich, so severely criticized by Hans Kelsen, dismissed by Carl Schmitt and ignored by Max Weber and other scholars of his time, is having the last laugh in the current condition of global society. His sociological method and emphasis on law as an order of rules spontaneously recognized by social associations appears appropriate for understanding the complexities of globalized law. It even led Gunther Teubner, a leading sociologist of global law, to remark that Eugen Ehrlich's sociology of law was perhaps wrong at the time of its writing at the beginning of the twentieth century, but turned out to be the most comprehensive and realistic response to our current globalized society, nicknamed 'Global Bukowina' by Teubner, and typical of 'global legal pluralism'.[49]

Living Law of a Global Civil Society

In this global context, Ehrlich's concept of living law is reformulated as signifying the process of spontaneous juridification and even the constitutionalization of different sectors of global society without polity, such as commerce, intellectual property, internet, sport, environment and so on. The well-established theoretical semantics differentiating between living and legislated law, respectively law in action and law in books, is supplemented by new distinctions, such as hard law/soft law, national government/transnational governance and state/civil global constitutionalism.

Ziegert, for instance, reinterprets Ehrlich's sociology of law and the concept of living law as the most persuasive critique of statist legal theory which corresponds to our current state of self-ordering and self-regulating global society and its legal system operating without the state.[50] He even considers Ehrlich's theory a general theory of society rather than just another theory of law. According to this reading of Ehrlich's living law, social order:

> … emerges as a relational and structural result of generalized, practised observation of others, that is, having respect for the actions and reactions of the

49 Gunther Teubner, '"Global Bukowina": Legal Pluralism in the World Society', in Gunther Teubner, ed., supra n. 8, 3.

50 Klaus A. Ziegert, 'World Society, Nation State and Living Law in the Twenty-first Century', in *Living Law: Reconsidering Eugen Ehrlich*, ed. Marc Hertogh (Oxford: Hart Publishing 2009), 223.

> other members of the association. This order cannot be singularly 'hijacked' or commandeered by any one individual. It develops over time, and becomes entrenched so deeply that the original, practical reasons for those 'actions and reactions' get lost in the cultural, intergenerational transmission. What there is to be 'vigorously' kept and preserved by the associations are the forms of relational conduct, that is, social norms.[51]

The social norms stabilize the inner order of association through social evolution and communicative experience. Social stability is conditioned by this self-regulatory primary order whose functionality – rather than a special apparatus of political enforcement – guarantees the effectiveness of valid norms. It is the factuality of social life rather than the normativity and/or rationality of a political order that facilitates the legitimacy of law. The living law dominates social life, and legal propositions and documents need to be recognized by these dynamic inner orders of human associations.

Ziegert reinterprets Ehrlich's conceptual separation of living law and lawyers' law as an example of the functional differentiation of society and a challenge for modern society that needs reflexively to reconstruct expert legal knowledge and legal propositions formulated by lawyers as part of living law.[52] He even treats Ehrlich's view of living law as:

> … a prophetic glimpse at the emerging world law of human rights … reminiscent of Kant's design of a cosmopolitan civil society of non-governmental 'associations' supported by law (international legal decision-making), together with the power play of states held in check by treaties. This civil society does not have nor needs to have a corresponding 'world government', but is anchored in and promoted by non-aggressive and humanitarian states …[53]

This optimistic assessment and surprisingly prescriptive 'civil' interpretation of Ehrlich's sociology of living law builds on the contrast between artificially integrated political order and spontaneously evolving global civil society.[54] Ehrlich's distinction between lawyers' law and living law can scarcely be reinterpreted as an example of functional differentiation because the living law, according to Ehrlich, dominates life, including the life of legal propositions, decisions and expert knowledge. The theory falls short of the heterarchies of a functionally differentiated society and its self-regulatory legal system because

51 Ibid., 227–228.

52 Ibid., 230.

53 Ibid., 235–236.

54 David Nelken, 'Ehrlich's Legacies: Back to the Future in the Sociology of Law?', in Marc Hertogh, ed., supra n. 50, 262–263.

Ehrlich expands the meaning of law by finding it everywhere in society and thus blurs its social boundaries and differentiation from other social normative orders.[55]

If living law depends on the life of associations and the recognition of their members, the meaning of law becomes semantically expanded beyond the point of obscurity. If every normative order is to be called law, what about the relationship between the legal order and other social normative orders? Is law really any order that people use and call 'law'?[56] And does not the whole distinction of lawyers' law and living law, respectively state law and non-state law, rather confirm the importance of the state as a law-making institution?[57]

From Global Living Law to Fragmented Societal Constitutionalism

Unlike the image of the living law's commonality of global civil society, supranational and transnational legal and political developments are characterized by fragmentation, asymmetries, structural irritations and collisions. These cannot be contained by some form of civil unification or cooperation between states and non-state agents at global level. Rapidly evolving subsystems of global society pursue their specific self-constitutionalization through functional differentiation and not by means of political integration facilitated by the deliberative political efforts and cooperation of state governments.[58]

Constitutionalizations of global law evolve not only without the state or any other global political authority but also as multiple processes of the differentiated social sectors of global economy, technology, science and so on.[59] The political constitutionalization of global society is just a 'constitutional illusion'.[60] A global polity has no constitution, and nation state constitutions are challenged by global self-constitutionalizations beyond the realm of constitutional law.[61] Instead of normative projects and politics, a truly radical theory of legal pluralism, therefore, needs to emerge as a theory of a global legal system which is functionally differentiated from global politics, economy or science. It is a system of internal

---

55 Marc Hertogh, 'From "Men of Files" to "Men of the Senses": A Brief Characterisation of Eugen Ehrlich's Sociology of Law', in Marc Hertogh, ed., supra n. 50, 2–8.

56 For this view, see, for instance, Brian Tamanaha, *A General Jurisprudence of Law and Society* (Oxford: Oxford University Press, 2001), 167.

57 See, for instance, Simon Roberts, 'Against Legal Pluralism', *Journal of Legal Pluralism and Unofficial Law* 42 (1998): 95–106, 105.

58 Gunther Teubner and A. Fischer-Lescano, supra n. 39, 1014.

59 Gunther Teubner, 'Constitutionalizing Polycontexturality', *Social and Legal Studies* 20(2) (2011): 216.

60 Andreas Fischer-Lescano, *Globalverfassung: Die Geltungsbegründung der Menschenrechte* (Weilerwist: Velbruck, 2005), 247.

61 Gralf P. Callies and Peer Zumbansen, *Rough Consensus and Running Code: A Theory of Transnational Private Law* (Oxford: Hart Publishing, 2010), 168–169.

paradoxes, deparadoxifying operations and fragmentations rather than a system of rules and doctrinal contestations.

Drawing on these notions of spontaneously evolving legal orders beyond political organizations and constitutionalism without the state, constituent power and polity, some scholars even reject the very idea of transnational or post-national constitutionalism and contrast it to a pluralist vision of global societal governance.[62] As Nico Krisch comments:

> [I]n pluralism, there is no common legal point of reference to appeal to for resolving disagreement; conflicts are solved through convergence, mutual accommodation – or not at all. It is a vision that takes societal fragmentation to the institutional level.[63]

Nevertheless, the concepts of law and constitutionalism can scarcely be so easily contrasted to the concepts of post-national governance and societal pluralism, if only because of the strong semantic tradition and common theoretical uses of the concept of legal and constitutional pluralism. Unlike Krisch and other scholars who completely renounce the concept of constitutionalism, Gunther Teubner, therefore, suggests that the process of functional differentiation in global society guarantees that the concurrent constitutionalizations of specific subsystems institutionalize their internal mechanisms of self-restraint. They thus effectively avoid the risk of society-wide expansion and constitutional interventions into other sectors of global society.

Nation state constitutions cannot be replicated at the level of global society: 'the constitutional totality breaks apart and is dissolved by a type of *constitutional fragmentation*'.[64] The legal system of global society is typified by a multiplicity of what Sciulli describes as societal constitutions[65] in which sovereign states may continue to have some operative capacity but characteristically lose their constitutive power within the system of international law and state constitutionalism.

Teubner adopted Sciulli's theory of societal constitutionalism for his theory of autopoietic law and reinterpreted it in the same original manner which informed his unorthodox reading of Luhmann's social theory of autopoietic systems and Ehrlich's sociology of law in the current state of 'global Bukowina'.[66] This theoretical move has made it possible for Teubner to pursue the goal of theoretical description and conceptualization of social differentiation and fragmentation at level of global law and society.

---

62 Nico Krisch, *Beyond Constitutionalism: The Pluralist Structure of Postnational Law* (Oxford: Oxford University Press, 2010).

63 Ibid., 69.

64 Gunther Teubner, supra n. 59, 220.

65 David Sciulli, *Theory of Societal Constitutionalism: Foundations of a Non-Marxist Critical Sociology* (Cambridge: Cambridge University Press, 1992).

66 Gunther Teubner, supra n. 49.

Drawing on the concepts of law as an autopoietic social system and the functional differentiation of modern society, Teubner pleads for a sociological theory of *societal constitutionalism* as a distinct position overcoming 'the obstinate state-and-politics-centricity'[67] of constitutional lawyers and political philosophers. This theoretical move is made possible by a general theory of social system differentiation which makes constitutional politics merely part of the functionally differentiated political system rather than an ultimate condition of societal unity.[68] The constitution of society consists of its differentiation, not its political integration.

Furthermore, the new research field of constitutional sociology supports general theories of social differentiation by providing for historical and empirical analyses between constitutional politics and other social subsystems and areas. Removing the process of constitutionalization from the fiction of the ultimate normative foundations of law, Teubner questions major orthodoxies of legal and political theory and asks constitutional and international law theorists to embrace not just the form of constitutionalism without the state but even more distant forms of the self-constitutionalization of sectors of private law and governance regimes.[69]

Societal constitutionalism, therefore, means the dissociation of constitutions and politics which, according to Teubner, has always been part of the sociology of law tradition. According to this perspective, different social systems, such as global law, politics or economy, often collide with each other and do not lead to some form of ultimate constitutional settlement of global society that would be able to replicate the national constitutionalization paradox by representing a politically sovereign global authority and symbolically expressing the totality of global society. Instead, this perspective represents a view of global law functionally differentiated from global politics and internally differentiated into a multiplicity of self-constituted and self-constituting subsystems.

On Global Systemic Self-Constitutionalizations: a Critique of Political Constitutions

Rethinking constitutionalization as part of social fragmentation and resisting the theoretical temptation of identifying society with normative unity guaranteed by a political constitution requires a different kind of imagination facilitated through Teubner's most original mixture of autopoietic systems theory, the classical terminology of sociology of law and a number of new concepts emerging in the rapidly expanding field of transnational law and constitutionalism.

67 Ibid., 3.

68 Niklas Luhmann, *Law as a Social System* (Oxford: Oxford University Press 2004), 404–412.

69 Gunther Teubner, supra n. 42, 1–2.

First of all, Teubner challenges the semantics of international law, the hierarchies of the nation state and its sovereign constitution of both the political system and the whole nation. According to him, the domain of international law is just a sectorally differentiated part of the global legal system in which political and legal sovereignty, both internal and external, cease to play the role of the essential precondition of legal communication. Due to the societal differentiation and globalization of functional systems including law and politics, which have been rapidly adopting transnational organizational forms and networks, the role of nation states, their borders and political constitutions, has been marginalized.

Globalization 'produces a tension between the self-foundation of autonomous global social systems and their political-legal constitutionalization'.[70] Instead of the process of political unification through general constitutionalization, one is now witnessing a profoundly pluralistic movement towards specific constitutionalizations of different transnational legal regimes, organizations and networks. According to Teubner, the state and its hierarchies are inadequate when dealing with non-state global social actors and the horizontal effects of fundamental rights guaranteed at supranational level and pursued through multiple transnational networks and institutions. He subsequently reformulates the process of global constitutionalization as a process in which:

> … [t]he constitution of world society does not come about exclusively in the representative institutions of international politics, nor can it take place in a unitary global constitution which overlies all areas of society, but, instead, emerges incrementally in the constitutionalisation of a multiplicity of autonomous sub-systems of world society.[71]

This process of global, yet fragmented, self-constitutionalizations without a state subsequently makes it theoretically possible to think of constitutionalism as the general societal processes of self-reference of non-state subjects unlimited by concepts of collective identity, shared political destiny and so on.

The modern semantics of state constitutionalism drawing on the image of society ultimately organized by the constitutional state needs to be replaced by the post-modern semantics of societal constitutionalism drawing on the image of functionally differentiated society consisting of specific autopoietic subsystems. The intrinsic tension between the political dimension of constitutions and their expressive symbolism covering the totality of society is reconceptualized as a non-representational politics of constitutionalization of autonomous sectors of global society pursued by both state and non-state agencies.[72]

Teubner is heavily critical of the state constitution as a politically expansive organization of the territorial distribution of power and the exclusive legitimate

70 Ibid., 43.

71 Gunther Teubner, supra n. 15, 8.

72 Gunther Teubner and Andreas Fischer-Lescano, supra n. 39.

claim to authority over people, resources and any autonomous social subsystems operating within the state's territory. The core of his argument is that these constitutions are socially expanding, yet territorially limited by the borders of the nation state. Contrary to these limitations, the self-constitutionalizations of specific functional systems, such as economy, science, religion, education or the media, operate irrespective of territorial borders, and their fragmented constitutions are determined by internal systemic operations and general codes of communication.

This clearly is a major conceptual breaking point. Should the concepts of constitution and constitutionalism refer exclusively to a specific organization of structural coupling and operations occurring between the legal and political systems, or should they signify any process of self-constitutionalization of internal operations of different social subsystems and sectors beyond law and politics? Would it not mean that constitutionalism is just another and, therefore, redundant name for the self-description and self-reference of functionally differentiated systems operating at the level of global rather than merely supranational European or national societies?

The New Constitutional Question and Subjects

Teubner's most fundamental attack on state constitutionalism is related to his claim that, in fact, it is transnational regimes, organizations and networks that become the new constitutional subjects, replacing the nation state constitutional semantics of a *demos*, its collective identity, the constituent/constituted power differentiation and the legitimacy arising from the democratic consensus and political pluralism. He repeatedly emphasizes that his major aim is to get rid of the substantive concept of constitution as a vehicle for the self-determination and self-identification of a collective actor, such as a nation and its self-founding myths. For him, the act of constitution is a matter of social communication between systems and not some form of legal recognition of the existence of a collective actor and its identity.

The 'new constitutional question',[73] therefore, is not a political one and covers non-political areas of global society in the process of constitutionalizing themselves. The global condition requires the rethinking of who is the constitutional subject of global societal constitutionalism. Unlike the hierarchies of the constitutional state established by paradoxical circularity between its constituent and constituted power subjects, Teubner promotes transnational regimes, organizations and networks as horizontally differentiated constitutional subjects of global constitutionalism without a state.

These new non-state and non-political subjects are presented as able to steer the self-constitutive processes and deliberations formerly associated with the state's constitutional subjects. Commenting on the rise of constitutionalism in the

73 Gunther Teubner, supra n. 42, 1.

economic system, its impact on welfare state and risks of its societal expansion, Teubner states that:

> [W]estern Europe is experimenting with a multiplicity of social constitutions granting the political constitution only the status of *primus inter pares*. Constitutions are everywhere in society: not just *ubi societas, ibi ius*, as Grotius once said, but *ubi societas, ibi constitutio*. Self-founding orders are developing at numerous places in society and are being stabilized by constitutional law. Law must accordingly develop a 'multilateral constitutionalism' that does not bind social orders unilaterally either to the constitution of the state or to the economy, but rather models specific constitutions that do justice to the peculiarities of the various orders.[74]

Societal constitutionalism is described as constitutional pluralism which, more importantly, attributes a strangely asymmetrical status to the political constitution. While claiming that constitutions are everywhere and arguing that the political constitution cannot unilaterally bind other social orders, it still is expected to 'model' specific constitutions beyond its jurisdiction.

However, this modelling function raises critical questions as regards political reflections of societal constitutionalism, limits and different models of its fragmentation, and asymmetries emerging from the differentiation of political and societal constitutions. Furthermore, it raises the question of the conceptualization of constitutional politics in functionally differentiated society and the limitations of any constitutionalist discourse, including societal constitutionalism, in social theories of global law and politics.

Drawing on Luhmann's description of the state constitution as politics' self-limitation of its own possibilities, historically accompanied by the increased need for structural compatibility with other social subsystems, Teubner generalizes this constitutional self-limitation as a problem facing all social subsystems, not just politics.[75] He subsequently launches an outright attack on legalism when he states that:

> [T]hough lawyers may not like to admit it, law does not play the primary role in state constitutions and other sub-constitutions. The primary aspect of constitutionalization is always to self-constitute a social system: the self-constitution of politics, the economy, the communications media, or public health. Law, in such processes, plays an indispensable yet merely supporting role. An exacting definition of societal constitutionalism would have to realize that constitutionalization is primarily a social process and only secondarily a legal process.[76]

74 Ibid., 35–36.
75 Ibid., 86–88.
76 Ibid., 103.

In this respect, Teubner is right when he describes Kelsen's normativism and Schmitt's decisionism as two theoretical extremes reducing constitution either to a legal phenomenon, or a power-politics phenomenon. It is true that constitution actually means a double phenomenon operating through the permanent linkage of societal power processes and legal processes. However, instead of adopting Luhmann's definition of the constitution as a distinct organization of structural coupling and irritations between the legal and political systems,[77] Teubner's concept of constitution now signifies external legal referencing to the general autopoietic operations of any functional system:

> [N]ot just politics, but other social systems, too, establish themselves through self-referential processes by which, ex nihilo, they constitute their own autonomy. Constitutions deal with the paradoxes of self-reference practically by externalizing them to the surrounding context. Social systems are never entirely autonomous: there are always points of heteronomy. If this externalization now occurs with the help of constitutions, the moment of heteronomy comes when the social system refers to the law. The 'self' of the social system is defined heteronomously by legal norms and it can define itself autonomously thereby … its identity is created in its constitution through the re-entry of external legal descriptions into its own self-description.[78]

Contrary to Luhmann's concept of strict autopoietic normative and operative closure, Teubner continues in his early criticisms of Luhmann's concept of system autopoiesis[79] and reconceptualizes the autopoietic closure by linking it to the concept of social reflexivity, law as a hyper-cycle, intersystemic conflicts and so on.

He suggests that legal normativity operates as an external description re-entering the system's self-description. However, this legal normativity re-enters a specific functional system, such as the economy or education, exactly as normativity and not as external cognitive information to be appropriated by the autopoietic system's internal norms and operations.

A societal constitution, therefore, is not structural coupling between the legal system and other social systems in its environment because, by definition, structural coupling 'is not a normative topic'.[80] It is heteronomy without any contribution to the social system's autopoiesis and/or co-evolution with other systems. Unlike the modern political constitution, it does not guarantee the structural coupling of the legal and other social systems.[81] Societal constitutions only provide for help in the systemic self-reference by heteronomous legal definitions.

77 Niklas Luhmann, supra n. 68, 404.

78 Gunther Teubner, supra n. 42, 65.

79 Gunther Teubner, *Law as an Autopoietic System* (Oxford: Blackwell, 1993), 31.

80 Niklas Luhmann, supra n. 68, 385.

81 Ibid., 409–412.

However, if the system's unifying self-referential operations merely use the legal semantics of constitutions as a metaphor, why bother about this marginal use of legal concepts if they actually describe the system's unity, produced by its specific non-legal binary coding and communication, such as profit or truth?

One can only agree with Teubner's view that a constitution is not a living law in the sense of the manifestation of the spirit of a people but a societal living process of 'the self-identification of a social system with the assistance of the law'.[82] Nevertheless, this 'assistance' can hardly be recognized as part of autopoiesis of a specific subsystem and the legal system's contribution to the self-constitution and self-reference of other systems can scarcely be considered constitutive in the autopoietic sense. As Luhmann summarizes, '... [t]he environment cannot insert operations of any other kind in the network of the autopoiesis of the system'.[83] Social systems can communicate about their environment but not with it.

Autopoiesis with a Human Face? Civil and Political Constitutions

According to Teubner, the radical concept of global societal constitutionalism without the state, polity and the symbolic image of ultimate social unity is difficult for constitutional and political theorists to digest because it would require 'breaking a taboo' of state-centred constitutionalism.[84] However, there is another taboo even Teubner does not break, that of *civility*. Teubner's theory of global legal pluralism surprisingly draws on the typically modern social science orthodoxy, namely the duality of hierarchically organized *political* constitutions and spontaneously evolving *civil* constitutions.[85]

The distinction between political and civil constitutions is not just a reflection of transnational globalized society and the international politics of sovereign states. In a similar vein to Ziegert's view of global civil society, Teubner reformulates the classical difference between society and the state in the context of the autopoietic systems theory of global legal pluralism by contrasting the instrumental rationality of legality and the bureaucratic administration of the state to the multiplicity of social subsystems and their specific modes of rationality.

Sectorial constitutions emerging in civil society are perceived as an antidote to the state constitutionalism. Avoiding normative politics' pursuit of the constitutional unification of civil society, Teubner identifies civility as fragmented areas of functionally differentiated society subject to centrifugal rather than centripetal and unifying societal tendencies. Teubner is convinced that the autonomy and civil self-constitutionalization of these sectors counter the risk of de-differentiation and the expansion of political instrumentalization and remarks:

82 Gunther Teubner, supra n. 42, 71.
83 Niklas Luhmann, supra n. 68, 465.
84 Gunther Teubner, supra n. 15, 8.
85 Ibid., 27–28.

> Strengthening the autonomy of spheres of action as a counter-movement to trends of de-differentiation seems to be the general response at work both in the traditional political constitutions and in the emerging civil constitutions. If it was the central task of political constitutions to uphold the autonomy of other spheres of action against the expansion of the polity, specifically in relation to political instrumentalisation, then, in today's civil constitutions, it is presumable to guarantee the chances of articulating so-called non-rational logics of action against the dominant social rationalisation trend, by conquering areas of autonomy for social reflection in long-lasting conflicts, and institutionalising them.[86]

The concept of civil constitutions is thus virtually another name for fragmented and fragmenting societal constitutionalism.[87] This civil field of societal constitutionalism is not just complementary but opposite to the sphere of state constitutionalism, and civility is thus understood in the state/civility antinomy elaborated by modern political and social normative theories. The civility of societal constitutionalism is further strengthened by the horizontal effect of human rights and their transnational regimes.

For Teubner, this self-constitutionalization of different societal sectors refers to non-state civil society's regimes, organizations and networks. They cannot be just expert processes of technical juridification without any constitutive meaning. They are, rather, the new constitutional subjects of the non-political, soft constitutional semantics which replace the hard political concepts of the democratic state, its people and constitutional power.

Heavily critical of normative political and constitutional theory, Teubner, nevertheless, has profoundly normative expectations of these new transnational constitutional subjects. For instance, regime constitutions may be starkly different from nation state political constitutions, yet they are oriented towards 'a global public interest'[88] – a concept almost impossible to explain within the conceptual framework of autopoietic systems theory if one does not limit it to the banality of the functional differentiation of global society. It may actually be perceived as the re-entry of normative conceptualizations and moral expectations of normative social and political theories. It resembles a form of the normative expectation of normative expectations, somewhat sarcastically described by Luhmann as 'morally motivated programmes of demands' which, in the name of 'humanity', are to support 'living law' to 'prevail against established conventions'.[89]

Teubner even reintroduces the regime's centre/periphery differentiation, which was refuted by Luhmann as a distinction signifying segmental rather than functional differentiation, to encompass informal institutions, organizations and

86 Ibid., 12–13.
87 Ibid., 8.
88 Gunther Teubner, supra n. 42, 157.
89 Niklas Luhmann, supra n. 68, 468–469.

actors operating beyond the central formal organization of a regime constitution.[90] However, this strange retro-semantics of state/society and centre/periphery distinctions in Teubner's theory of societal constitutionalism effectively mean that the dynamics of the functional differentiation of global legal and global societal constitutionalism continues to be exposed to the persisting segmental differentiation of formally organized centres and informally evolving and interacting social peripheries.

These theoretical problems are further exposed by Teubner's call for a 'hybrid regulation' combining the internal regulation of functional systems with external pressure from other social spheres, in particular, public discussions, protests, movements, NGOs and trade unions, to guarantee the effective self-limitation of the functional systems. According to him:

> … [p]olitical-legal regulation and external social influences can only succeed if they are transformed into the self-regulation of systemic dynamic. This requires massive interventions from politics, law and civil society: interventions, however, which, as a matter of fact, are translated into self-limiting impulses and transformed into a regime constitution.[91]

However, this conclusion effectively means that the self-regulation of global societal constitutionalism is safeguarded by global societal interventions in legal rationality rather than by legal autopoiesis.

No More Experts? Systemic and Sectorial Differentiation

Another problematic aspect of Teubner's societal constitutionalism is the internal differentiation of social systems into spontaneous and organized professional spheres. Though this particular difference makes it possible for Teubner to identify different constitutional arenas, the specific distinctions of consumers and corporations (in the economy), respectively public opinion and government (in politics), it also raises the question of the possibility of the systemic closure and autopoiesis of societal constitutions, yet again.

Teubner calls the differentiation of the spontaneous and organized sphere 'a starting point for societal constitutionalism'[92] and reflexive politics because it opens up new possibilities and reflections of dissent and disputes. In spontaneous areas, the various function-specific constituencies and social sectors have distinct modes of operations which are reflexive of system operations, yet very different from the highly organized capacities of expert knowledge. However:

---

90 Gunther Teubner, supra n. 59, 222–223.

91 Ibid., 225.

92 Gunther Teubner, supra n. 42, 89.

> [T]he organized sphere of decision-making certainly does not receive any clear signals from the spontaneous sphere. It is condemned to freedom – and only once the critical decisions have been made, the specific mechanisms of responsibility begin to work that reside in democracy or in the market.[93]

The very differentiation of the organized and spontaneous spheres is part of the concept of systemic reflexivity and communicative tensions emerging between civil society and expert communication. Societal constitutionalism's goal, therefore, is to move beyond the sphere of expert knowledge communicating through highly specific and specialized systemic codes. The self-limitation and self-constitutionalization of different functional systems is thus achieved through societal mobilization of consumer groups, eco-activism, public interest litigation, human and animal rights protests, humanitarian aid networks and other forms of spontaneously created areas of civil society campaigning.

Professional organizations and their expert knowledge are challenged and need to engage in its self-limitation because of irritations caused by the demands of civil society activism and the general public. The internal systemic differentiation of the organized and spontaneous spheres thus leads to the reflexive learning pressures between expert and civil society knowledge, respectively the hard laws of organizational operations and the soft laws of public pressure, recommendations and protests. Societal constitutionalism thus consists of perturbations and irritations between these two constitutional spheres of any functional system.

The sectorial differentiation of different spheres of functional systems is closely related to the problem of double reflexivity of functional systems. In this context, Teubner proposes yet another definition of societal constitutions as 'structural coupling between the reflexive mechanisms of the law (that is, secondary legal norm creation in which norms are applied to norms) and the reflexive mechanisms of the social sector concerned'.[94] Teubner believes that a constitution emerges in every social system which has its reflexivity supported by legal norms. Constitutional processes thus emerge as an institutionalized co-evolution between the two social systems, and constitutions should be termed 'binding institutions' between law and the social sphere.[95]

Unlike the process of juridification which means enacting only primary norms for behavioural control, this societal constitutionalization always involves, in the Hartian sense, secondary 'norms of norms', that is, norms prescribing the identification, setting, amendment and regulation of primary norms. Like political constitutionalism, societal constitutionalism is impossible without these two reflexive processes which keep the societal rationalities of other systems both autonomous and juridified via already (juridically) reflexive legal processes.[96]

93 Ibid., 90.
94 Ibid., 105.
95 Ibid.
96 Ibid., 105–106.

This concept of constitutionalization as double reflexivity is not problematic in itself. However, Teubner introduces an additional form of reflexivity which requires social subsystems to take account of their 'public responsibility'.[97] At this point, the internal differentiation of the organizational and spontaneous spheres is exposed to a critique that it actually does not consist of the internal autopoietic operations and functions of social subsystems and therefore needs to be reformulated as the specific operation of the politics of civil protest and dissent reflected and internalized by other social systems.

The very distinction of the organization and spontaneous spheres is far from the process of functional differentiation due to its spatial/sectorial semantics and striking resemblance to the early modern sociological distinction of society and community (in which society was identified with high levels of professionalism, expertise and rational organization while community signified the process of spontaneous social evolution). The contrast between the bureaucratically organized rational state and spontaneously evolving and consensually cooperating society was typical of nineteenth-century political and legal theory; the establishment of sociology and, later, sociology of law as new scientific fields was one of its most remarkable consequences.

In Teubner's theory, the differentiation between civil and political constitutions and the general differentiation of the spontaneous and organizational spheres of the self-constitutionalization of social systems remain exposed to this normative retro-semantics of sociological and social theory.

In the Name of the Noble Savage? Cultural Polycentrism in Global Societal Constitutionalism

According to Teubner, the functional differentiation of global society and conflicts of different system rationalities leads to constitutional fragmentation. However, there is a second fragmentation emerging at global level which is caused by cultural polycentrism and the divergences of different world cultures. This fragmenting of functional systems and of regional cultures involves the difference and conflicts between culturally embedded traditional knowledge and highly specialized expert knowledge produced by modern functional systems.[98]

Unlike the vast majority of other adherents of autopoietic social systems theory, Teubner seeks to reconcile functional differentiation and the concept of culture when it comes to the protection of traditional cultures and their knowledge. He does not consider culture a mere reservoir of collective memories and past events meaningful for society's present,[99] and his major concern is the social exploitation

97 Ibid., 110.

98 Ibid., 163.

99 Niklas Luhmann, *Theory of Society. Volume 1* (Stanford, CA, Stanford University Press, 2012), 349.

and destruction of traditional knowledge by functional systems, organizations, networks and the expert knowledge of world society.

According to Teubner, constitutional theory:

> … has to change its focus from conflicts between subsystems within functional differentiation to the conflicts between functionally differentiated globality and the social embeddedness of regional cultures.[100]

This particular collision in global societal constitutionalism is thus analysed from a predetermined normative position, demanding the external imposition of limits on globalized modernity which threatens local cultures, and respect for these cultures.

The language becomes less clear when Teubner calls for 'the development of hybrid legal forms within modern law that represent a peculiar compromise between regional-cultural identities and modern-day legal mechanisms of protection'.[101] Inter-constitutional collisions related to cultural polycentrism are thus to be sorted by another hybridization which is mainly described in the common normative political language and ethics of 'responsibility', 'compromise' and 'sensitivity' to cultural differences.

The post-humanist radical message of autopoietic theory thus gets blended by the humanist ethics of globality and concepts completely strange or marginal to the process of functional differentiation. Those who believed that Teubner's constitutional fragmentations represent a persuasive critique of identity politics are left puzzled by the theorist's requirement that legal protection must be guaranteed not only for traditional knowledge, but also its embedding in the local culture.[102]

This is also the only point of reference to sovereignty in societal constitutionalism, when Teubner calls for 'shared sovereignty' enabling the coexistence of modern politics and the self-determination of indigenous groups. In the most moralistic and passionate call, which is alien to autopoietic systems theory, Teubner demands that the development of these groups 'should not be exposed to the grasp of functional differentiation'.[103]

In this context, one subsequently needs to ask how the blind process of social evolution through functional differentiation may be steered at global level to exclude some segments of world society from its systemic operations. Is it possible to have governance of the world society's functional differentiation in which cultural segment differentiation could take over the functional differentiation of society? Is not Teubner's 'Beelzebub'[104] of the state replaced by the Furies of cultures?

---

100 Gunther Teubner, supra n. 42, 165.

101 Ibid., 166.

102 Ibid., 168.

103 Ibid.

104 Ibid., 86.

The Impossibility of Closure of Global Law by the External Semantics of Civility

Teubner's use of the concept of civility is not linked to some prescriptive notion of a global civil society based on the notion of an ethical human life. Nevertheless, it indicates the possibility of some form of overarching commonality in the sectorally and functionally differentiated global society. The 'civil' operates as a precondition of the self-constitutionalizations of different sectors of global society and thus resembles the tradition of civil society as a basis of the differentiation of economy, politics, family and other sectors of modern social life.[105]

Teubner's theory of the civil self-constitutionalizations of different sectors of global society is a peculiar mixture of self-referencing legal autopoiesis and the constitutive civility of non-state actors as its external reference. The concept of post-sovereign civil constitutions without the constitutional state relies on external reference to the notion of civility rather than the self-reference of globally pursued legality. Global civility is expected to operate in the same manner as a 'civil religion', limiting constitutional power by external reference to a set of political and social values.

The external reference to the civility of self-constitutionalization effectively means that the global legal system can never fully achieve its systemic differentiation and operative closure. Legality is not the only medium of the global legal system and the whole concept of societal constitutionalism is unthinkable without the external semantics of civility which is particularly burdened by the difference between the organized state and spontaneously evolving society. Civility becomes a stabilizer of the most general process of societal constitutionalization.

The concepts of civil constitutions in particular and societal constitutionalism in general are profoundly influenced by the idea of the self-constitution and self-regulation of civil society spontaneously evolving and gradually reducing the power and instrumental rationality of the state. The concept of civility represents a specific normative project rather than merely blind social processes of functional differentiation. Teubner establishes a sophisticated theory of autopoietic subsystems of functionally differentiated global law but also pursues the typically modern theoretical goal of eliminating political power and sanction from the definition of law. Structural pressures of legal and political globalization allegedly lead to the abandonment of Schmitt's concept of political sovereignty and Kelsen's concept of the basic norm but also need to keep using the typically modern concept of civility. This is the only way a heterarchical, polycentric and spontaneously evolving global civil society can structurally prevail over political hierarchies and bureaucratic organizations emerging at national, subnational, supranational and transnational levels of global society.

Nevertheless, one can ask what is meant by the 'civility' of functional differentiation and constitutionalization in, for instance, global science, technology

105 Ibid., 16.

and sport. Is the evolution of the global *lex mercatoria*[106] and *ius humanitatis*[107] just a more sophisticated version of the early modern process of the evolution of civil society analysed at the dawn of political modernity by, for instance, Adam Fergusson? Will it lead to the global political establishment of a self-organized and spontaneously evolving civil society unconstrained in its forms by the state's organization and its limiting hierarchies?

Teubner's theory of societal constitutionalism actually replicates some classic distinctions associated with Ehrlich's difference between living law and lawyers' law, especially the contrast between society and community, organization and spontaneity, human alienation and organic bonds. Indeed, this segmental differentiation of modern society can be discovered in a number of theories and philosophies of society and politics of Ehrlich's time, for instance in the Marxist critique of modern industrial capitalism and utopian hopes of a post-revolutionary classless society and socialist beliefs in economic and political self-organization. It also was typical of various forms of modern nationalism and ethno-politics drawing on 'the decline of civilization' and the need to protect communal bonds and national traditions against the destructive forces of modern industry and bureaucratic political organizations. It permeated modern nationalism and political struggles for national self-determination as well as the socialist belief that the state can be converted from an organ superimposed upon society into one subordinate to it.

The spontaneity of social and legal evolution is preferred to the iron cage of the state's official legality and bureaucratic organization. Montesquieu and Savigny's silently operating social forces appear to be much more significant than legislated laws. These elements of the classical difference between politically organized *society* and spontaneously evolving *community* are detectable even in highly sophisticated theories of legal pluralism, despite their heavy reliance on theoretical notions of administrative efficiency and depoliticized forms of social steering. Theories of global legal pluralism and self-constitutionalized sectors of global law paradoxically replicate this classical sociological distinction and, therefore, are both uniquely inspired and haunted by the spectre of Ehrlich's sociology of law and its paradoxes, prescriptions and limitations.

106 Gunther Teubner, 'Breaking Frames: Economic Globalisation and the Emergence of Lex Mercatoria', *European Journal of Social Theory* 5 (2002): 199.

107 Boaventura de Sousa Santos, supra n. 2, 301–311.

Chapter 5
Power in Sovereignty and its Popular Legitimation: On the Semantics and Contingency of Popular Sovereignty

In this chapter, I further expand my critique of societal constitutionalism and argue that it cannot eliminate power politics. Power structures are pluralistic in modern society and the nation state and supranational or transnational organizations are just some of their manifestations.

Teubner and Foucault's criticisms of politics of constitutional sovereignty and power are used as a starting point of my argument, contrasted to one another but also critically assessed as two different forms of the same fallacy substituting sovereignty for the social norm. Teubner's claim that constitutions evolve outside the political system of modern society undermines the importance of structural coupling between politics and law in the modern constitutional state as well as beyond its organizational framework. Unlike Teubner, Foucault rejects sovereignty as a model of juridically legitimized politics obfuscating the permanent state of war, extremities of violence in society and omnipresent social domination as subjugation. However, this view inadequately reduces the complexity of social reality by translating it to the omnipresent power discourse.

Critically drawing on Teubner and Foucault's work, I analyse sovereignty as part of multiple power structures with distinct forms of legitimation. Apart from techniques of democratic self-government, the concept of popular sovereignty involves the self-description of society as the self-constituted democratic polity of the sovereign people. This interplay between power structures and the prescriptive aspect of sovereignty as a legitimation strategy opens the possibility of self-description and mobilization of modern political society and its coeval structuration into nation states. However, the problem of popular sovereignty and democratic legitimation is not limited to the nation state structures and informs the emergence and legitimation dilemmas of supranational or transnational organizations as well.

The self-description of society as a democratic polity reflects on the typically modern tension between democracy as a contingent form of government and democracy as an imagined definite form of social totality. It is already present in Tocqueville's early analysis of democracy as government depending on a shared civic culture which, nevertheless, is historically and socially contingent itself. The notion of the sovereign people as polity representing the collective foundations and moral expressions of society and thus legitimizing power of government is paradoxically countered by the fact that these foundations and expressions need to be communicated by this government and its power structures. Democratic polity legitimizes power of government, yet the same power constitutes such polity and its laws facilitate the semantics of popular sovereignty both materialized and limited by the rule of law.

The semantics of society as democratic polity is thus an internal construct of the structurally coupling legal and political systems to enhance and legitimize power in the modern state and beyond its legal and political structures. Popular sovereignty of *demos* subsequently cannot be taken as the existential precondition of constitutional politics ultimately legitimizing political power. There is no polity without the systems of positive law and politics. The image of morally embedded and fully integrated polity under the sovereign popular will is just an outcome of the power abstraction and historical reconfigurations in the functionally differentiated organization of the constitutional state and more recent supranational and transnational legal and political organizations.

Societal Constitutionalism as Fear of the Political? Confronting Beelzebub of Political Constitutions

Theories of legal and constitutional pluralism make a fascinating story of a revival of social theory in mainstream jurisprudence and theory of law.[1] They show that law, like other normative orders, is determined by its social reference and response to the 'practical regulatory requirements of communal life'.[2] Despite numerous criticisms of the Weberian concept of law and power by theorists of legal pluralism, this view is surprisingly close to Max Weber's early sociological findings that structural preconditions of the law's existence are not exclusively limited to the state and political sovereignty.[3] Unlike the Weberian sociology of law, sociological theories of legal pluralism and societal constitutionalism, however, are typical of one particular failure – the failure of methodological and normative depoliticization.

To understand this depoliticization and normative ambitions hidden in conceptual antinomies and theoretical paradoxes of theories of legal pluralism, one has to analyse, for instance, Teubner's differentiation of *le politique* and

1 See especially Pospíšil's work inspired by Weber's concepts of power and domination. Leo Pospíšil, *Anthropology of Law: A Comparative Perspective* (New York: Harper and Row, 1971); similarly, see Sally F Moore, *Law as Process: An Anthropological Approach* (London: Routledge, 1978).

2 Roger Cotterrell, 'Transnational Communities and the Concept of Law', *Ratio Juris* 21(1) (2008): 13.

3 Max Weber, *Economy and Society: An Outline of Interpretive Sociology. Vol I* (Berkeley, CA: University of California Press, 1968), 313–317.

la politique.[4] While institutionalized politics, state constitutions and the expert knowledge of governing technocrats allegedly threaten to monopolize politics, societal constitutions facilitate a high degree of social autonomy. Instead of formalizing society in the medium of law, they use it to refer to social processes external to the political and legal form. Societal constitutionalism thus involves a paradox of criticizing the political and legal form of *la politique* while using its concepts to describe non-political processes of self-limitation and self-constitution of different social systems and sectors of global society. The paradox of the political self-denial and external expansion of the concept of constitution is a hallmark of societal constitutionalism which both completely depoliticizes the concept of constitution and gives it the most prominent political role of *le politique* by relocating it to a higher level of theoretical abstraction and identifying it with both functional differentiation and societal alternatives to institutionalized politics.

Teubner especially calls for the following methodological modifications: disconnection of the constitution from statehood (thus opening the semantics of constitutionalism for transnational regulatory regimes); decoupling the constitution from institutional politics (thus opening the possibility of identifying other areas of global civil society as possible constitutional subjects together with transnational regimes); decoupling the constitution from the medium of power (thus making other media of communication in other specific systems possible constitutional targets).[5]

Teubner's concepts of fragmented global legal pluralism and societal constitutionalism actually represent a grand critique of power politics and politics in general. Political constitutions are referred to as 'Beelzebub',[6] casting out the devil of the power expansion of the political system by its self-limitation. Teubner feels comfortable when discussing non-state social orders and private transnational regimes as constitutions but desperately seeks to avoid the typical constitutionalist language of constituent and constituted power, and even suggests avoiding the classical political and philosophical concept of 'self-determination' in societal constitutionalism.[7]

When discussing the classical differentiation of constituent and constituted power, Teubner even resorts to the physics-driven conceptualizations of a 'communicative potential' and 'social energy'[8] which merely steers the reciprocal irritations between society and individuals, respectively communication and consciousness, and thus does not represent a specific semantic contribution to the legal and political autopoiesis. However, such an approach reduces the problem of the modern democratic constitutional subject, which is communicated precisely

4 Gunther Teubner, *Constitutional Fragments: Societal Constitutionalism and Globalization* (Oxford: Oxford University Press, 2012), 114–116.

5 Ibid., 60.

6 Ibid., 86.

7 Ibid., 61.

8 Ibid., 62–63.

in the difference between constituent and constituted power, to the constitution's external referencing and 'the area of perturbation where individual consciousness encounters social communication'.[9] This interface of individual consciousness and social communication does not indicate any constitution of the people as a collective with political identity or intersubjective communicative power.

Beelzebub's power remains the same devilish instrument for Teubner even if it comes in the angelic guise of discourse ethics. In fact, he is so uneasy about the differentiation of constituent and constituted power that he wants to leave it to psychologists, medical doctors and priests.[10] Any possibility of a sociological examination of the constituent/constituted power differentiation as specific self-referentiality in both politics (through the medium of power) and law (through the medium of constitutional normativity) is thus lost.

Nevertheless, Teubner's concept of societal constitutions cannot be easily dismissed as just another project of global civil society and a theory of depoliticization by societal constitutionalism and global governance. It involves the possibility of reformulating constitutional sovereignty as a process of permanent self-constitutionalization by the functionally differentiated systems of globalized law and politics. It also opens the possibility of rethinking sovereignty as part of the functional differentiation that is typical of coupling and structural irritations emerging between globalized law and politics and the symbolic self-descriptions of different polities.

So heavily drawing on Savigny and Ehrlich's concept of legal science examining the forces silently operating behind legislated laws, theories of societal constitutionalism and legal pluralism, however, need to be confronted by the persistent Weberian question of power, legality and legitimacy of the modern state and other, especially supranational and transnational political organizations. The concept of legitimacy as the transformation of social power into political domination represents a modern sociological response to the political and jurisprudential problem of sovereignty as the transformation of *potentia* to *potestas*. The sovereignty question, therefore, is to be reformulated as a sociological question of power structures and the semantics of their legitimation within and beyond the state which cannot be ignored by ever more refined and detailed legal pluralism studies of horizontal legal networks, their global constitutionalizations and spontaneous social evolution.[11]

Sovereignty, Power and the State in Global Legal Pluralism

As regards functional differentiation and asymmetries in legal and political globalization, Luhmann treated the legal system of global society as 'a special

9 Ibid., 63.

10 Ibid., 62–63.

11 John Hoffman, *Beyond the State: an Introductory Critique* (Cambridge: Polity Press, 1995).

case'[12] and warned against overlooking huge legal differences in different parts of the globe. In the absence of globally centralized legislation and decision-making, a global legal order, according to Luhmann, evolves through the generalized semantics of human rights and their violations. Legal globalization is facilitated by the general expectation that states, these differentiated 'segments' of the global political system,[13] are responsible for their compliance with human rights and make them an intrinsic part of legislation and law enforcement.[14] The divergence in legal developments at the level of global society, nevertheless, is so significant that it raises the very question of the functionality of a global legal order.[15]

Unlike Luhmann, Teubner never doubts the unity of the global legal system and the autopoiesis of its operations beyond the state and international law structures and organizations. Despite this theoretical optimism, global legal plurality, nevertheless, hardly can be interpreted mainly as non-state spontaneous and heterarchical social evolution and constitutionalization, because: a) the state and its hierarchical practices and power continue to be part of the process of legal globalization; b) the process of globalization comes with its specific power configurations and hierarchies beyond the state organization.

Power has not disappeared as the political medium in globalized society.[16] It cannot be removed from global politics by depoliticized governance like caffeine from coffee beans by decaffeination.

Similarly, the trend towards internal heterogeneity and decentralization of the state[17] leads to the reconfiguration of state power rather than its replacement by horizontal forms of depoliticized governance and societal constitutionalism. The state 'is a central player even in producing its own downsizing'[18] in the process of globalization. State power practices and strategies can lead to both the renationalization and transnationalization of politics in global society. States thus redefine themselves in the global 'meta-power game'.[19]

The state's decentralization and globalization give rise to internal legal pluralism which, however, replicates and even expands state power practices. For instance, private security companies may be granted extensive powers to conduct

---

12 Niklas Luhmann, *Law as a Social System* (Oxford, Oxford University Press 2004), 481.

13 Ibid., 487.

14 Ibid., 482.

15 Ibid., 488.

16 Robert O. Keohane and Joseph Nye, *Power and Interdependence: World Politics in Transition* (Boston, MA: Little, Brown, 1977).

17 Michael Jacobsen and Stephanie Lawson, 'Between Globalization and Localization: A Case Study of Human Rights versus State Sovereignty', *Global Governance* 5 (1999): 205.

18 Boaventura de Sousa Santos, *Towards a New Legal Common Sense. 2nd edition* (London: Butterworths, 2002), 94.

19 Ulrich Beck, *Power in the Global Age: A New Global Political Economy* (Cambridge: Polity, 2005), 168.

surveillance of electronic communication and data of whole populations and act outside the rule of national and international law.[20] In this context, Sousa Santos, for instance, profoundly disagrees with Teubner's decentred, depoliticized and spontaneously evolving heterarchical sociological concept of global law without the state[21] and comments that:

> [T]he depoliticization of the state and destatization of social regulation … show that under the same name – the state – a new, larger form of political organization is emerging, articulated by the state itself, and composed of a hybrid set of flows, networks, and organization, in which state and non-state, national and global elements combine and interpenetrate.[22]

The state, which used simultaneously to occupy communicative space within the legal and political systems and dominate the organization of their structural coupling, becomes just another organization of global society facilitating the operations of supranational and transnational politics and law.[23] Nevertheless, the continuing operative capacity of the state as a distinct form of social organization has not entirely vanished even in the polycentric and pluralistic globalized world.[24]

Furthermore, moving beyond the limits of state politics-centred constitutionalism does not change the political character of collectively binding decisions and decision-making processes associated with any kind of constitutionalism. Global constitutionalism simply cannot dispose of its politics[25] because power persists as an autonomous medium of global social communication. It, therefore, needs to be theorized against the background of global transformation of statehood and structural coupling between politics and law in the constitutions of nation states and beyond them.

In this context, it has to be emphasized that state and politics are two distinct categories and the nation state is just one of many forms of modern contingent power structures.[26] Instead of the pronounced end of state sovereignty in global

20 See, for instance, Andrew C. Orr, 'Unmanned, Unprecedented, and Unresolved: The Status of American Drone Strikes in Pakistan under International Law', *Cornell International Law Journal* 44 (2011): 729.

21 Boaventura de Sousa Santos, supra n. 18, 57.

22 Ibid., 489.

23 See, for instance, Robert H. Jackson, *Quasi-States: Sovereignty, International Relations and the Third World* (Cambridge: Cambridge University Press, 1990), 16–25.

24 Neil Walker, 'The Idea of Constitutional Pluralism', *Modern Law Review* 65 (2002): 317–318.

25 Hans Lindahl, 'Societal Constitutionalism as Political Constitutionalism: Reconsidering the Relation between Politics and Global Legal Orders', *Social and Legal Studies* 20(2) (2011): 234.

26 Chris Thornhill, 'Constitutional Law from the Perspective of Power: A Response to Gunther Teubner', *Social and Legal Studies* 20(2) (2011): 246.

society, sovereign states continue to operate as power organizations in political and legal constellations of global society. The international state pluralist order coexists with transnational orders and cosmopolitan idealistic aspirations in globalized politics and law.[27] The nation state still is the most common form of political organization not just in the supranational system of European society but even in global society characterized by a great variety of international, supranational and transnational institutionalizations and organizations.[28] The sovereign state's power only becomes part of much more complex supranational and transnational power structures and asymmetries.

In this social condition, the state sovereignty question may be reformulated in the following words: What power do sovereign state authorities have in the Europeanized and/or globalized legal and political systems? What is the relationship between these authorities and other authorities enforcing the laws and making political decisions in supranational and transnational organizations and networks?

The simple fact that global society falls short of any form of global political sovereignty concentrated in a single transnational organization does not justify theoretical conclusions of the end of sovereignty. The sovereignty question always has involved the problem of legitimation and neither Europeanization nor globalization changed it. Unstructured, contingent and socially pervasive power creates its legitimation strategies and establishes legitimate frameworks of its operations – national, supranational and transnational.[29]

The modern state's paradox of constitutionalism as the permanent communication of political sovereignty through the medium of legality cannot be resolved by the legal pluralist claim that constitutionalism is just another name for the juridification of functionally differentiated sectors of global society completely dissociated from the power operations and asymmetries of constitutional politics. The constitutionalization of different sectors of global society is a process of increasing rather than limiting the power operations regulating these sectors. The global systemic plurality of functionally differentiated society, therefore, calls for theoretical reconsideration and reconceptualization of the modern notion of constitutional sovereignty as part of the genealogy and semantic transformation of contingent power structures emerging in globalized society and its systems of positive law and politics.

27 Andrew Hurrell, *On Global Order: Power, Values, and the Constitution of International Society* (Oxford: Oxford University Press, 2007).

28 Robert J. Holton, *Globalization and the Nation State* (Palgrave: Macmillan1998).

29 Jens Bartelson, *A Genealogy of Sovereignty* (Cambridge: Cambridge University Press, 1995), 217–219.

Enter Power, Exit Law?: Societal Power beyond Politics and its Critique

Instead of the distinction between societal and political constitutions, another one needs to be introduced and critically assessed to comprehend the persistence and persuasiveness of sovereignty in Europeanized and globalized society as well as its historical transformation, namely the distinction between state and capillary constitutions and power.

Capillary power permeating all social areas has its 'capillary constitution' which permeates the state constitution, yet its specific mode of self-imposition is beyond the state constitution's control. Teubner recalls Derrida and Foucault's view of capillary power achieved beyond juridical power and political sovereignty through scientific disciplines and technology,[30] yet never explores its political context and impact. Foucault, however, contrasted power as capillary transgression of social institutions to the constitution of right organization and judicial techniques of social control. Rather than societal spontaneity and self-regulation, it is the extremity of power at its outer limits and violent interventions that defines its capillarity and societal pervasiveness.[31]

This position may be summarized as 'enter power (in various guises); exit law'.[32] Capillary power, by its definition, rules out the possibility of some constitutional containment and rule-based settlement. It signifies expansive societal power unbound by any rules, customs and regulatory regimes. It is a model of the power of extremity directly contrasted to the power based in the sovereignty of either monarchical or democratic right and judicial exercise.[33]

The history of power is far too complex and extreme to be contained by interests, customs, laws or the juridical fiction of sovereignty and its institutional settlement. Power is not a state of affairs and something that agencies can possess and exercise as force. It has the relational character and thus only can be comprehended as the interplay between opposing terms and techniques and the war raging at the periphery – multiple capillaries of the social body.

According to Foucault, modern society is constituted by internal wars as the precondition of its survival and protection. Civil war, so much abhorred by legal and political theorists in early modernity, cannot be eliminated by any sovereign power. Constitution of the sovereign state from the war-like state of nature only masks the fact that the civil state is the continuation of civil wars by other means.[34] Wars and struggles continue in the laws and political institutions which are officially legitimized by their capacity to regulate and limit power.

30 Gunther Teubner, supra n. 4, 85–86.

31 Michel Foucault, *'Society Must Be Defended'. Lectures at the College de France, 1975–76* (New York: Picador, 2003), 27–28.

32 Ben Goulder and Peter Fitzpatrick, *Foucault's Law* (Oxon: Routledge, 2009), 13.

33 Michel Foucault, supra n. 31, 28.

34 Ibid., 98.

This state of permanent social wars signifies a retreat from the political constituent notion of the sovereign nation to the medical notion of population and/or the biological notion of racially defined and internally divided nation.[35] Indeed, Foucault notes that the nation is characterized by the state, its potential and capacities. 'The nation is the State' – it is constituted by its ability of self-administration through state control.[36] However, the nation is not just a juridical category of self-rule which is the necessary precondition of the formation of constitutional government and the delegation of power. It is equally defined by its historical existence and social functions and apparatuses, such as the army, justice, the church and the administration.[37]

These social functions and apparatuses are much more important for understanding the production and circulation of power in the body of modern society than abstract images of the political nation and the legal fiction of state sovereignty.[38] They determine who is the enemy of society and which strategies and wars need to be launched to defend society against these enemies within its body.

The rise of modernity is subsequently described by Foucault as the diminishing role of the rule of law and political sovereignty which get replaced by new and more effective modes of disciplinary power over individual bodies and populations. The problem of sovereign authority governing the state territory and its individual inhabitants was replaced by the problem of various authorities administering populations and shaping their selves through 'governmentality'.[39]

Foucault's concept of the juridico-discursive power in the first volume of *The History of Sexuality* is therefore profoundly different from the power of limiting legality. It is an expansive and formative bio-power.[40] This contrast draws on Foucault's earlier view that 'power produces; it produces reality; it produces domains of objects and rituals of truth'.[41] A genealogy of power thus needs to critically highlight this jurisprudential production of sovereignty and the sovereign right as 'truth'[42] of modern politics emerging in the medieval Western legal system.

---

35 Peter Fitzpatrick, *Mythology of Modern Law* (London: Routledge, 1992), 150–154.

36 Michel Foucault, supra n. 31, 223.

37 Ibid., 219.

38 Bernard Yack, 'Popular Sovereignty and Nationalism', *Political Theory* 29(4) (2001): 517.

39 Michel Foucault, 'Governmentality', in *Power. Essential works of Foucault 1954–1984, Vol. 3*, ed. James D. Faubion (London: Penguin, 2000), 201.

40 Michel Foucault, *The Will to Knowledge: The History of Sexuality, Vol. 1* (Harmondsworth: Penguin, 1979), 83.

41 Michel Foucault, *Discipline and Punish: The Birth of the Prison* (Harmondsworth: Penguin, 1991), 194.

42 Michel Foucault, 'Truth and Power', in *Power/Knowledge: Selected Interviews and Writings 1972–1977*, ed. Colin Gordon (New York: Pantheon, 1980), 121.

According to Foucault, the sovereign right disguises the actual multiplicity of techniques of social domination by the institutionalized and centralized system of the sovereign rule.[43] This critical view considers the complex conceptualization and semantics of sovereignty as a mere discourse production of truth, the function of which is both the obfuscation of the multiplicity of subjugations taking place in society and the legitimation of the particular form of politically institutionalized and socially centralized subjugation.[44] The sovereign right is an instrument of social domination, yet domination is not just:

> … the brute fact of the domination of the one over the many, or of one group over another, but the multiple forms of domination that can be exercised in society; so, not the king in his central position, but subjects in their reciprocal relations; not sovereignty in its one edifice, but the multiple subjugations that take place and function within the social body.[45]

While Weber considers domination a legitimate exercise of power based on social obedience and acceptance, Foucault defines domination in terms of techniques of subjugation involved in social discipline.[46] Underneath the code of legality, disciplinary power supervises and produces normality by non-legal and more effective means of disciplinization.[47] This is the reason why, according to Foucault, the problem of sovereignty as the obedience of individuals submitting to the legitimate right of ultimate, centralized and institutionalized power needs to be replaced by the study of polymorphous techniques and procedures of subjugation in society.[48]

Sovereignty of the Social Norm

In modern society, 'the juridical is increasingly incapable of coding power, of serving as its system of representation'.[49] Instead of the system of positive law, it is now the power and expansion of the social norm that are important for the

---

43 Nikolas Rose and Peter Miller, 'Political Power Beyond the State: Problematics of Government', *British Journal of Sociology* 43(2) (1992): 176–177.

44 Alan Hunt, 'Foucault's Expulsion of Law: Toward a Retrieval', *Law & Social Inquiry* 17(1) (1992): 1.

45 Michel Foucault, supra n. 31, 27.

46 Victor Tadros, 'Between Governance and Discipline: The Law and Michel Foucault', *Oxford Journal of Legal Studies* 18 (1998): 80.

47 Alan Hunt and Gary Wickham, *Foucault and Law: Toward a Sociology of Law as Governance* (London: Pluto Press, 1994).

48 Michel Foucault, 'Omnes et Singulatim: towards a Criticism of "Political Reason"', *The Tanner Lectures on Human Values 1981* (Salt Lake City, UT: University of Utah Press, 1981), 221.

49 Michel Foucault, supra n. 40, 89.

order and discipline of modern society. The rise of socially productive bio-power corresponds to 'juridical regression'.[50]

Capillary power extends beyond the limits of the sovereign state and its official laws and functions as a disciplinary power of social norms.[51] Views and conceptualizations of Hobbes and Machiavelli, these generally recognized founding fathers of modern political theory, need to be abandoned because they are grounded in the realm of institutionalized politics and its legal form of the legitimate right. As Foucault comments:

> ... rather than asking ourselves what the sovereign looks like from on high, we should be trying to discover how multiple bodies, forces, energies, matters, desires, thoughts, and so on are gradually, progressively, actually and materially constituted as subjects, or as the subject.[52]

Machiavelli's image of the Prince's politics of absolute power exempt from the laws and Hobbes's concept of Leviathan with the legal right to sovereignty are dismissed as 'false paternities'[53] because they exactly raise the question of how a multiplicity of individual wills gets transformed into a unity and single political will and body. Absolute power of sovereignty constitutes one political subject.

Foucault, however, contrasts this image of the political subject constituted by sovereignty to the multiple subjects constituted by polymorphous power techniques emerging at the periphery of and beyond the limits of institutional politics and its constitutional form.[54] He presents a sweeping critique of juridical theories of power and sovereignty.[55] Inadequacy of the juridical focus on absolute power is summarized in the following words:

> From the Middle Ages onward, the essential role of the theory of right has been to establish the legitimacy of power; the major or central problem around which the theory of right is organized is the problem of sovereignty. To say that the problem of sovereignty is the central problem of right in Western societies means that the essential function of the technique and discourse of right is to dissolve the element of domination in power and to replace that domination, which has to be reduced or masked, with two things: the legitimate rights of the sovereign on the one hand, and the legal obligation to obey on the other.[56]

---

50 Ibid., 144.

51 Michel Foucault, supra n. 42, 122.

52 Michel Foucault, supra n. 31, 28.

53 Ibid., 59.

54 Carole Smith, 'The Sovereign State v Foucault: Law and Disciplinary Power', *The Sociological Review* 48 (2000): 283.

55 Anthony Beck, 'Foucault and Law: The Collapse of Law's Empire', *Oxford Journal of Legal Studies* 16 (1996): 489.

56 Michel Foucault, supra n. 31, 26.

Indeed, the sovereignty model of society drawing on the simple differentiation between the sovereign and its subjects is useless for depicting complexities of modern political power and its legitimation. Reciprocity of political will established by the fictional social contract is too weak and the habit of obedience hardly can be separated from other techniques of social domination and subjugation.

Foucault's dissolving of the state by power politics[57] and denunciations of sovereignty, nevertheless, do not mean a complete denial of the state and law's functionality within the power constellations of modernity.[58] Law rather becomes a battlefield and tactics[59] and the normative force of bio-power can be channelled through constitutions, legal codes and the legislature's constant activities.[60]

This adoption of the power of the norm by the system of legality due to which 'the law operates more and more as a norm',[61] is described by Francois Ewald as a shift from the concept of law as the expression of sovereign power to the concept of *social law*[62] regulating the welfare of society and facilitating its production of normality and governmentality.[63]

Despite Foucault's frequent denunciations of sovereignty and law, the question of sovereignty persists in his work.[64] In the discussion of the relationship between sovereignty and governmentality, he famously commented that the transition from the rule of law to the societal discipline and policing actually makes the problem of sovereignty 'more acute than ever'.[65] In his analysis of governmentality, Foucault even remarks:

> ... [w]e should not see things as the replacement of a society of sovereignty by a society of discipline, and then of a society of discipline by a society, say, of government. In fact we have a triangle: sovereignty, discipline, and governmental management, which has population as its main target and apparatuses of security as its essential mechanism.[66]

---

57 Jens Bartelson, *The Critique of the State* (Cambridge: Cambridge University Press, 2004), 175–176.

58 Gary Wickham, 'Foucault, Law, and Power: A Reassessment', *Journal of Law and Society* 33(4) (2006): 596.

59 Michel Foucault, *Security, Territory, Population. Lectures at the College de France, 1977–78* (Basingstoke: Palgrave Macmillan, 2007), 99.

60 Francois Ewald, 'Norms, Discipline, and the Law', in *Law and the Order of Culture*, ed. Robert Post (Berkeley, CA: University of California Press, 1991), 144.

61 Michel Foucault, supra n. 40, 144.

62 Francois Ewald, 'A Concept of Social Law', in *Dilemmas of Law in the Welfare State*, ed. Gunther Teubner (Berlin: Walter de Gruyter, 1988), 40.

63 Francois Ewald, supra n. 60, 138.

64 Ben Goulder and Peter Fitzpatrick, supra n. 32, 58–59.

65 Michel Foucault, supra n. 59, 107.

66 Ibid., 107–108.

Instead of the simple contrast between law and norm, the continuing mutual interdependence[67] of the legal form and the social norm's power is typical of modernity.

Sovereignty is no more the central concept of legal and political theory.[68] It became part of a police science in modernity. Foucault's critique of sovereignty is part of his more general critique of political modernity which is surprisingly close to the post-humanist systems theory.[69] However, it is compromised by the following shortcomings: it draws on the centre/periphery distinction by focusing on capillary extremities of power techniques and contrasting them to the centre of institutionalized politics; furthermore, it considers power the ultimate productive and omnipresent mode of social relationships and communication which is everywhere and has 'no outside';[70] and, finally, it ignores the semantics of sovereignty as a socially and politically mobilizing, productive and legitimizing force of modern society opening radically new forms of this society's self-description and self-reflection.

Foucault's interpretation of Hobbes's *Leviathan* actually draws on common knowledge that the legally legitimized sovereign right to exercise power is not the exclusive form of domination in modern society which is typical of the multiplicity of power relationships operating irrespective of the code of legality and institutionalized power politics. Foucault's view of power thus 'amounts to restating some elementary sociological commonplaces'[71] and classic sociological theories of social regulation, control and discipline.

The distinction between capillary and institutionalized power is useful for understanding the forms of social subjugation and domination operating independently of the legality/illegality distinction.[72] However, this contrast often leads to reductive criticisms of political institutions and their legal form

67 Nikolas Rose and Mariana Valverde, 'Governed by Law?', *Social & Legal Studies* 7 (1998): 542.

68 Kevin Walby, 'Contributions to a Post-Sovereigntist Understanding of Law: Foucault, Law as Governance, and Legal Pluralism', *Social & Legal Studies* 16 (2007): 551.

69 Axel Honneth, 'Foucault's Theory of Society: A Systems-Theoretic Dissolution of the *Dialectic of Enlightenment*', in *Critique and Power: Recasting the Foucault/Habermas Debate*, ed. Michael Kelly (Cambridge, MA: The MIT Press, 1994), 165.

70 Michel Foucault, 'Sex, Power, and the Politics of Identity', in *Essential Works of Foucault 1954–1984, Vol. 1: Ethics*, ed. Paul Rabinow (London: Penguin, 2000), 167.

71 Steven Lukes, *Power: A Radical View. Second Edition* (Houndmills: Palgrave Macmillan, 2005), 97.

72 For this evaluation, see especially Gary Wickham and George Pavlich, eds, *Rethinking Law, Society and Governance: Foucault's Bequest* (Oxford: Hart Publishing, 2001).

as distorting the real and much more sinister functions and apparatuses of social domination and control.[73]

Foucault's contribution to the genealogy of modern social power and evolution of alternative forms of social discipline, control and knowledge is invaluable and the distinction between the rule of political law and the power of social norms reveals both legitimation and enforcement limitations of state sovereignty. Nevertheless, the techniques and apparatuses of administration cannot simply be contrasted to the history of political sovereignty. They, rather, are its intrinsic part.[74]

Furthermore, Foucault's critique of sovereignty makes it impossible to understand its general political appeal and power of social mobilization and legitimation. In the following part of this chapter, it is therefore necessary to theoretically focus on exactly the interplay between power structures and the prescriptive aspect of sovereignty as a legitimation strategy opening the possibility of self-description and mobilization of modern political society and its recent parallel structuration into nation states and supranational or transnational organizations.

A Theory of Sovereignty as a Command Structure of Society

In an early criticism of the emerging science of sociology, Friedrich Nietzsche wanted it replaced by a 'theory of command structures'.[75] Foucault's view is part of this intellectual tradition. Like Nietzsche, Foucault finds power and commands everywhere including philosophies of modern politics and law as manifestations of the will to power/knowledge. He was always fascinated by Nietzsche's concept of power which excluded freedom and truth.[76]

The history and present state of social and legal science thus continues to be split between the study of social customs, mores and their historical change, which originally fascinated the Romantic artists and philosophers, and the study of power, its authorizations, institutionalizations and genealogies.[77] While the former has always been close to ethnology and anthropology and inspired theories of legal pluralism and societal constitutionalism, the inspirations and critical evaluations of political theory and philosophy of power opened up the possibility of a sociological analysis of the structures and dynamics behind social relationships and asymmetries of which politics and law were just the two of many manifestations.

---

73 Charles Taylor, 'Foucault on Freedom and Truth', *Political Theory* 12(2) (1984): 158–160.

74 Francois Ewald, supra n. 62.

75 Wolf Lepenies, *Between Literature and Science: The Rise of Sociology* (Cambridge: Cambridge University Press, 1988), 239.

76 Steven Lukes, supra n. 71, 91.

77 Scott Lash, *Sociology of Postmodernism* (Oxon: Routledge, 1990), 10–11, 123–152.

Sociology, therefore, would be unthinkable without political and legal science terminology.[78] The academic journeys of Max Weber, Emile Durkheim, Robert Michels and many other scholars drew on this conceptual and methodological symbiosis which needs to be cultivated even in the emerging sociology of constitutionalism and constitutional sovereignty. This field of sociology of law thus cannot rely on Ehrlich's concept of living law and societal recognition of legal rules as their only source of legal validity. The function of power, its manifestations, institutionalizations, varieties, transformations, different forms of symbolic legitimation and social communication are intrinsic parts of the sociological perspective of law and constitutionalism, including constitutional sovereignty.

Max Weber's sociology signifies a new approach to power, the modern state, its rule of law and constitutional sovereignty.[79] According to Weber, power is a basic element of social life, society consists of a wide range of positive and productive power relationships and the state is merely one of many manifestations of power in modern society which is a result of social evolution and historical development.

Instead of taking it as a precondition of the existence of society and its persistence and unity, Weber defines state sovereignty as one of many manifestations of power in modern society which cannot be taken as a guarantee of its social integration and a symbol of its ultimate unity and moral bonds. It is belief in the state's legitimacy, a minimum of voluntary compliance and a social interest in obedience that makes the state's physical coercion possible and legitimate.[80]

The legitimacy of the modern state is based on the idea that its officials can exercise their powers only according to established rules and that they, equally, are selected according to pre-existing rules. The state's power separation regulated by a constitution is the modern state's legitimate form.[81] Nevertheless, as Weber noted:

> [C]onceptions of the 'rightness of the law' are sociologically relevant within a rational, positive legal order only in so far as they give rise to practical consequences for the behavior of law makers, legal practitioners, and social groups interested in the law.[82]

The systems of modern positive law and politics are legitimate only if they correspond to the abstract postulates of modern rationalist humanism and its 'canon

---

78 For a classic volume, see Seymor M. Lipset, ed., *Social Science and Politics* (Oxford: Oxford University Press, 1969).

79 Anthony Giddens, *Politics, Sociology and Social Theory: Encounters with Classical and Contemporary Social Thought* (Cambridge: Polity Press, 1995), 15–56.

80 Max Weber, *Economy and Society I* (Berkeley, CA: University of California Press, 1978) 212–213.

81 Max Weber, *Economy and Society II* (Berkeley, CA: University of California Press, 1978) 652–653.

82 Ibid., 866.

of the ends of "Nature's" will'.[83] However, this legitimacy is not guaranteed by the definition and prescriptive character of these postulates. This 'correct' and 'right' law is legitimate only to the extent to which it has practical social consequences in legal and political life.[84] In other words, society must be convinced that these postulates are right and political and legal officials must act according to them.

According to Weber, politics, indeed, is part of the eternal struggle for power[85] which defines all areas of social life. For instance, economic competition is another power struggle and the study of the national economy deals with power distribution within the economic system and its impact on the nation state as the organization of the nation's power. The state is a territorial political organization establishing a political community by monopolizing and legitimizing violence. It regulates the interrelations of the inhabitants of the state territory in the most general way and has the following basic functions: legislative, police, administration of justice, military administration and other forms of administration of social life, such as education, welfare, public health and so on.[86]

The state and its functions do not indicate some universal structural and functional preconditions of all societies. They are an outcome of historical development. As Weber comments:

> … [t]he monopolization of legitimate violence by the political-territorial association and its rational consociation into an institutional order is nothing primordial, but a product of evolution.[87]

In fact, the state is a particular institutionalization and legitimization of politics emerging in modernity and coinciding with rationalization of social life:

> For the purpose of threatening and exercising such coercion, the fully matured political community has developed a system of casuistic rules to which that particular 'legitimacy' is imputed. This system of rules constitutes the 'legal order', and the political community is regarded as its sole normal creator, since that community has, in modern times, normally usurped the monopoly of the power to compel by physical coercion respect for those rules.[88]

---

83 Ibid., 868.

84 Roger Cotterrell, 'Legality and Political Legitimacy in the Sociology of Max Weber', in *Legality, Ideology and the State*, ed. D. Sugarman (London: Academic Press, 1983), 69.

85 See Max Weber, 'The Nation State and Economic Policy', in *Political Writings* (Cambridge: Cambridge University Press, 1994), 16.

86 David Beetham, *Max Weber and the Theory of Modern Politics. 2nd revised edition* (Cambridge: Polity, 1985), chs 4 and 5.

87 Max Weber, supra n. 81, 904–905.

88 Ibid., 904.

Modernization thus involves the co-evolution of a rational legal order and its political guarantee by the state using legality for its rational legitimation. This rise of modern legality to political pre-eminence coincides with the dissolution of the old communal bonds and differentiation of modern society, especially its economy. The system of positive law turns out adequately to protect steadily widening social interests in modern differentiated societies.

The legal system and the state are thus structurally differentiated but mutually benefit from this differentiation by enhancing their operative capacity in modern society.[89] The modern differentiation of economy, law and politics equally leads to their increasing interdependence. As Weber comments:

> ... [t]he constant expansion of the market ... has favored the monopolization and regulation of all 'legitimate' coercive power by one universalist coercive institution through the disintegration of all particularist status-determined and other coercive structures which have been resting mainly on economic monopolies.[90]

Modern politics is guaranteed by the legal system but legality is not its primary source as claimed by so many theories of the rule of law and the constitutional state. Weber even concludes that the most fundamental questions of politics are left unregulated by the modern system of positive law and must be resolved through the medium of political conventions and internal rationality of the political system.[91] This differentiation of political and legal rationality makes it impossible to reduce political issues to legal categories and vice versa.

The Abstraction of Power as Liberty in Modern Constitutional Statehood

Using the sociological perspective, power is commonly defined as a capacity and therefore needs to be distinguished from its exercise and institutionalization.[92] However, it is not merely a conflict and problem-solving capacity because the most efficient use of power is prevention and neutralization of such conflicts and problems before they arise in society.

Recalling Spinoza's distinction between *potestas* and *potentia*, Steven Lukes seeks to eliminate the great variety of metaphorical and analytical uses of the concept of power including Foucault's notion of omnipresent power strategies to which there is no social outside. Lukes directly links power to the concept of domination, yet does not treat domination as mere subjugation when he states:

89 Roberto M. Unger, *Law in Modern Society: Toward a Criticism of Social Theory* (New York: Free Press, 1976), 58–62.

90 Max Weber, supra n. 80, 337.

91 Ibid., 330.

92 Steven Lukes, supra n. 71, 12.

> Power as domination is the ability to constrain the choices of others, coercing them or securing their compliance, by impending them from living as their own nature and judgement dictate.[93]

Nevertheless, power is not just a capacity different from its exercise. It also is manifest in its exercise.[94] State power may be backed by the use or threat of force, yet its exercise is far from these simple coercive measures.[95] It involves complex reasons of actions beyond the Weberian notion of politics as a socially dominating struggle for power. Political institutions do not have their exclusive origins in conflict between social actors over the monopoly of power.

Furthermore, power is not implicated in all spheres of society. Its exercise is largely operating without explicitly stated reasons and intentions and proceeds as a type of 'background practices'[96] granting legitimation. Political power is then different from non-political power relationships evolving in modern society without legal codification and political institutionalization. Political power, therefore, needs to be analysed as an intrinsic part of the functionally differentiated political system and its background practices and operations including structural coupling with the system of positive law in modern society.

The historical construction of modern states thus cannot be simply identified with a process of heightening political force and coercion and constituting other forms of social domination and subjugation. During the process of modern state-building, power, in fact:

> ... was refined as a differentiated social object ... utilized in increasingly constant procedures, and ... defined and applied in legal formulae that could be used, in internally replicable manner, to regulate very different questions across wide social boundaries.[97]

The process of growing political abstraction through generalized and uniformly applicable employment of political power meant that the European sovereign states underwent the process of self-consolidation by specific structural changes. These changes include the establishment of institutional mechanisms for integrating powerful private groups into the administrative apparatus, the development

---

93 Ibid., 85.

94 John Searle, *Making the Social World: The Structure of Human Civilization* (Oxford: Oxford University Press, 2010), 146.

95 George H. Sabine, 'The Concept of the State as Power', *Philosophical Review* 29(4) (1920): 301.

96 John Searle, supra n. 94, 155; Searle also refers to 'background abilities' in his earlier work *The Construction of Social Reality* (London: Penguin 1995), 127.

97 Chris Thornhill, *A Sociology of Constitutions: Constitutions and State Legitimacy in Historical-Sociological Perspective* (Cambridge: Cambridge University Press, 2011), 158.

of more regular boundaries between state and other social spheres, such as the economy and religion, the establishment of control and limitation of social issues that had to be filtered through the political system and the employment of power as 'a uniform commodity' organized in distinct procedures.[98]

The state and its constitution started to function as 'an artificial device for holding together what has emerged as the self-reinforcing dynamics in the political system and the legal system'.[99] Because of these structural changes, sovereign states became public actors using power in society through general principles and public procedures which allowed them 'to apply and reproduce power in abstracted inclusionary fashion and to withdraw the internal basis of political power from incessant contest'.[100] However, the legal image of the subjects of this power as bearers of general subjective rights and the constitutional construction of these rights as uniform attributes of legal subjects resulted in the expansion of political power and, as Chris Thornhill, for instance, remarks, rights evolved 'as inner elements of power's abstracted autonomy'.[101]

The original use of general rights by states to replace feudal societal particularism led to political and legal monism, and sovereignty of the state could abstract itself as a public order under the rule of general laws.[102] At the same time, the growing functional differentiation of modern societies led to the increasing dependence on generally articulated public laws and formal rights, reflected and culminating in the Enlightenment doctrines of natural and universal rights and liberties.

Modern sovereign states effectively separated themselves from other social spheres and transformed their constitutional orders into an internal power apparatus. At this point in modern European history, rights and constitutions – as the most legitimate form of political power and their normative and ideological contexts – began to play a formative role in the creation of the modern democratic state. They actually represented a revolutionary form of modern power applying itself throughout society at an unprecedented level of abstraction, generalization, autonomy and inclusion.

Modern revolutions, therefore, are both rights revolutions and constitutional revolutions, and the popular sovereignty doctrine is but the final moment in the modern process of the political construction of the sovereign constitutional state.[103] In the revolutionary constitutional principle of national inclusion, political power finally became both an abstracted and inclusive social resource and the whole

98 Ibid., 159.

99 Niklas Luhmann, supra n. 12, 365.

100 Chris Thornhill, supra n. 97, 159.

101 Ibid., 161.

102 Daniel Philpott, *Revolutions in Sovereignty. How Ideas Shaped Modern International Relations* (Princeton, NJ: Princeton University Press, 2001).

103 Theda Skocpol, *States and Social Revolutions* (Cambridge: Cambridge University Press, 1979).

constitutional formation was reconfigured under the principles of universal rights and popular sovereignty. The revolutionary constitutions thus transformed society:

> … from a diffusely structured array of particular status-defined groups, diversely and pluralistically related to the state, into an evenly ordered mass of – in principle – functionally autonomous individuals, selectively included in and excluded from political power. The relations between these individuals, then, were increasingly mediated through the state: that is, through rights guaranteed by the state as a centre of representative sovereignty.[104]

Constitutions represent a power-building model while power ensures its constitutional self-constraint. They are a vehicle of both political legitimacy and organization of politics in modern society. They are 'functional preconditions for the positive abstraction of political power and … highly probable preconditions of institutions using power: that is, states'.[105]

Modern societies are functionally differentiated and pluralistic, and constitutions ensure that modern political institutions augmenting power are both public in the sense of social inclusion and limited in terms of their expansion into other spheres and segments of society. The normative foundations of political legitimacy and legal validity need to be sociologically reinterpreted as power expansion, and identify the social reasons for the reliance of political institutions on abstract principles of constitutional laws.

Legitimacy is not achieved by constitutional protection and the enforcement of political ideals and generalized principles of legal validity. It is not produced by political acts and decisions consistent with a body of theoretical normative judgements. Legitimacy, rather, is obtained through complex and contingent processes of specific semantic changes and constitutional formations as functional societal preconditions of modern political power. It is an outcome of the societal functions of normative political forms and legitimate political power is:

> … power exercised in accordance with public laws, applied evenly and intelligibly to all members of society (including those factually using power), which are likely to give maximum scope to the pursuit of freedoms that are capable of being generally and equally appreciated by all social actors.[106]

Only a social theoretical approach can explain the paradox of modern societies producing the highest level of power and social liberty at the same time.[107] Constitutions function as maximizations of power reserves in modern society

104 Chris Thornhill, supra n. 97, 218.

105 Ibid., 372.

106 Ibid., 7.

107 Peter Wagner, *A Sociology of Modernity: Liberty and Discipline* (London: Routledge, 1994).

and, at the same time, 'in multiplying power, they also (normally) produce and multiply social freedom'.[108] They, therefore, hardly can be seen as mere reservoirs of deductive ideals and prescriptions. Liberty is not the ultimate purpose of constitutional settlements. It is, rather, a contingent outcome of constitutional functions.

Democratization of Politics: On the Self-Legitimization of Power as Popular Sovereignty

A social theoretical perspective of sovereignty must accommodate both Nietzsche's call for a theory of command structures and the need to study the social variety of their legitimation. Weber's early sociological analysis of the modern state already described the constitutional state's capacity to distribute power in modern society. It also highlighted the problem of legitimacy as the general historical process of societal differentiation and the specific process of belief formation and power persuasion.

While Foucault's critique of the notion of the nation as a juridical category of self-rule helps to identify non-juridical and politically non-institutionalized forms of power in modern society, it neglects exactly the productive power of the notion of *demos* and popular sovereignty as a legitimation strategy drawing on the image of the ultimate social body with the unlimited capacity of inclusion and exclusion of individuals, groups, political techniques, programmes and ideas. In the final sections of this chapter, the concept of popular sovereignty, therefore, is analysed as a distinct form of legitimation of power generated by the modern political system which, furthermore, involves the self-description of modern society through symbolic representations of political authority and its legal constitution as an imagined democratic polity of the sovereign people.

Modernization of politics means its democratization. This process involves fundamental semantic changes in the concept of sovereignty but also pragmatic changes in its metaphorical use. Former subjects of sovereign power – inhabitants of a territory of the state – now become members of a new imagined polity – the sovereign democratic nation.[109] They expect to exercise the same sovereignty to which they are subjected.

Modernization as democratization and the rise of nationhood and the sovereign political people led to the fundamental changes in the political semantics introduced by Hobbes and other scholars of the seventeenth and eighteenth centuries.[110] The social contract ceased to be perceived as just a device creating a sovereign rule and

108 Chris Thornhill, supra n. 97, 375.

109 For the link between modernity and nationalism, see, for instance, Liah Greenfeld, *Nationalism: Five Roads to Modernity* (Cambridge, MA: Harvard University Press, 1992).

110 Quentin Skinner, 'Hobbes on Representation', *European Journal of Philosophy* 13(2) (2005): 155.

guaranteeing social stability, peace and liberties of the sovereign's subjects. Now, the need for authority and rule became identical with the demand of individual liberty and rights. Liberty and authority became just two sides of the same coin – the self-governing people.

In this context, Montesquieu's famous remark about the confusion between the power of the people and the liberty of the people[111] may be reinterpreted as an example of different self-descriptions of popular sovereignty, the function of which is to limit the expansive semantics of either political power, or legal normativity associated with modern constitutional sovereignty. Liberty is impossible to guarantee if sovereignty of the people is unbound and unlimited by the constitution of civil rights and freedoms.[112] Nevertheless, power legitimized by sovereignty of the people may always redefine and reconsider the extent of the legal protection of individual liberties.

Constitutional rights and liberties mean nothing if they are not self-constructed and self-constituted by the people. What has been described by normative political theory as the struggle between the aristocratic principle of liberty and the democratic principle of sovereignty or 'the thousand-year-old duel fought between sovereignty and liberty, between Power and the freeman',[113] may subsequently be reformulated as the very structure of constitutional sovereignty permanently translating political will to the legal norms and vice versa.

The sovereign will of the people guarantees a right aim and a right judgement in modern democracies.[114] Through this evolution of the modern political semantics, a political will of the sovereign gets linked to the general popular will and the modern state becomes the democratic state. The creation of the people as the new sovereign legitimized by its absolute and unlimited will is a self-referential and self-descriptive act drawing together the modern political tendency of both despotism and liberty. Whereas the divine will takes the form of eternal laws, the popular will, despite Rousseau's concept of the transcendental general will, has no such stability and, apart from constantly referring to the principle of the common good and natural justice, is contingent and may be changed by the successive laws and decision-making of democratically elected bodies.[115]

---

111 Charles de Montesquieu, *The Spirit of the Laws* (Cambridge: Cambridge University Press, 1989), 155–156.

112 Brian Tamanaha, *On the Rule of Law: History, Politics, Theory* (Cambridge: Cambridge University Press, 2004), 47–59.

113 Bertrand de Jouvenel, *On Power. Its Nature and the History of Its Growth* (Boston, MA: Beacon Press, 1962), 318.

114 Bertrand de Jouvenel, *On Sovereignty. An Inquiry into the Political Good* (Indianapolis, IN: Liberty Fund, 1997), 107–115.

115 Patrick Riley, *The General Will before Rousseau: The Transformation of the Divine into the Civic* (Princeton, NJ: Princeton University Press, 1986).

Contingency of popular sovereignty and democratic government cannot be mitigated by elevating the masses, political majority and its representative bodies to the status of the divine will. In this respect, Herbert Spencer commented:

> The great political superstition of the past was the divine right of kings. The great political superstition of the present is the divine rights of parliaments. The oil anointing seems unawares to have dripped from the head of the one on to the heads of the many, and given sacredness to them also and to their decrees.[116]

The most significant change in the concept of sovereignty now identified as popular sovereignty is thus the enhancement of power generated from within society. It is no longer individuals and political bodies who exercise sovereignty by limiting all other power agencies within the framework of institutionalized politics. In modern times, sovereignty signifies the self-administering and steering capacity of society that is self-governed by the popular will and legitimized by the common good of the whole polity. The constant making and unmaking of the modern sovereign state as well as supranational and international organizations actually contributes to this enhancement and expansion of power.[117]

Contingency of Popular Sovereignty: Notes on Tocqueville's Proto-Sociology of Politics and Civility

When Montesquieu wrote his treatise on the spirit of the laws, the fascination by the social and cultural multitude was matched by the common perception of sovereign authority as fundamentally important for the process of law-making and the overall organization of political life. The spirit of the laws referred to the particularity of human cultures but the very concept of political power and the exercise of a sovereign rule were considered independent variables of politics. A sovereign ruler, indeed, had to respect the spirit of the laws but this job was not fundamentally different from the Hobbesian sovereign's obligation to protect those whose acts of will led to the civil association and the constitution of sovereign power.[118]

Nevertheless, it was Tocqueville who first noticed the paradoxical truth about modern political democracy governed by the constitutional rule of law, namely that its stability depends on citizens being aware that they can change the laws

---

116 Herbert Spencer, *The Man Versus the State: With Six Essays on Government, Society, and Freedom* (Indianapolis, IN: Liberty Fund, 1982), 123.

117 Robert O. Keohane, *Power and Governance in a Partially Globalized World* (London: Routledge, 2002), 71.

118 Andrew Arato and Jean Cohen, *Civil Society and Political Theory* (Cambridge, MA: The MIT Press, 1992), 87–88.

at any time because they have made them.[119] Popular sovereignty, therefore, finds itself under the jurisdiction of contingent non-transcendental social law.[120] Though Rousseau and Robespierre's notions of politically enforced civil religion profoundly differed from Tocqueville's emphasis on personal commitment to both individual liberty and the public order of democracy, the intrinsic contingency of the democratic political system is strikingly present even in Rousseau's famous statement that each man 'in giving himself to all gives himself to none'[121] which summarized the identification of liberty with authority of the general will and considered this will a process of constant willing of all members of polity.

Now, sovereignty is reformulated as the democratic self-reference and self-description of self-governing citizens.[122] The democratic self-rule embodying political equality of all citizens turns out to be the structural precondition of the modern political system. The republican notion of liberty as personal autonomy and a lack of political domination can materialize only if it establishes the political sphere of participating and deliberating citizens. The concept of politics as socially active involvement and participation – politics of active republican citizenship – is considered the most effective protection against arbitrary rule and domination.[123]

However, Tocqueville asked the most intriguing question of how democratic societies can persist despite their profoundly pluralistic nature.[124] He believed that citizens had to share the same civic virtues, mores and faith in the democratic process and institutions because no democratic society could survive without these common bonds of civic culture irreducible to individual goals and interests.[125] Studying democracy and its civic culture subsequently required a completely new approach, emphasizing the social conditions of modern political life and the novelty of social and moral experiences caused by the gradual development of democracy.

Because a sovereign ruler is the people living in its self-governed polity, politics becomes a study matter for a sociologist and Tocqueville highlights

119 Werner J. Dannhauser, 'Some Thoughts on Liberty, Equality and Tocqueville's *Democracy in America*', *Social Philosophy and Policy* 2(1) (1984): 141.

120 For similarities with the autopoietic systems theory, see especially Francois Ewald, 'The Law of Law', in *Autopoietic Law: A New Approach to Law and Society*, ed. Gunther Teubner (Berlin: Walter de Gruyter, 1988), 45.

121 Jean-Jacques Rousseau, *Discourse on Political Economy and the Social Contract* (Oxford: Oxford University Press, 1994), 55.

122 For this exceptional similarity between Tocqueville's political sociology and Luhmann's systems theory, see Claus Offe, *Reflections on America: Tocqueville, Weber and Adorno in the United States* (Cambridge: Polity Press, 2005), 17.

123 Richard Bellamy, *Political Constitutionalism: A Republican Defence of the Constitutionality of Democracy* (Cambridge: Cambridge University Press, 2007), 154–175.

124 Alexis de Tocqueville, *Democracy in America* (Chicago, IL: University of Chicago Press, 2000), 7.

125 See also Bernard Yack, 'The Myth of the Civic Nation', in *Theorizing Nationalism*, ed. Ron Beiner (Albany, NY: State University of New York Press, 1998), 103.

three theoretical variables as essential for the study of the coming social and political age of equality, namely the factual conditions, the institutions and laws and the subjective dispositions of society. While the factual conditions drew on Montesquieu's studies of historical, geographic and other external aspects of political life, and the institutions and laws recalled the Hobbesian language of politics, the subjective dispositions of particular customs, sentiments and expectations of members of a particular political society indicated a radical shift in political science.[126] According to Tocqueville, the power of intersubjective and commonly shared customs eventually determined social and political developments and the functioning of normatively imposed institutions.

Social structural preconditions, such as the lack of historically rooted inequalities acquired by birth, frequent elections and exercising political rights had been extremely important for the American democracy,[127] yet this democracy could only flourish because its citizens loved it as much as they loved their private religion. The public devotion to liberty had been as strong as the private devotion to religious belief. However, this public devotion to liberty had been supported by a belief that secular and religious powers must be kept away from each other and religious authority must not end up in the hands of politicians.[128]

Popular Sovereignty as the Simultaneous Legitimation and De-legitimation of Power

Tocqueville's view that a common *civic culture* and faith in shared civic virtues and mores is a precondition of democratic society informs a classic sociological view that modern politics is impossible to be exclusively founded on the instrumental rationality of individual actors negotiating the most acceptable ways of securing individual goals and interests. Modern tension between democracy as a form of government and democracy as a form of social life[129] is reflected in the generalization of moral values and legal norms which lead to the semantic creation of a new point of politics – the nation as the sovereign people using its political will to enforce generally binding legal rules in its polity.[130]

---

126 Annelien de Dijn, *French Political Thought from Montesquieu to Tocqueville: Liberty in a Levelled Society?* (Cambridge: Cambridge University Press, 2008), 150–151.

127 Sheldon S. Wolin, *Tocqueville between Two Worlds: The Making of a Political and Theoretical Life* (Princeton, NJ: Princeton University Press, 2001), 305.

128 For more recent discussions of civil religion and Tocqueville, see especially Ronald Beiner, *Civil Religion: A Dialogue in the History of Political Philosophy* (Cambridge: Cambridge University Press, 2011), 249–258.

129 Jacques Ranciere, 'Does Democracy Mean Something?', in Jacques Ranciere, *Dissensus* (London: Continuum, 2010), 47.

130 Frederick M. Barnard, 'National Culture and Political Legitimacy: Herder and Rousseau', *Journal of the History of Ideas* 44(2) (1983): 231.

However, the sovereign people and its polity is not the substance of power but one of its conceptualizations in modern politics and law. The legitimation of power through its democratic constitutionalization is part of the general tendency of power to self-justification and a drive to accept the social state of things as understandable and therefore acceptable for those living in it. The paradoxical differentiation of constituent and constituted power – this unique semantic invention of the political sovereign of the people that does not decide anything itself and transfers all decision-making processes to the normative realm of political constitution – thus needs to be reconceptualized as coeval processes of the constitutional self-limitation of power and power dynamics beyond the realm of constitution which, nevertheless, recursively influence the conceptualizations and symbolization of basic constitutional categories such as the people, the citizen, constitutional sovereignty, constitutional rights, their transnational legal regimes and so on.[131]

Tocqueville's early analysis of democracy already draws on the paradox of government founded by a historically and socially contingent civic culture which recursively requires governmental enforcement and support. Democratic polity of the sovereign people representing the moral foundations of society and legitimizing power of government is paradoxically countered by the fact that the fundamental values and moral expressions require the support of government and its power structures. Governmental power legitimized by the image of democratic polity actually constitutes this polity. Its laws facilitate the semantics of popular sovereignty both materialized and limited by the rule of law. Polity is thus constituted by the structurally coupling legal and political systems to enhance and legitimize power in society. There is no polity without the systems of positive law and politics.[132]

'[T]he "power of the people" simultaneously legitimizes and de-legitimizes itself'.[133] It found its strong manifestation within the sovereign constitutional state as a historically specific organization facilitating communication between modern politics and the system of positive law. Nevertheless, as the reader could see in the opening part of this book, it applies to national polities as well as supranational and transnational polities and even affects moral and political speculations about global cosmopolitan community – cosmo-polity.

---

131 R.B.J. Walker, 'Sovereignty, Identity, Community: Reflections on the Horizons of Contemporary Political Practice', in *Contending Sovereignties: Redefining Political Community*, eds R.B.J. Walker and Saul H. Mendlovitz (Boulder, CO: Lynne Rienner, 1990), 159.

132 For the polity formation through systemic communication in the context of international relations, see especially Alexander Wendt, 'Collective Identity Formation and the International State', *American Political Science Review* 88(2) (1994): 384.

133 Jacques Ranciere, supra n. 129, 53.

Though cosmopolitan community may be important rhetorically and semantically, it hardly can govern any government in an operative sense.[134] Supranational and transnational organizations, therefore, facilitate their specific forms of communication between law and politics and incorporate legitimation alternatives beyond the nation state and its symbolic images. Nevertheless, these alternatives cannot completely avoid legal and political communication reflecting on the notion of self-governing polity of free and equal citizens actively participating in these supranational and transnational legal and political organizations.

Modern law and politics – local, national, European or global – are thus permanently exposed to the irresolvable questions of who is the people, what is the difference between an individual and a citizen, what establishes the difference of private and public life, how to overcome intrinsic tensions between social and legal justice, legitimacy and legality and so on. Neither legal normativity nor political decision fully grasp the social contingency underlying the modern concept of popular sovereignty. The autopoietic social systems of positive law and politics, therefore, can only steer communication about these issues within and beyond democratic statehood which, rather than identifying the foundational norms and principles of politics, only raises more questions stimulating further political and legal communication without moral and existential foundations.

---

134 Edward L. Rubin, *Beyond Camelot: Rethinking Politics and Law for the Modern State* (Princeton, NJ: Princeton University Press, 2005), 225.

PART III
Theories and Systems

Chapter 6

The Evolution of the EU's Political and Legal Autopoiesis: On the Self-Reference of European Polity

The concept of polity generally signifies a politically organized society, its form and process of government. It assumes a system of legitimately exercised political power. In modern democratic polity, power circulates between the people, party politics, administration and public opinion communicated through mass media.[1] While the principle of popular sovereignty – sovereignty 'by the people' – provides the system with democratic legitimacy, political parties struggle to win power by winning a majority of the votes 'of the people' and thus form a government administering specific policies 'for the people' which can be recursively evaluated by the public, affect political preferences and thus contribute to the future processes of political majority-building.

This power circulation does not exist in the European Union. The EU political system circulates power by the self-referential operations of its administrative organization. State organization is missing but alternative forms of governing and processes of decision-making are no less powerful. The absence of two out of Lincoln's three characteristics of democratic government,[2] namely, government 'of the people' and 'by the people', makes the EU's political system one which primarily operates 'for the people' or, better, 'for the peoples of the EU'. It is impossible to characterize the Union in common terms of territoriality, government, population and (in case of democratic statehood) popular legitimacy. In the absence of EU democratic government, the complex forms and processes of the Union's political decision-making are commonly labelled as a system of *European governance*. Good and efficient governance is considered a major force integrating the emerging *European polity* despite the absence of EU statehood and democratic government.[3]

---

1 Niklas Luhmann, *Die Politik der Gesellschaft* (Frankfurt: Suhrkamp, 2002), 258.

2 Abraham Lincoln, *Speeches and Writings: Volume 2: 1859–1865* (New York, NY: Library of America, 1989).

3 Christian Joerges and Renaud Dehousse, eds, *Good Governance in Europe's Integrated Market* (Oxford: Oxford University Press, 2002); Leon Lindberg and Stewart Scheingold, *Europe's Would-be-Polity: Patterns of Change in the European Community* (Upper Saddle River, NJ: Prentice-Hall, 1970); Sonja P. Riekmann, Monika Mokre and Michael Latzer, eds, *The State of Europe: Transformations of Statehood from a European Perspective* (Cambridge: Cambridge University Press, 2005).

The process of European integration, therefore, is one of the most persuasive examples of the paradoxical constitution of polity beyond the democratic state organization, yet constantly searching for its efficiency and democratization as two general forms of legitimation of power in modern society. The democratic deficit and legitimation debates, rather than limiting, actually enhance the EU's political and legal communication and thus contribute its societal evolution with all its paradoxes, crises and asymmetries.

Furthermore, the growing systemic complexity of European political institutions, laws and administrative regulations has led to the creation of new political concepts, metaphors and legal fictions. Their purpose is to grasp internal tensions, structural irritations and systemic paradoxes within the European Union and thus to respond to its recent developments. The Union currently represents *the unity of conceptual contradictions*. Apart from the concept of divided sovereignty, the slogan 'widening is deepening' introduced in the 1990s and the appropriated self-description of the EU as 'unity in diversity', political concepts, such as 'polity without statehood' and 'differentiated integration', have been adopted to describe current operative paradoxes of European politics and law.

In the next two chapters, the semantics and structures of the European Union are thus analysed to show both the potential and limits of the concept of sovereignty in post-sovereign society. This chapter describes the emergence of self-referential European politics and law in three separate steps. In the first step, political and legal theory of the EU integration and its paradigmatic changes are analysed vis-à-vis the EU's legal and political integration and functional differentiation. It especially is highlighted by the Union's legitimation dilemma and its recent legal reflection in the Lisbon 'Reform' Treaty. Summarizing major theoretical debates regarding the European polity, its legal form and governance, the chapter subsequently argues that the general theory of autopoietic social systems synthesizes the temporal, functional and self-referential aspects of European integration and avoids the epistemological trap to identify the particular concept of polity, its organizational restraints and institutional hierarchies with the general concept of society.

Although the Union transgresses its nation state segmentation, the notions of statehood and popular sovereignty continue to inform legal and political semantics of the EU and specific responses to the Union's systemic tensions, such as the policy of differentiated integration legislated by the EU flexibility clauses. Nevertheless, this policy also shows a much more profound social dynamics of differentiation which does not internalize the concept of the European polity as an encompassing metaphor of society but makes it part of self-referential and self-limiting semantics of the functionally differentiated European political system. In the final part of this chapter, the EU political system, therefore, is described as self-referential, internally differentiated between European institutions and Member State governments and functionally differentiated from the system of European law.

Between Neofunctionalist and Intergovernmentalist Debates: the European Polity, its Theoretical Conceptualizations and Legitimacy

Since the early stages of European integration in the 1950s,[4] normative theoretical debates regarding European integration and the emergence of the European polity have been informed by the theoretical conflict between neofunctionalist[5] and intergovernmentalist approaches.[6] In general, neofunctionalist political theories assume that European governance will eventually constitute a supranational federalized EU statehood or some alternative supreme form of European political and constitutional integration. In contrast, intergovernmentalist perspectives see European integration continuing to be bound by Member State interests and priorities.

Despite many differences, both theoretical approaches consider statehood and state sovereignty[7] a driving force of European integration – neofunctionalists as a desired goal of the European federalist imagination and constitution-making and intergovernmentalists as an institutional framework embedded in the nation state, accounting for the scale and style of European political and legal integration. The neofunctionalist paradigm in EU political studies takes European governance as a force of instrumental rationality which can recursively constitute the democratized European polity. The centrality of technocratic bureaucracy and expert knowledge strongly influenced the early stages of European integration and federalist visions of the 1950s.[8] Drawing on the power of instrumental reason and pluralist theories of international politics, neofunctionalists believe that different EU agencies, interest groups and corporations can forge links across national boundaries and create political pressure in favour of progressive integration within the Member States.[9] The EU institutions and their integration policies are expected to inspire the 'functionalist spillover' and further integration demands among relevant interest groups and agencies.[10]

---

4 Ernst B. Haas, *The Uniting of Europe: Political, Social and Economic Forces 1950–1957* (Stanford, CA: Stanford University Press, 1958).

5 For the multilevel neofunctionalist perspective, see, for instance, Liesbet Hooghe, ed., *Cohesion Policy and European Integration: Building Multi-level Governance* (Oxford: Oxford University Press, 1996).

6 For the intergovernmentalist perspective, see especially Andrew Moravcsik, *The Choice for Europe: Social Purpose and State Power from Messina to Maastricht* (Ithaca, NY: Cornell University Press, 1998).

7 Richard Bellamy and Dario Castiglione, 'Building the Union: The Nature of Sovereignty in the Political Architecture of Europe', *Philosophy and Law* 16 (1997): 421.

8 Kevin Featherstone, 'Jean Monnet and the "Democratic Deficit" in the European Union', *Journal of Common Market Studies* 32 (1994): 149.

9 Stephen George, *Politics and Policy in the European Union* (Oxford: Oxford University Press, 3rd edition, 1996), 38.

10 Robert Keohane and Stanley Hoffmann, 'Institutional Change in Europe in the 1980s', in Robert Keohane and Stanley Hoffman, eds, *The New European Community: Decisionmaking and Institutional Change* (Boulder, CO: Westview Press, 1991), 1, 20.

The neofunctionalist legitimacy of European integration is the one driven by the *outcomes* of élite-led policies rather than democratic procedures.[11] On the other hand, intergovernmentalists insist that one can understand EU integrative dynamics by explaining Member State *negotiations* rather than referring to the imaginary political projects.[12] The intergovernmentalist approach links integration policies to the logic of demand and supply and perceives democratic legitimacy as a problem and political value typical of the nation state. The demand for integration is 'a function of domestic preference formation' while the supply is 'a function of interstate bargaining and interstate strategic interaction'.[13] Intergovernmentalism is based on the public choice theory according to which democratically constituted Member States can carry out a cost-benefit calculation whether to accept or reject integration policies. The importance of democratic legitimacy is upheld by preserving the central role of Member States in European integration.[14]

Disputes between neofunctionalists defending the multilevel governance model and intergovernmentalists arguing in favour of the Member State-centric model of European governance often have a strong political and ideological context and significantly influence EU legislation and policy-making. They commonly perceive the problem of the EU's legitimation as a central theoretical issue and cling on to normative expectations of the European public and political élites. Different theories of EU integration thus aim at utilizing legitimacy by conforming EU politics and administration to external criteria of public efficiency and/or generally shared values and obligations. For this purpose, normative theories of EU integration reinvent and recycle political semantics of statehood, sovereignty, civil society, public accountability, democratic participation of citizens and/or their absence at EU level.

EU Legal and Political Structures: Preliminary Remarks on the Lisbon Treaty and the EU's Legitimacy

Before analysing EU legal documents and multilevel governance policies, it is necessary to re-emphasize a profound difference between semantics and structures

11 William Wallace and Julie Smith, 'Democracy or Technocracy? European Integration and the Problem of Popular Consent', in *The Crisis of Representation in Europe*, ed. Jack Hayward (London: Frank Cass, 1995), 140.

12 Andrew Moravcsik, 'Preferences and Power in the European Community: A Liberal Intergovernmentalist Approach', *Journal of Common Market Studies* 31 (1993): 473.

13 Paul Craig, 'The Nature of the Community: Integration, Democracy, and Legitimacy', in *The Evolution of EU Law. 2nd edition*, eds Paul Craig and Gráinne de Búrca (Oxford: Oxford University Press, 2011), 19–20.

14 Alan Milward, *The European Rescue of the Nation State* (Berkeley, CA: University of California Press, 1992).

of specific social systems.[15] The difference also informs structures and semantics of the EU as a specific kind of autopoietic organization.[16]

Semantics usually change with a change in social structures but this coeval process is accompanied by many discrepancies and communication noises. In the current EU state of semantic confusion and structural transformation, it is thus of primary importance 'to account for the semantic contents of the categories that we apply to new and disturbing phenomena in our social reality'.[17] In this section, I therefore highlight this close relationship between EU legitimation semantics so strongly disputed by different social and political theories and their structural reflections in the EU legal and political systems.

After the 'system consolidating' period of the Treaty of Amsterdam (1999), which was preceded by the 'policy-generating' Single European Act (1987) and the 'polity-creating' Maastricht Treaty of European Union (1993),[18] the Union's constitution-making (2000–05) failed in its reflexive polity-transformation attempts at democratizing the constituent power beyond the Member States.[19] Nevertheless, the detailed legalistic frameworks drafted by successive treaties in the 1990s could not avoid addressing the question of whether EU nations have been building a new kind of profoundly *democratized European polity*.[20]

The European Commission linked the concept of governance to the new polity emerging within the EU in 1990s European public debates.[21] It thus introduced the political themes of who is actually governed by EU governance, how, in whose name and to what end.[22] Indeed, it is true that democratic procedures and institutions have been a precondition of EU membership and thus are embedded in nation

15 Niklas Luhmann, *Law as a Social System* (Oxford: Oxford University Press, 2004), 143–147.

16 For the notion of an autopoietic social organization and its role in an autopoietic system, see, for instance, John Mingers, *Self-Producing Systems: Implications and Applicatioins of Autopoiesis* (Dordrecht: Springer, 1994), 138.

17 Peer Zumbansen, 'Semantics of European Law', *European Law Journal* 5 (1999): 114.

18 Alexander Stubb, *Negotiationg Flexibility in the European Union* (Basingstoke: Palgrave, 2002), 25.

19 Erik O. Eriksen, ed., *Making the European Polity: Reflexive Integration in the EU* (London: Routledge, 2005).

20 John Clarke, 'Reconstituting Europe: governing a European people?', in *Remaking Governance: Peoples, Politics and the Public Sphere*, ed. Janet Newman (Bristol: The Policy Press, 2005), 28.

21 Alec Stone Sweet and Wayne Sandholtz, 'Integration, Transnational Governance and the Institutionalization of the European Polity', in *European Integration and Supranational Governance*, eds Alec Stone Sweet and Wayne Sandholtz (Oxford: Oxford University Press, 1998), 1; Paul Craig and Carol Harlow, eds, *Lawmaking in the European Union* (Dordrecht: Kluwer, 1998).

22 Thomas Banchoff and Mitchell P. Smith, eds, *Legitimacy and the European Union: The Contested Polity* (London: Routledge, 1999).

states. Responding to the Constitutional Treaty's ratification failure and building on the democratic legitimacy commitment already incorporated in the Treaty of Amsterdam and the Treaty of Nice,[23] the current Lisbon Treaty, nevertheless, opens by an explicit proclamation turning the EU's biggest fear, the democratic legitimacy and its deficit, into a political desire. It directly links the Union's governance and its efficiency driven 'legitimacy by outcomes' to the legitimacy by democratic values and procedures in its preamble in the following words:

> DESIRING to enhance further the democratic and efficient functioning of the institutions so as to enable them better to carry out, within a single institutional framework, the tasks entrusted to them.[24]

At the level of general proclamations and principles, the Treaty thus makes the Union considerably more committed to the discourse of democratic legitimation and/or its absence. The legalist language of the EU accommodates the need to democratize representation, political participation, openness and accountability of EU institutions. The legal provisions of the Treaty, therefore, expose the Union much more to the political discourse of democratic legitimation and/or its absence which will be examined in detail in the next chapter.

Nevertheless, it already may be stated that the EU operating according to the legal provisions of the Lisbon Treaty is very different from a democratic polity drawing on the principles of democratic will-formation and the majority rule. Its maximum 'reform effect' can be the construction of a polity operating on the enhanced principles of democratic representation of views, interests and preferences of citizens of the Union. Instead of its radical democratization, the system of European governance thus continues to be an example of *negotiated governance* which has been agreed by the national governments of Member States.

Negotiated governance and the continuing central role of Member States effectively rules out any chance of building supranational European statehood governed under a constitution. More than three decades ago, even such a strong advocate of European federalism as Leo Tindemans already warned against the

---

23 Beate Kohler-Koch and Berthold Rittberger, eds, *Debating the Democratic Legitimacy in the EU* (Lanham MD: Rowman & Littlefield, 2007).

24 Preamble of the Treaty of Lisbon amending the Treaty on European Union and the Treaty establishing European Community, Consolidated Version of the Treaty on European Union, *Official Journal of the European Union*, 9th May 2008, C115/15. In the text approved at the Intergovernmental Conference in Brussels in December 2007, there is an explicit remark tracing this commitment back to the Treaty of Amsterdam and the Treaty of Nice: 'Desiring to complete the process started by the Treaty of Amsterdam and by the Treaty of Nice with a view to enhancing the efficiency and democratic legitimacy of the Union and to improving the coherence of its action …'CIG 14/07, Brussels, 3 December 2007.

utopian nature of European statehood as potentially damaging faith in Europe.[25] Instead of drafting a constitutional formula for Europe, which would imitate institutional settings of the modern nation state, the 1975 *Tindemans Report on European Union* focused on a series of unification efforts in the areas of foreign policy, economic and social policy, fundamental civil rights and institutional governance-driven alternatives of political, momentum-based, ready-made concepts of federal unification. In this context, Tindemans commented two decades later:

> Much as I would like to see a definitive federal union materialize overnight, I do not believe that it can happen or, at least, not in one sudden, gigantic step. If we were closer to some sort of popular high tide in support for the federalist model in the 1940s and 1950s, we were undoubtedly further away in 1974–5, and we are indisputably yet further away now.[26]

After the failure of EU constitution-making and the Lisbon Treaty's polity-building self-constraints, the emphasis on spontaneity in the unification of Europe and the impossibility of ignoring that democratic legitimacy is embedded in the Member States became a lot more significant. European integration has become ever more dependent on democratization of its institutions and EU democratization has become subject of evolution rather than a constitutional leap of faith in the European *demos* in waiting.

These trends imply two crucial questions, namely, how far the Union's powers and jurisdiction can be extended without questioning the democratic sovereignty of Member States and to what extent effective European governance can expand without the institutional support of democratically legitimate political government.

Beyond Statehood: Social Constructivism and Functional Differentiation of the EU

The semantic persistence of statehood, democratic legitimacy and political sovereignty in both official documents and critical theories of EU integration shows persuasive force of the modern state as a concept used by the political system to describe its unity and to make its operations understandable as autonomous and independent of operations of other social systems, such as economy, law

25 Leo Tindemans, 'Letter to European Council colleagues', sent on 29 December 1975, at 8; the letter later annexed to 'European Union. Report by Mr Leo Tindemans, Prime Minister of Belgium, to the European Council', *Bulletin of the European Communities*, Supplement 1/76 (1976).

26 Leo Tindemans, 'Dreams come true, gradually: The Tindemans Report a quarter of a century on', in *The European Union beyond Amsterdam: New Concepts of European Integration*, ed. Martin Westlake (London: Routledge, 1998), 139.

and religion.[27] Nevertheless, structural complexities of EU supranational and transnational governance should rather warn us against simplistic criticisms of the EU's non-existent statehood drawing on the notion of political sovereignty. These complexities, however, should equally warn us against naïve parallels between European multilevel governance and the goal of democratic polity-building legitimizing further EU integration.

Within the context of private law, Hugh Collins, for instance, persuasively illustrated how the emerging European law structures have been disintegrating national institutions and autonomous structures of political authority and cultural identity. Sceptical about an 'ever closer Union' unified by one system of EU law, Collins concludes that the existing theoretical separation between public and private law has lost its explanatory value and is to be replaced by functionalist and contextualist theories of law better responding to the contingent and fragmented European social reality.[28]

Transgressing normative and semantic limitations of the notions of statehood and constitutional sovereignty, theoretical views of the Union, its governance and polity-building accommodate different perspectives capable of explaining the historical process of the Europeanization of national societies, the growing fragmentation of the EU and the functional differentiation of European politics and law. Evolutionary, constructivist and functional differentiation theories of EU law and politics have recently been emerging to semantically respond to structural changes of the EU and to make the Union understandable in both legal and political terms.

A: Evolutionary Perspectives

Evolutionary metaphors have been playing a significant role in social and political science reflections on European integration for some time. For instance, Martin Westlake introduces the paradigm of evolution theory to describe the spontaneity and the lack of intentionality in the process of European polity-building, constitution-making and legal integration.[29] According to his argument, the Union's constitutionalism is organic and evolutionary and as such may run in both progressive and regressive directions. While nation state constitution-making is typical of particular designs, deliberations and final settlements enacted after public reasoning and democratic decision-making, the European constitutional settlement has never been considered final. Instead, it favours a never-ending

27 For further details see, for instance, Michael King and Chris Thornhill, *Niklas Luhmann's Theory of Politics and Law* (Basingstoke: Palgrave, 2003), 77.

28 Hugh Collins, 'European Private Law and the Cultural Identity of Member States', *European Review of Private Law* 3 (1995): 353.

29 Martin Westlake, 'The European Union's 'blind watchmakers': The process of constitutional change', in Martin Westlake, ed., supra n. 26, 16.

process of organically reworking and reinterpreting the Union's legal framework and existing treaties.

According to the evolutionary perspectives,[30] European integration is a long-term evolutionary process, drawing on integrative drives but equally respecting existing political limitations and cultural boundaries.[31] European political leaders, their actions, discourses, disputes, constitutional proposals and blueprints are not part of a trivial system of rational choices, causes and consequences. The Union is governed by a constant flow of compromises and negotiated decisions. These are often the contingent result of the last-minute 'pressure-cooker atmosphere'[32] of intergovernmental conferences, meetings of the European Council, administrative decisions of the Commission and landmark judgments of the Court. However, mechanisms of the organic evolution of European constitutionalism and polity eventually determine EU deliberations, settlements, decisions, judgments and inter-institutional agreements. These mechanisms are described as 'blind watchmakers', momentarily selecting the best-fitting operations and decisions without any future 'intelligent' plan, purpose or knowledge of possible consequences.[33]

Unlike the nation state's constitutional and political changes, the Union's changes are more frequent, unintentional and cumbersome. European progressive integration and post-national, constitutionalism-based polity[34] are being built by temporary settlements determined by legal restraints and political circumstances at the time, such as the accession of different governments in individual Member States. Thus, the Union evolves organically, but also contingently. Selection processes are cumulative and their contingency translates into the systemic complexity of the evolving European legal and political systems.

B: Constructivist Perspectives

The fact that the Union falls short of having a state-like engineered political system and designed constitutional settlement raises the question of its political and legal 'deficits' in legitimacy, accountability, constitutionality, democracy and so on.[35] Among many theoretical elaborations and responses, social constructivist

30 For a global law evolutionary perspective, see Marc Amstutz, 'Global (Non-)Law: The Perspective of Evolutionary Jurisprudence', *German Law Journal* 9 (2008): 465.

31 Daniela Piana, 'An Evolutionary Approach to the Constitutionalism of an Enlarged EU: Why will Cognitive and Cultural Boundaries Matter?', in *Spreading Democracy and the Rule of Law? The Impact of EU Enlargement on the Rule of Law, Democracy and Constitutionalism in Post-communist Legal Orders*, eds Wojciech Sadurski, Adam Czarnota and Martin Krygier (Dordrecht, Springer, 2006), 219.

32 Martin Westlake, supra n. 29, 26.

33 Ibid., 18.

34 See, for instance, Jo Shaw, 'Postnational Constitutionalism in the European Union', *Journal of European Public Policy* 6 (1999): 579.

35 See, for instance, Svein Andersen and Kjell Eliassen, eds, *The European Union: How Democratic Is It?* (London: Sage, 1996).

approaches to EU governance and polity claim that the deficit discourse is theoretically flawed because of its continuing reliance on the idea of statehood and the concept of polity as a nation state-based society.

Social constructivism is close to the neofunctionalist paradigm despite constructivists' criticism of the utilitarianism and positivist methodology embraced by neofunctionalists. Some theorists even claim that neofunctionalism is a precursor of constructivist approaches in political theory.[36] According to the constructivist view, the EU is more than an intergovernmental regime and constitutes its distinct forms of multilevel governance by transnational policy agents, shared interests and more or less informal administrative procedures and practices.[37] This functional framework of the EU creates long-term political and social change in Europe – it leads to the formation of new *polity*.

This polity-building is perceived by constructivists as a process of structuration[38] and construction[39] of an area of increasing social interaction in which shared legal rules and formal decision-making procedures are inseparable from a multitude of informal common practices, mutual learning processes and the behaviour patterns of social actors.[40] For instance, Shaw and Wiener suggest studying the evolution and emergence of EU policy-making practices and their subsequent transformation into legally stipulated rules.[41] Methodologically oscillating between theoretical constructivism and socio-legal realism, they analyse the process of transforming the norms of European governance into the EU official legal domain. One example of this is the legal concept of European citizenship which allegedly evolved from an embedded set of EU ideas and policy objectives.[42] Other examples can be found in the areas of a common market, fundamental rights, security and justice.

---

36 Ernst B. Haas, 'Does Constructivism Subsume Neo-functionalism?', in *The Social Construction of Europe*, eds Thomas Christiansen, Knud E. Jorgensen and Antje Wiener (London: Sage, 2001), 27–29.

37 Markus Jachtenfuchs and Beate Kohler-Koch, 'Governance and Institutional Development', in *European Integration Theory*, eds Antje Wiener and Thomas Diez (Oxford: Oxford University Press, 2004), 97.

38 Anthony Giddens; for the use of Giddens's theory of structuration in the context of European law, see Francis Snyder, *New Directions in European Community Law* (London: Weidenfeld & Nicholson, 1990).

39 For the philosophical context, see especially John R. Searle, *The Construction of Social Reality* (New York: Free Press, 1995); for the sociological context of constructivism, see especially the classic work of Peter L. Berger and Thomas Luckmann, *The Social Construction of Reality* (Harmondsworth: Penguin, 1966).

40 Jeffrey T. Checkel, 'Social Construction and European Integration', in Thomas Christiansen, Knud E. Jorgensen and Antje Wiener, eds, supra n. 36, 57–58.

41 Jo Shaw and Antje Wiener, 'The Paradox of the "European Polity"', in *The State of the European Union Vol. 5: Risks, Reform, Resistance, and Revival*, eds Maria G. Cowles and Michael Smith (Oxford: Oxford University Press, 2000), 66.

42 Antje Wiener, 'The Embedded Acquis Communautaire: Transmission Belt and Prism of New Governance', *European Law Journal* 4 (1998): 294.

The embedded structure of the *acquis* consists of the social processes (and cultural ideas) that precede legal enactment and stipulation.[43] The EU deficit discourse and all its prescriptive connotations can apparently be eliminated if legal concepts are linked to their social environment. Shaw and Wiener define the concept of EU law's social environment as an area covering rational policy-making as well as social and historical contingencies.[44] Their approach belongs to the rich sociological and socio-legal tradition according to which understanding legal concepts means understanding their practical meaning and social or political uses.

In the constructivist approach, the governance-driven construction of the European polity is conceptualized as the evolution of social and cultural practices, discourses, identities and patterns and their subsequent internalization by the legal system. The social is gradually reflected and *adopted* by the legal.

C: Differentiation Perspectives

Apart from the constructivist perspective, which considers EU law part of the more general system of EU governance, there are other conceptualizations of European law, governance and polity inspired by theories of social differentiation. Drawing on the constructivist distinction of formal rules and informal practices, these approaches define European governance as a system of 'soft laws' which is profoundly different from the official *acquis* as a system of 'hard laws'.[45] According to this view briefly discussed in the first chapter in the context of EU constitutionalization by *Juristenrecht* of epistemic communities, law is a differentiated social system of official rules, institutional settings and specific forms of communication establishing the difference between legality and illegality. Governance is its social environment which, however, does not generate and inform the content of legal rules. It is based on soft laws which are, in fact, contrasted to the EU official legal system. Governance uses the operations of the legal system but also seeks 'to overcome the *impasses* the legal code has on offer'.[46] The rule of law is challenged by governance because one of governance's aims is the de-juridification of political society.[47]

---

43 Jo Shaw and Antje Wiener, supra n. 41, 69.

44 Ibid.

45 For critical evaluation see, for instance, David M. Trubek and Louise G. Trubek, 'Hard and Soft Law in the Construction of Social Europe: the Role of the Open Method of Co-ordination', *European Law Journal* 11 (2005): 352–362; see also Ulrika Mörth, ed., *Soft Law in Governance and Regulation: An Interdisciplinary Approach* (Cheltenham: Edward Elgar, 2004).

46 Christian Joerges, 'Constitutionalism and Transnational Governance: Exploring a Magic Triangle', in *Transnational Governance and Constitutionalism*, eds Christian Joerges, Inger-Johanne Sand and Günther Teubner (Oxford: Hart Publishing, 2004), 341.

47 Edgar Grande and Louis W. Pauly, eds, *Complex Sovereignty: Reconstituting Political Authority in the Twenty-first Century* (Toronto: Toronto University Press, 2005), 3.

New modes of governance[48] evolve outside the legal system and gradually substitute for the traditional law-mediated and state-controlled modes of modern politics. Constitutionalism becomes reflective of this self-regulatory capacity of new European governance.[49] These and many other views are common to both constructivist and differentiation theories of European governance and law. However, unlike the constructivist approaches which treat the difference between European official 'hard' legality and informal 'soft law'-based governance in terms of precedence and embeddedness, soft/hard law differentiation approaches *oppose* governance to law. Governance and law are considered to be systems coevally emerging at the level of European society – the latter using legality as its medium and the former using the specific medium of administrative efficiency. Soft laws involve administrative decrees and practices that are examples of the increasing bureaucratization of European society and its stabilization by procedural legitimation.[50] These decrees emanate from the comitology-based[51] European offices and the decisions of their officials whose legitimacy cannot be formulated in terms of democratic power but only redefined within the context of the EU's operative, purpose-oriented administration.[52] EU governance by comitology and soft laws draws on legitimation by objectives – it is expected to be 'good governance' in terms of its efficiency and accountability.[53]

Soft laws are instruments that 'may provide for the necessary flexibility and may help to cope with political realities'[54] of the Union. They are used instead of EU legislation as a means of differentiating the legal instruments of the EU and thus of contributing to the effectiveness of EU institutions. In other words, EU soft laws have a 'para-law' function[55] of interpretative and application techniques of officially legislated laws. They are not part of the internal operations of the EU

48 Joanne Scott and David M. Trubek, 'Mind the Gap: Law and New Approaches to Governance in the European Union', *European Law Journal* 8 (2002): 1.

49 Neil Walker, 'EU Constitutionalism and New Governance', in *Law and New Governance in the EU and the US*, eds Gráinne de Búrca and Joanne Scott (Oxford: Hart Publishing, 2006), 29–35.

50 Linda Senden, *Soft Law in European Community Law* (Oxford: Hart Publishing, 2004), 68.

51 Carl F. Bergström, *Comitology: Delegation of Power in the European Union and the Committee System* (Oxford: Oxford University Press, 2005).

52 Gráinne de Búrca, 'The Quest for Legitimacy in the European Union', *Modern Law Review* 59 (1996): 359.

53 Christian Joerges, 'Good Governance through Comitology?', in *EU Committees: Social Regulation, Law and Politics*, eds Christian Joerges and Ellen Vos (Oxford: Hart Publishing, 1999), 311.

54 Linda Senden and Sacha Prechal, 'Differentiation in and through Community Soft Law', in *The Many Faces of Differentiation in EU Law*, eds Bruno De Witte, Dominik Hanf and Ellen Vos (Antwerpen: Intersentia, 2001), 182.

55 Ibid.

legal system despite their support of particular instructions and recommendations.[56] Soft laws do not have any legal justification and belong to the administrative mode of political communication. They are steering instruments of both 'pre-law' and 'post-law' functions[57] highlighting structural irritations between European law and politics. EU soft laws consequently turn out to be stabilizing mechanisms of the increasingly differentiated EU legal and political systems because they provide a minimum unity in the application of EU rule of law.[58]

From Evolutionary and Constructivist Approaches to the Autopoietic Social Systems Theory of the EU

Brief comments on recent theoretical approaches to European integration and polity-building show the need to elaborate and interconnect systematically the evolution, construction and differentiation of the European Union. In other words, *time*, *environment* and the *self-reference* of European integration have become defining topics in European legal and political studies. Furthermore, the notion of state law has been gradually replaced by various concepts of societal law which accommodate legal pluralistic views discussed in the fourth chapter and appreciate differences and the presence of more than one legal order in a social field.[59] As Roger Cotterrell remarked: '[I]n more recent times, legal pluralism has often been invoked in socio-legal studies of Europe. ... It may be that Europe is now a particularly important laboratory in which the reshaping of the very idea of law is taking place'.[60]

Socio-legal perspectives and legal pluralistic approaches are commonly employed by 'new governance', 'legal regimes' and 'soft law' studies. Drawing on Cotterrell's remark, legal semantics ('the idea of law') is changing in Europe in response to emerging structures of social plurality and fragmentation recognized by EU law which is irreducible to commonly acknowledged legal pluralism of parallel legal regimes of the EU and its Member States. This pluralism involves a mixture of legal and non-legal social norms rather than merely the coexistence of different legal regimes.[61]

---

56 Francis Snyder, 'Soft Law and Institutional Practice in the European Community', in *The Construction of Europe – Essays in honour of Emil Noel*, ed. Stephen Martin (Dordrecht: Kluwer, 1993), 197.

57 Linda Senden and S. Prechal, supra n. 54, 188–189, 192.

58 Linda Senden, supra n. 50, 366.

59 John Griffiths, 'What is Legal Pluralism?', *Journal of Legal Pluralism and Unofficial Law* 32 (1986): 1.

60 Roger Cotterrell, 'Images of Europe in Sociolegal Traditions', in *European Ways of Law*, eds Volkmar Gessner and David Nelken (Oxford: Hart Publishing, 2007), 23–24.

61 Roger Cotterrell, *Law's Community: Legal Theory in Sociolegal Perspective* (Oxford: Clarendon Press, 1995), 309–311.

Legitimacy of European law can hardly be reduced to its efficiency and utility while any references to the common European public values, unifying federal statehood and *demos*-based political identity sound premature, if not futile and dangerously utopian. The EU's failed constitution-making process was not only an example of technical legal difficulties of accommodating the principle of divided sovereignty into a new constitutional formula. In fact, it revealed a profoundly pluralistic nature of the EU which, instead of following the public law logic of ultimate constitutional integration, has been experiencing social processes of further pluralization, fragmentation and differentiation, most recently during the process of drafting and ratifying the Lisbon Treaty.

The discussed theorizations of evolution and construction of European integration and polity successfully show that European law and politics (but also other social systems of economy, science, technology and so on) evolve in the EU's process of functional differentiation. For instance, addressing the social and political embeddedness of legal concepts as the distinction between informal practices and formal rules facilitates understanding the distinction between legal texts and their policy contexts. Similarly, the distinction between hard and soft laws recently elaborated within EU legal and political studies reveals the level of separation of legal and political operations at EU level.[62] The research emphasis on the social context of EU legal institutions supports the view that law, like any other social system, evolves through the process of differentiation from its social environment. The construction of its internal structures equally entails the construction of its environment.

The above discussed theoretical efforts clearly indicate that it is necessary to break away from old theoretical and political EU semantics and adopt a new approach. In other words, those efforts and perspectives need to be synthesized and accommodated within a general social theory capable of grasping complexities of social (not just political) constructivism together with general evolutionary processes of functional differentiation. Furthermore, this theory should successfully capture the pluralistic complexity of the EU legal system and eliminate typically modern mistakes of identifying society with political community, its state and ultimately shared values.

The paradigm of autopoietic systems theory offers this synthesis and its complex social science semantics ultimately leads to a better understanding of operative closure, mutual differentiation and the intensity of current structural coupling between European law and politics. It also helps to better understand the role and limits of EU laws in the emergence and construction of the differentiated post-sovereign and post-national European polity.

Another reason why to adopt the evolutionary epistemology of the autopoietic social systems of European politics and law is that, unlike rational action and/ or institutionalist views, it eliminates the political and ideological contexts

62 Francis Snyder, *New Directions in European Community Law* (London: Butterworths, 1990).

of neofunctionalist theories because of the emphasis on operative rather than normative aspects of functionalist social theory. Furthermore, it abandons the common view of the centrality of institutional settings, decision-making powers and administrative competences. Instead of the notion of a system as constantly replicating the same and subjecting different elements to one equilibrium, social systems, such as law and politics, are described as actually evolving and reproducing themselves by differentiating from the social environment and reconstituting meanings and their surpluses which 'provide the chance to include new differences and new constraints and thus to increase the ability to constrain the initial situation via differentiation'.[63]

Using the epistemology of autopoietic systems theory, it is possible to describe the European Union as an autopoietic system organization functionally differentiated into systems of law, politics, economy, education and so on. These systems operate by producing meaning surpluses that further differentiate the initial situation, increase the systems' complexity and thus constitute their self-reproduction by self-referring to internal varieties of meaning production. What looks like an incomprehensible plethora of ad hoc rules, fluid institutional settings and contingent decisions turns out to be the complexity of operations guaranteeing the external and internal differentiation, self-reference, self-reproduction and self-regulation of both European law and politics. In the following sections of this study, I therefore introduce some concepts of the autopoietic systems theory to reconceptualize both EU politics and law as internally and functionally differentiated self-regulatory and self-referential social systems.

Differentiated Integration as Part of Self-Referential European Governance and its Juridification

Nevertheless, before engaging in theoretical generalizations and outlining autopoietic semantics of self-referential and self-regulatory EU law and politics, it is necessary to examine whether there are any specific EU policies and evolutionary trends supporting such theoretical changes and claims. I believe that the policy of enhanced cooperation, most recently drafted by the Lisbon Treaty and commonly described as the process of differentiated integration, is such an example of the EU's political response to its increasing functional differentiation and social fragmentation.

Although the process of differentiated integration has been part of European integration since the 1950s, its importance has grown vis-à-vis recent developments within and outside the EU. The ambitions of some European countries for progressive unification, especially the establishment of a currency union (the European Monetary Union) and the abolition of border controls (the

63 Niklas Luhmann, *Social Systems* (Stanford, CA: Stanford University Press, 1995), 189.

Schengen Zone), were not welcomed by all EU Member States at the time. Instead of a common integration trajectory accompanied by temporary opt-outs by individual countries in specific areas, the very process of integration started to be associated with the need for institutional and organizational flexibility in the 1990s.

Reflecting these changes, the concepts of 'differentiated integration', 'flexible integration', 'closer cooperation' and 'enhanced cooperation'[64] have evolved from political and academic debates on the speed, direction and purpose of European integration, especially the ambitious calls for a 'hard core' of Member States willing and capable of closer political integration.[65] The idea of differentiated integration was originally promoted by countries such as Germany and France that favoured progressive integration and called for a core group of Member States that would not be held back by other Member States reluctant to join the ever closer Union project.[66] In their view, the rigidity of integration of all Member States in all areas at the same time was to be abandoned in favour of an 'avant-garde' integration of the willing states which would operate as a source of inspiration for the rest of the EU. Nevertheless, the principle of flexibility, which would legally operationalize the political possibility of differentiated integration of the EU, was finally incorporated in the Amsterdam Treaty as a functional response to what Ralf Dahrendorf described as a 'remarkable institutional failure'[67] vis-à-vis further European integration.

---

64 See, for instance, Monica Den Boer, Alain Guggenhühl and Sophie Vanhoonacker, eds, *Coping with Flexibility and Legitimacy after Amsterdam* (Maastricht: European Institute of Public Administration, 1998); Jörg Monar 'Schengen and Flexibility in the Treaty of Amsterdam: Opportunities and Risks of Differentiated Integration in EU Justice and Home Affairs', in *Schengen, Judicial Cooperation and Policy Cooperation*, ed. Monica de Boer (Maastricht: European Institute of Public Administration, 1997), 9; Jörg Monar, 'Justice and Home Affairs in the Treaty of Amsterdam: Reform and Price of Fragmentation', *European Law Review* 23 (1998): 320; Karlheinz Neunreither and Antje Wiener, eds, *Amsterdam and Beyond: Institutional Dynamics and Prospects for Democracy in the European Union* (Oxford: Oxford University Press, 2000); Filip Tuytschaever, *Differentiation in European Union Law* (Oxford: Hart Publishing, 1999).

65 The term was coined by two top German conservative politicians Karl Lamers and Wolfgang Schäuble in their paper presented before the Christian Democratic Union/ Christian Social Union Group in the Lower House of Parliament of Germany in September 1994. See Karl Lamers and Wolfgang Schäuble, 'Reflections on European Policy', The Christian Democratic Union/Christian Social Union Group, Bonn, 1 September 1994.

66 See Karl Lamers, 'Strenthening the Hard Core', in *The Question of Europe*, eds Peter Gowan and Perry Anderson (London: Verso, 2000), 104; see also Daniel Levy, Max Pensky and John Torpey, eds, *Old Europe, New Europe, Core Europe* (London: Verso, 2005).

67 Ralf Dahrendorf, 'A Third Europe?', Third Jean Monnet Lecture, delivered in Florence on 26 November 1979; quoted from Alexander Stubb, supra n. 18, 35.

From the legal perspective, the concept of differentiated integration may read like an anomaly.[68] Legality is commonly associated with the general application of rules, unity of legal authority and equal treatment of all subjects. The rule of law-based EU presumes the uniform interpretation and application of European laws. All powers conferred by Member States and remedies facilitated by European institutions are expected to be governed by generally applicable and enforceable legal rules. It is, therefore, not surprising that EU legal bodies have been hostile to the flexibility principle and differentiated integration and that, for instance, 'the Court of Justice has shown a disinclination to allow the presence of differentiated or partial arrangements to undermine the coherence and uniformity of the legal order it has created'.[69]

Because legalization of the differentiation principle raises the problem of the universality of European legality, the policy of differentiated integration can only be legalized by European treaties as a legal exception in the form of the *flexibility clauses* which are typical of international law rather than the hybrid transnational EU legal system. In this manner, legal provisions related to opt-outs from a particular EU policy need to restate that provisions, measures and decisions related to that policy area shall not affect the competences, rights and obligations of non-participating states.[70]

Different levels of commitments for different groups of states have often been considered merely a temporary side-effect of an otherwise strong and centripetal integration policy of *one* Union to rule *all* Member States by the same system of law. European opt-out legislation, such as the British and Danish protocols in the context of Economic and Monetary Union (EMU),[71] had not been intended as a blueprint for the Union's official legal design, drawn according to the principle of differentiated integration, but to resolve problems in specific policy areas arising from further unification that was not completely endorsed by all Member States at the same time.

According to the persistent logic of progressive integration, these exemptions were negotiated as temporary measures to provide unwilling Member States with more time to adjust and accept new integration policies before adopting them like

---

68 Neil Walker, 'Sovereignty and Differentiated Integration in the European Union', *European Law Journal* 4 (1998): 375–378.

69 Jo Shaw and Antje Wiener, supra n. 41, at 86.

70 See, for instance, Protocol No. 4 on the position of the United Kingdom and Ireland annexed to the (Amsterdam) Treaty on European Union and to the Treaty establishing European Community (signed in Amsterdam on 2 October 1997). The Protocol guarantees opt-outs of both countries from the Schengen-related *acquis*. For further details, see Stefan Griller et al., *The Treaty of Amsterdam: Facts, Analysis, Prospects* (Wien: Springer, 2000), 514–518.

71 Paul Beaumont and Neil Walker, eds, *Legal Framework of the Single European Currency* (Oxford: Hart, 1999).

the rest of the Union's Member States.[72] The original function of the flexibility clauses was to contribute to the final achievement of one overarching integrative pattern facilitated by the body of European laws. However, the indefinite design and persistence of some clauses, such as the Irish and UK opt-outs from the Schengen Zone or the UK opt-outs from the Union's protection of social rights, have gradually weakened the original idea of flexibility as a transitional measure and made it an intrinsic feature of European legal integration.[73]

The EU's differentiated integration was historically transformed from the political practice familiar within EU institutions into a rule of intergovernmental negotiations and the guiding European treaty principle. After the enactment of the Amsterdam and Nice treaties incorporating the principle of flexibility and differentiated integration, the European Union emerged as a supranational body integrating its Member States well beyond the framework of international law but granting them a sufficient level of national sovereignty to decide whether they choose to opt in or out of specific integration policies.[74] In fact, the Maastricht Treaty on European Union had already effectively established a 'multi-speed Europe' by enacting the Economic and Monetary Union (EMU) and the Schengen Zone. The institutionalization of differentiated integration by the Amsterdam Treaty subsequently enabled the Member States to develop progressive forms of multilevel integration under conditions defined by the legal language of the Treaty.[75] In other words:

> … while Maastricht showed that unwilling member states cannot be forced to integrate, Amsterdam made clear that the reluctant countries cannot keep the others from further deepening. After the accession of three neutral countries in 1995 and in view of the long, heterogeneous queue of candidates, the Treaties finally acknowledged Europe's diversity.[76]

---

72 See, for instance, Olivier De Schutter, 'Anchoring the European Union to the European Social Charter: the Case for Accession', in *Social Rights in Europe*, eds Gráinne de Búrca, Bruno De Witte and Larissa Ogertschnig (Oxford: Oxford University Press, 2005), 111–152.

73 Bruno De Witte, 'Future Path of Flexibility: enhanced cooperation, partial agreements and pioneer groups', in *The European Union: An Ongoing Process of Integration*, eds Jaap W. de Zwaan, Jan H. Jans, Frans, A. Nelissen and Steven Blockmans (Cambridge: Cambridge University Press, 2005), 141–152.

74 John A. Usher, 'Enhanced Cooperation or Flexibility in the Post-Nice Era', in *Accountability and Legitimacy in the European Union*, eds Anthony Arnull and Dan Wincott (Oxford: Oxford University Press, 2002), 97.

75 Ingolf Pernice, 'Multi-level Constitutionalism in the European Union', *European Law Review* 27 (2002): 511.

76 Sieglinde Gstöhl, 'The European Union after Amsterdam: Towards a Theoretical Approach to (Differentiated) Integration', in Maria G. Cowles and Michael Smith, eds, supra n. 41, 42.

The original institutionalization of differentiated integration in the Amsterdam Treaty, ratified in 1999, and subsequent amendments to it in the Nice Treaty, ratified three years later, was primarily a response to growing political differences and fragmentation regarding the speed and scale, but also purpose, direction and limits of EU integration.[77]

Similarly, recent EU enlargement processes and accession talks multiplied these differences and proved that differentiated integration was the only realistic way of dealing with economic, political, administrative, legal and international differences in Europe.[78] The cultural diversity, economic or legal compatibility and political heterogeneity issues became much more pressing after two unprecedented enlargements – the first, in 2004, opening the EU to ten new accession states, eight of which were post-communist democracies from the former Soviet bloc (the Czech Republic, Estonia, Hungary, Latvia, Lithuania, Poland, Slovakia and Slovenia), plus two others (Cyprus and Malta), and the subsequent enlargements in 2007, admitting Bulgaria and Romania, and 2013, admitting Croatia, despite these countries' economic underdevelopment and significantly lower level of democratic and administrative accountability even in comparison to the other post-communist states admitted in 2004.[79]

Differentiated integration was an intrinsic part of the Copenhagen conditionality process which was inspired by the Maastricht Treaty and significantly affected economic, political and international developments in candidate states, especially in the early stages of accession talks.[80] Successive enlargement processes, therefore, show that the flexibility clauses are not only internal legal measures processing the political opt-outs of Member States refusing to join specific policies of EU. They also provide an operative framework for integrating candidate states without imperilling the existing state of European integration and the efficiency of different policies, such as the Euro zone, free movement of labour, immigration, agriculture subsidies and so on.

Member States – Segments of the European Political System

The EU's differentiated integration illustrates how Member State governments continue to exercise their power at EU level and thus secure their national interests

77 Giorgio Gaja, 'How Flexible is Flexibility under the Amsterdam Treaty?', *Common Market Law Review* 35 (1998): 855.

78 Fraser Cameron, 'Widening and Deepening', in *The Future of Europe: Integration and Enlargement*, ed. Fraser Cameron (London: Routledge, 2004), 1.

79 Jan Delhey, 'Do Enlargements Make the European Union Less Cohesive? An Analysis of Trust between EU Nationalities', *Journal of Common Market Studies* 45 (2007): 253.

80 Tim Haughton, 'When Does the EU Make a Difference? Conditionality and the Accession Process in Central and Eastern Europe', *Political Studies Review* 5 (2007): 233.

within the general system of European governance.[81] Differences in the bargaining power of national governments profoundly influence the operative power of European institutions.[82] Furthermore, the EU's burden of a governing bureaucracy without democratic accountability highlights the Union's traditionally ambivalent relationship to popular politics which is 'a testimony not just to the élite character of the EU's invention and development, but also to the fears of an incursionary democratic politics of Europe (whether regressive or emancipatory)'.[83]

The structural difference between Member State governments and European governance has always informed all major debates regarding the paradigmatic shift and the experimental character of European integration.[84] However, this paradox of Member State governments communicating their goals through the channels of EU governance has actually been a source of the Union's growing operational capacity resulting in the emergence of the European self-referential political system. National interests get reformulated as European interests and, as such, are subsequently pursued and protected by EU institutions irrespective of their country of origin.

The European political system is internally differentiated into individual segments – territorial nation states,[85] the political systems of which are based on democratic procedures and legitimacy. Apart from the Europeanization of national politics, *the nation state segmentation of the EU* means that democracy primarily remains a matter for Member State political systems, their territorial enforcement and limitations. For instance, any project in favour of a supranational parliament elected directly by all citizens of Member States according to democratic procedures common to nation states would be impossible to implement at the EU level. The majority will of the citizens of Germany and France would immediately make the will of the citizens of Luxemburg and Slovenia irrelevant.

Differences between individual states supporting supra-state integration are as important as their overall similarity and common interest in demanding integration.[86] Within the self-referential system of European politics, Member States continue to operate as a political *opposition* which, by adjusting the communication of national interests to the European political semantics, can counterbalance the power of EU institutions and thus be part of the more general and self-reinforcing dynamics of European transnational governance.

The Union has definitely transgressed, yet not made redundant the modern political *organization* of societies into nation states, relying on the semantics

81 Paul Taylor, *The European Union in the 1990s* (Oxford: Oxford University Press, 1996).

82 Andrew Moravcsik, supra n. 12.

83 John Clarke, supra n. 20, 28.

84 Brigid Laffan, Rory O'Donnell and Michael Smith, *Europe's Experimental Union: Rethinking Integration* (London: Routledge, 1999).

85 Niklas Luhmann, *Theories of Distinction: Redescribing the Descriptions of Modernity* (Stanford, CA: Stanford University Press, 2002), 107.

86 Niklas Luhmann, supra n. 1, 227.

of popular sovereignty, democratic legitimacy, citizenship and constitutional rights even in the post-sovereign EU structures. The Member State organizations have gradually made the system of EU political governance adopt the goal of democratization. The old nation state semantics of democratic legitimacy thus leads to the structural changes of the EU. Furthermore, democratization calls change the Union's self-description and support its political semantics of an autopoietic political system operating beyond the nation state and/or international politics. Governance democratization policies became an intrinsic part of the EU political system and the goal of enhancing democratic legitimacy was adopted by European treaties and other legal documents.

The complexity of political structures and semantics of the EU is illustrated even in much more technical and legalistic contexts, such as the controversial subsidiarity principle which 'can, on the one hand, suggest a desire to reduce EU-level intervention into national policy, or, on the other hand, the normatively more attractive and positive desire to enhance self-government and to involve those most directly affected by decision-making as fully as possible in the process'.[87]

As the policy of differentiated integration indicates, national societies politically represented by the state organization keep their importance in the highly integrated EU.[88] The question of to what extent the Union's institutional framework can replicate the system of democratic decision-making and legitimacy typical of its Member States remains a major source of political controversies, disputes, optimistic projects and sceptical remarks.[89] The nation state's democratic legitimacy and accountability function as a source of the *politicization* of otherwise depoliticized technocratic and instrumental European governance.[90]

The Union of European *Governance* and National *Governments*: On the Internal Differentiation of the European Political System

Despite its nation state segmentation, the current EU is commonly described as a multilevel polity both independent and reflexive of Member State political systems. It can generate authoritative decisions through its self-regulatory system

87 Gráinne de Búrca, 'Legal Principles as an Instrument of Differentiation? The Principles of Proportionality and Subsidiarity', in Bruno De Witte, Dominik Hanf and Ellen Vos, eds, supra n. 54, 133.

88 Gary Marks, Liesbet Hooghe and Kermit Blank, 'European Integration since the 1980s: State-Centric versus Multi-Level Governance', *Journal of Common Market Studies* 34 (1996): 341.

89 Albert Weale, 'Democratic Legitimacy and the Constitution of Europe', in *Democracy and Constitutional Culture in the Union of Europe*, eds Richard Bellamy, Vittorio Bufacchi and Dario Castiglione (London: Lothian Foundation Press, 1995), 81.

90 Jiří Přibáň, *Legal Symbolism: On Law, Time and European Identity* (Aldershot: Ashgate, 2007), 116–128.

of governance and make them respected by interdependent nation state polities.[91] Although national governments remain strong participants in the processes of European governance, Member States have lost much of 'their former authoritative control over individuals in their respective territories'.[92] The Union's evolution 'from policy to polity' and the constitution of 'politics like any other'[93] indicate the emergence of a European political system with autonomous institutions and a structure independent of national politics.[94] The system is 'an exercise in enlarging the operation of social engineering while creating new structures of opportunity above the state level, without conforming to the contours of a system-wide hierarchy that is typical of the component polities'.[95]

European governance generally means the capacity of social networks to enhance interactions and to organize EU politics into a self-referential system which, unlike conventional political hierarchies, permanently negotiates shared goals, purposes and general rules of governing.[96] It has no sovereign authority, represents an alternative to both spontaneous market regulations and organizational hierarchies and thus signifies more general recent changes in the political system, methods and processes of governing in which practicality dominates over ideology and self-organizing networks over state bureaucratic authority.[97]

EU history of differentiated integration illustrates how strong governance-driven legitimation by efficiency and expert knowledge can be and how it can, up to a certain point, successfully neutralize calls for institutional democratization and political reform.[98] Nevertheless, the emphasis on instrumental rationality and legitimation by expertise makes European governance a challenge to the political authority of democratically elected legislative and administrative bodies. Within the EU context, this challenge is either successfully suppressed by the Union's institutions, or made part of complex relations between those institutions and the

---

91 For the analysis of different functional subsystems of European governance, see Gary Marks, Fritz W. Scharpf, Philippe C. Schmitter and Wolfgang Streeck, eds, *Governance in the European Union* (London: Sage, 1996).

92 Liesbet Hooghe and Gary Marks, *Multi-Level Governance and European Integration* (Oxford: Rowman & Littlefield, 2001), 2.

93 Dimitris N. Chryssochoou, *Theorizing European Integration* (London: Sage, 2001), 96.

94 Laura Cram, 'The European Commission as a Multi-Organization: Social Policy and IT in the EU', *Journal of European Public Policy* 1 (1994): 195.

95 Dimitris N. Chryssochoou, supra n. 93, 97.

96 Bob Jessop, 'Governance and meta-governance: on reflexivity, requisite variety and requisite irony', in *Governance as Social and Political Communication*, ed. Henrik P. Bang (Manchester: Manchester University Press, 2003), 142.

97 Roderick A.W. Rhodes, 'The New Governance: Governing without Government', *Political Studies* 44 (1996): 652.

98 Michael Zürn and Christian Joerges, eds, *Governance and Law in Post-National Constellations: Compliance in Europe and Beyond* (Cambridge: Cambridge University Press, 2005).

EU Member States as democratically constituted social organizations. European supranational and transnational governance then expands and accelerates the general tendency of governance networks towards self-regulation without government and towards autopoieticaly communicated power beyond the state.[99]

On Polity-building, the EU's *Betweenness* and the Functional Differentiation of European Law and Politics

Despite general calls for its democratization, governance as a system of implementing collectively binding decisions is primarily focused on performance indicators and legitimized by outcomes rather than by democratic procedures and deliberations.[100] Its structure is polycentric, involves a multiplicity of decisions and governing agencies and contributes to 'the hollowing out of the state'[101] because individual networks of governance successfully preserve their autonomy and self-regulation and resist any attempts at centralized political guidance. Possibilities of political intervention in a self-regulated and self-referential society are very limited and cannot change self-stabilizing steering operations of governance.[102]

Apart from the evolution of the self-referential system of EU politics and its internal differentiation and segmentation, the policy of differentiated integration legally formulated by the flexibility clauses illustrates the level of functional differentiation of European law and politics. EU law is an instrument of EU politics and its legal restraint at the same time.[103] This means that the functional differentiation of European law and politics also leads to their growing interdependence. Within the EU context, it is possible to detect the general process of the *juridification of politics* which is typical of functionally differentiated modern societies. From the very beginning, the unification of Europe has been progressing as a continuous process of legalizing integration by enacting a series of European treaties and cultivating the growing body of the *acquis communautaire*.[104] Since the Treaty of Rome, European integration has been based on the principle of legal unification beyond the common practices and limits of international law. Juridification has been another name for

99 Marie-Laure Djelic and Kerstin Sahlin-Andersson, eds, *Transnational Governance: Institutional Dynamics of Regulation* (Cambridge: Cambridge University Press, 2006).

100 Guy Peters and Jon Pierre, 'Multi-level Governance and Democracy: A Faustian Bargain?', in *Multi-level Governance*, eds Ian Bache and Matthew Flinders (Oxford: Oxford University Press, 2004), 75.

101 Roderick A.W. Rhodes, 'The Hollowing Out of the State', *The Political Quarterly* 65 (1994): 138.

102 Andrew Dunsire, 'Tipping the Balance: Autopoiesis and Governance', *Administration & Society* 28 (1996): 299.

103 Niklas Luhmann, *Law as a Social System* (Oxford: Oxford University Press, 2004), 365.

104 Kenneth Armstrong, 'Legal Integration: Theorizing the Legal Dimension of European Integration', *Journal of Common Market Studies* 36 (1998): 155.

unification. It means that the actions of both Member States and EU institutions can be generally scrutinized and equally challenged by all legal subjects.

However, this process has been inseparable from the coeval process of the political *instrumentalization of law* which is, for instance, detectable in the use of European treaties for the purpose of further political integration. In their coding, the political instrumentalization of law and the legal limitation of political power meet as coeval processes typical of mutually differentiated systems of modern politics and law. European politics determines which laws become valid but European laws are preconditions of the making of European politics. Despite the structural absence of political statehood and the lack of political coding in terms of democratic government and opposition, the European political system has enough operative capacity to be self-portrayed and self-represented in a rule-of-law-like formula based on the tautology that 'the rule and the law are the same'.[105] However, this level of semantic self-reference in European politics would be impossible without European legality which has been a grand instrument for the realization of EU political goals.

Using the European legal system's notions and communication, the European polity can describe itself as the rule of law established polity. The European polity is thus an intrinsic part of the conceptual framework of the European political system which summarizes external boundaries and self-limitations of EU politics but also effectively and self-referentially internalizes the notions of European constitutionalism and legality.[106]

The difference between the legal semantics of the flexibility clauses and the political semantics of differentiated integration shows how European legality and politics have managed to benefit systemically from being insulated from each other's interventions. The EU flexibility clauses reaffirm the political and legal sovereignty and right of Member States to either stay out of a specific EU integration domain, or join it after political deliberation and decision-making at national level in the future. The clauses are expected to outline the legally tolerable differences of integration.[107] They contribute to the 'betweenness'[108] of the Union struggling to accommodate national governments and European governance, international diplomacy and transnational politics, markets and social welfare, constitutional rights and jurisdictional limitations and so on.[109]

105 Niklas Luhmann, supra n. 15, 370–371.

106 Carolyn Rhodes and Sonia Mazey, eds, *The State of the European Union, Vol. 3: Building a European Polity?* (Boulder, CO: Lynne Rienner Publishers, 1995).

107 Neil Walker, 'Theoretical Reflections on Flexibility and Europe's Future', in *Constitutional Change in the EU: From Uniformity to Flexibility*, eds Gráinne de Búrca and Joanne Scott (Oxford: Hart Publishing, 2000), 9.

108 Brigid Laffan, 'The European Union: A Distinctive Model of Internationalization', *Journal of European Public Policy* 5(2) (1998): 236.

109 Caitriona Carter and Andrew Scott, 'Legitimacy and Governance Beyond the European Nation State: Conceptualising Governance in the European Union', *European Law Journal* 4(4) (1998): 429.

For legal scholars, officials and judges, the betweenness of the Union represents a set of challenges associated with its 'non-state' pluralistic character, especially the absence of supreme legal authority and the impossibility of logically establishing the normative hierarchy of EU and national legal systems.[110] Despite numerous efforts by the European Court of Justice to pursue the vision of EU law as superior to the Member States' legal systems, national institutions, especially constitutional and supreme courts, persist in preserving the supremacy of national constitutions and their jurisdiction as final guardians of citizens' rights and freedoms.

The process of political integration increases the complexity of the legal system and thus inevitably contributes to the coeval process of legal *fragmentation.* The whole development subsequently can look like another strain on the EU's institutional framework and 'a Pandora's box with a high degree of uncertainty as to how, where and when the flexibility clauses will be used'.[111]

The European legal system has to operationalize differentiated integration by enacting the flexibility clauses politically negotiated by the Member States. Its operation has to conform to the Union's objectives and its approval by the European Commission is conditioned by the fact that these same objectives cannot be achieved by the Union as a whole.[112]

The clauses do not create a jurisdictional crisis or paralysis. In fact, they enhance the operational complexity of the European legal system and thus strengthen EU legal semantics.[113] The European legal system, therefore, allows the Member States to exercise their constitutional sovereignty even in the highly integrated and sovereignty-limiting institutional setting of the EU.[114] Legal operations guarantee the current political dynamics of the Union and the principle of legally predefined differentiation empowers the willing Member States to enhance their mutual cooperation while guaranteeing the benefits of the existing levels of integration to all members of the Union.[115]

The flexibility clauses enacted by the European treaties can be treated as enhancements of the autopoietic operability of the European legal system. In other words, the clauses are not a threat to current European integration but its very expression at a time of growing complexity in the Union's political, legal, economic and other social settlements. They enhance the level of autonomy and self-regulation of the EU's legal system, contribute to legal self-reference and

110 Deidre Curtin, 'The Constitutional Structure of the Union: A Europe of Bits and Pieces', *Common Market Law Review* 30(1) (1993): 17.

111 Alexander Stubb, supra n. 18, 143.

112 Article 10 of the Treaty of Lisbon amending the Treaty on European Union and the Treaty establishing European Community, CIG 14/07, Brussels, 3 December 2007.

113 Stephan Leibfried and Paul Pierson, eds, *European Social Policy: Between Fragmentation and Integration* (Washington, DC: Brookings Institution Press, 1995).

114 Neil Walker, supra n. 68, 355.

115 Filip Tuytschaever, supra n. 64.

mark further differentiation in the legal system and the governance-based system of European politics.

The EU as Supranational Social Organization of Legal and Political Autopoiesis

The differentiated integration of the EU operates as integrated differentiation. The EU internalizes both the supremacy of European laws and the constitutional sovereignty of its Member States. It is a system of multilevel interdependence between national and European institutions. While constituent national governments do not wish to constitute a European statehood, the EU's constitutional domain as a self-referential system of laws significantly limiting national jurisdictions has been established for several decades. The system of national negotiations and intergovernmental conferences reallocates traditionally nation state powers to the Union but also enhances the autonomy of negotiating Member State governments.[116] Sovereignty is shared and divided between national and European bodies and no European institution can claim supreme legislative authority. The ever closer Union is rephrased as an 'ever closer fusion'.[117]

The legal institutionalization of differentiated integration by incorporating the flexibility clauses in EU treaties primarily minimizes the risk of the pursuit of progressive integration by individual Member States outside the treaty framework. The acceptable level of differentiation is determined within the system of EU treaties and other legal documents. It is based on the functionality of specific governance arrangements for cooperation and mutual coordination among varying sets of participating countries.[118]

The Union's pluralistic complexity and functional differentiation of horizontally linked social systems means a departure from the nation state as a unified system of representative authority in full territorial and political control.[119] Its framework rules out the possibility of a new political centre or authoritative hierarchy. Its internal dynamic is that of a 'self-regulated pluralistic society'.[120] The heterarchy of EU politics and law indicates that any form of progressive integration necessarily leads to the growing differentiation and diffusion of the political authority and jurisdiction of EU bodies.

The EU's differentiated integration significantly enhances EU legal and political autopoiesis. Normative conceptualizations of the European polity by

116 Andrew Moravcsik, supra n. 12, 507.

117 Wolfgang Wessels, 'An Ever Closer Fusion? A Dynamic Macropolitical View on Integration Processes', *Journal of Common Market Studies* 35(2) (1997): 274.

118 Wolfgang Streeck, 'Neo-voluntarism: A New European Social Policy Regime', in G. Marks et al., eds, supra n. 91, 70.

119 Richard Bellamy and Dario Castiglione, supra n. 7.

120 Dimitris N. Chryssochoou, supra n. 93, 27.

references to the foundations, values and original federalist goals of founding fathers of European integration, which can be witnessed in both recent history of the European Convention and early history of European federalism of the 1950s drawing on the Treaty of Rome, are of little use. They only reveal the scale of the EU's democratic deficit and continue to associate the concept of society with institutional hierarchies, normative orders and territorial limitations which is inadequate because of operative complexities and horizontal differentiations of the EU. However, the EU is functionally differentiated into social systems, each of them internally differentiated, unable to operate outside its own borders and self-reproduced – autopoietic. The European polity, therefore, can hardly signify ultimate normative foundations, values and goals of the EU. It, rather, needs to be treated as just one of many fragmented concepts signifying the functional differentiation and self-reference of the European political and legal systems.

Chapter 7

Desiring a Democratic European Polity: The Post-Sovereign EU Governed by Sovereign Member States

Political themes of who is actually governed by EU institutions, how, in whose name and to what end[1] turned out inescapable vis-à-vis progressive European political integration, its commitment to democratic principles and impact on democratic institutions and legitimacy of Member States. Within the context of European governance, the tension between instrumental *legitimation by outcomes* (based on policy effectiveness) and symbolic *legitimation by values* (based on the principles of democratic representation and participation)[2] has always been articulated through the often criticized but popular 'common benefit' discourse.[3] However, in the 1990s the 'permissive consensus' between the citizens of EU countries and Eurocratic élite administrative decisions was gradually replaced by a 'constraining dissensus' regarding the future direction and legal or constitutional settlement of European integration.[4]

Despite the wealth of debates on supranational governance, post-sovereignty, constitutionalism and the EU as a polycentric polity,[5] the semantics of popular democracy and national or European sovereignty remains an important reference point in political debates and conflicts within the context of both the EU and its Member States. It marks important political, juridical, economic and collective identity problems emerging coevally with globalization and Europeanization and

---

1 Thomas Banchoff and Mitchell P. Smith, eds, *Legitimacy and the European Union: The Contested Polity* (London: Routledge, 1999).

2 Fritz W. Scharpf, *Governing in Europe: Effective and Democratic?* (Oxford: Oxford University Press, 1999).

3 Giandomenico Majone, 'Europe's 'Democratic Deficit': The Question of Standards', *European Law Journal* 4 (1998): 5.

4 Myrto Tsakatika, 'The European Union and the democratic limits of governance', in *Governance and Civil Society in the European Union, Volume 1: Normative Perspectives*, eds Carlo Ruzza and Vincent Della Sala (Manchester: Manchester University Press, 2007), 31.

5 See, for instance, Marlene Wind, 'The European Union as a polycentric polity', in *European Constitutionalism Beyond the State*, eds Joseph H.H. Weiler and Marlene Wind (Cambridge: Cambridge University Press, 2003), 103.

the impossibility of continuing to build EU legitimacy on governance-driven efficiency rather than democratic accountability.[6]

The question of 'who governs the Union?' has often been overshadowed by the question of 'how is the Union governed'? However, theoretical and political reflections of ever growing European integration cannot escape the question of 'who governs' and 'who is governed' by the EU. In other words, European governance is not just a matter of instrumentality and different techniques but also a matter of questions of democratic rules and their adoption by European polity. Following these persistent issues, this chapter opens by summarizing the democratic principle commitments formulated by the Lisbon Treaty and their impact on the character of European governance and European polity. The most recent EU attempts at democratizing its forms of governance are subsequently contextualized by outlining historical links between the EU's institutional framework and the notion of European polity.

Democratic Legitimacy and European Integration

Since the 1950s, administered and expertly driven prosperity, stability, procedural justice and shared political interests and values of Member States have been the added value that legitimized the process of European integration. In the 1990s, democratic mobilization supplanted the existing processes of technocratic legitimacy and the European public was expected to engage in 'ever closer' post-Maastricht Union. When, however, the populations of several Member States rejected the Constitutional Treaty, democratization proved an obstacle to further integration. In the first decade of the twenty-first century, the split between the EU's calls for democratization and the crisis of functionality thus became ever more acute.

Theories of EU governance often underestimate the importance of democratic decision-making and reduce the problem of legitimacy to efficiency. Nevertheless, the process of democratization hardly can be discarded as a secondary problem at supranational EU and/or global level. However, this call for democratization paradoxically weakens administrative legitimacy by technocratic governance of EU experts and makes the EU a significantly more conflict-driven polity replicating a number of problems and conflicts historically associated with the modern democratic state and its political sovereignty. The post-sovereign EU, therefore, cannot avoid the modern politics of popular sovereignty and, in the absence of a democratically constituted institutional framework, it needs to

6 For the view that EU does not need demos but efficiency, see Jens Steffek, 'Sources of Legitimacy Beyond the State: A View from International Relations', in *Transnational Governance and Constitutionalism*, eds Christian Joerges, Inger-Johanne Sand and Gunther Teubner (Oxford: Hart Publishing, 2004), 81.

enhance its democratic legitimacy by strengthening political communication between democratic Member States and supranational EU political institutions.

The problem of democracy is general and the European Union is just one of its many specific contexts. During EU constitution-making, political constructivist notions of European democratic polity-building and federal statehood in waiting were frequently courted by European politicians and academics. At the beginning of the new millennium, the EU was engaged in the self-generating process of supranational form of constitutionalism which was expected to legally strengthen the principle of democratic legitimacy at EU level and thus justify the concept of 'ever closer Union' within the context of political and legal integration.

Reflecting on what actually happened during EU constitution-making process and its subsequent rejection by the French and the Dutch referenda in 2005, the most remarkable phenomenon was a contrast between the official EU language of public enthusiasm and the wall of private distrust of citizens in individual Member States. Ambitious statements made by Euro-enthusiastic politicians were accompanied by a dismissal of any criticisms and discontents regarding the state and future of the EU as 'anti-European', 'Eurosceptic' and even 'Europhobic'. A journey from one currency to one EU politics and one European polity governed by a constitution was considered an iron law of European integration. Echoing the Marxist logic of a political and ideological superstructure catching up with an economic substructure, advocates of ever more progressive integration assumed that the Constitutional Treaty could be enacted in the same manner like the Euro currency and even be enthusiastically welcomed by the peoples of the EU, if not by the European people – *demos* – in waiting.

After the failure of the constitutional experiment, the Lisbon Treaty was drafted and all Member States except Ireland, which was constitutionally obliged to call a referendum, avoided the process of ratification by this form of direct democracy. Nevertheless, the Lisbon Treaty was rejected by the first Irish referendum of 2008 and, while the European Council kept a low profile regarding renegotiations of the Treaty with the Irish government,[7] the Treaty suffered further ratification complications in the Czech Republic and was reviewed by constitutional courts in Germany and other Member States. The current state of the Union, therefore, persuasively illustrates that the process of economic integration does not automatically lead to supranational political integration and a constitutional momentum of state-building.

Furthermore, the process of transferring ever more power to the Union without adequate political accountability and democratization has recently been exploited by nationalist populist leaders in a number of Member States.[8] According to those politicians, the very fact of cultural and socio-political differences among

7 *Presidency Conclusions of the Council of the European Union*, CONCL 4, No. 14368/08, 16 October 2008.

8 Jiří Přibáň, *Legal Symbolism: On Law, Time and European Identity* (Aldershot: Ashgate, 2007), 123.

EU nations makes any project of a functioning polity impossible and dangerous from the perspective of national cohesion, integrity and sovereignty.[9] The Union's impossibility to equally recognize its political potential, tasks and limits invites adherents of the dark legacy of European ethno-nationalism to represent themselves as the guardians of nation state democratic institutions and popular sovereignty itself against the supranational undemocratic Union.

The populist right and left hugely benefited from the process of European integration driven by dreams rather than political reality.[10] This current ideological battleground is a semantic reflection of the Union's intrinsic structural paradoxes which increasingly call for political reforms of the Union and enhancement of its supranational democratic legitimacy.

In this context, several questions are of primary importance regarding the Lisbon Treaty and its incorporation of the principle of democratic legitimacy and representative democracy. Does the treaty successfully avoid the conceptual obscurantism of EU constitution-making mixing international law principles with hierarchies typical of federal or confederative statehood? Does the treaty mean both significant enhancement of the Union's democratic legitimacy and a final demise of the political dream of EU constitutional statehood and European polity founded and legitimized by the existence of European *constituent power*? In other words, can the Union democratize its institutions while abandoning the project of building the sovereign European *demos* by legal means and administrative governance?

Desiring the Democratic Union?: the Lisbon Treaty's Incorporation of Democratic Values and Principles

While it is true that nation state constitutionalism and democratic politics are just one of many contextualizations of European politics and constitutionalism today, they simply cannot be rejected as 'dated and artificial',[11] because the constitutional democratic sovereignty of the Member States remains a constitutive part of the EU's political and constitutional domain and supranational EU power structures urgently call for their democratic self-legitimation.

The 'true nature' of European constitutionalism without a constitution can hardly be just 'the balancing of diverse and often conflicting interests and fears'.[12] The question of the EU polity subsequently raises the problems of political

9 Bertrand Benoit, *Social-Nationalism: An Anatomy of French Euroscepticism* (Aldershot: Ashgate, 1997).

10 For this incapacity, see Ralf Dahrendorf, *Der Wiederbeginn der Geschichte. Vom Fall der Mauer zum Krieg im Irak* (München: C.H. Beck, 2004), ch. 9.

11 Miguel P. Maduro, 'Europe and constitution: what if this is as good as it gets?', in *European Constitutionalism Beyond the State*, eds Joseph H.H. Weiler and Marlene Wind (Cambridge: Cambridge University Press, 2003), 74.

12 Ibid., 75.

inclusion and exclusion as well as the boundaries of the EU polity[13] and its effect on the constitutional polities of Member States. Translating the sociological constitution of society as the unity of social plurality and multitude into the EU context, one is immediately reminded of the failed Constitutional Treaty preamble speaking of 'unity in diversity' that has subsequently been reformulated in Article 2 of the Lisbon Treaty stating that

> The Union is founded on the values of respect for human dignity, freedom, democracy, equality, the rule of law and respect for human rights, including the rights of persons belonging to minorities.
>
> These values are common to the Member States in a society in which pluralism, non-discrimination, tolerance, justice, solidarity and equality between women and men prevail.[14]

This general proclamation of the value foundations of the EU is further supplemented by another 'unity in diversity' statement in Article 3(3) of the Lisbon Treaty according to which the Union

> … shall promote economic, social and territorial cohesion, and solidarity among Member States.
>
> It shall respect its rich cultural and linguistic diversity, and shall ensure that Europe's cultural heritage is safeguarded and enhanced.[15]

The Lisbon Treaty text thus contains the paradoxes, contingencies and potential of the EU political domain beyond state and popular sovereignty. Political and legal unity is to be based on profound territorial pluralism, and the imagined polity of European citizens is to be built on the reimagined and transformed nations and communities of the EU. Although it has proven impossible to replicate at the EU level the systemic complexity and normative preconditions of democratic legitimacy that exists in the politics of Member States, EU institutions are based on, and actively promote, the values of democracy, equality and respect for human rights.

The Lisbon Treaty clearly is a retreat from ambitious plans of progressive integration by the process of constitution-making. The other name of the Lisbon Treaty – 'the Reform Treaty' – indicates that the process of progressive integration needed to be revised and reformed after the Constitutional Treaty's rejection by the French and Dutch citizens in 2005. The Lisbon Treaty's framework is an example of such coeval legitimation through technocratic efficiency and democratization.

---

13 Hans Lindahl, 'European Integration: Popular Sovereignty and a Politics of Boundaries', *European Law Journal* 6(3) (2000): 253–256.

14 Consolidated Version of the Treaty on European Union, *Official Journal of the European Union*, 9th May 2008, C115/17.

15 Ibid.

The Treaty's call for the improved efficiency and democracy of EU institutions, however, reveals a structural discrepancy between the EU's politics of supranational governance, which primarily neutralizes conflicts by administrative reason and technocratic expertise, and the ever growing difficulties Member States encounter in attempting to transfer the powers of their democratically legitimate political institutions to the EU.

Analysing the principle of democratic legitimacy and representation, it is important to emphasize that the Lisbon Treaty is neither a constitutional document of self-determination of the democratic European nation, nor an act of a democratically representative political body. If one can use the term at all, the Union's *constituent power* lies with the peoples of the EU collectively as represented by their national parliaments and governments in their political diversity. It is an international law treaty strengthening the current state of European economic and political integration and opening new options of further integration.

This retreat from constitutional ambitions is confirmed by the abandonment of the original idea behind a constitutional treaty according to which a new treaty was intended to replace all previous legal foundations of the EU and operate as a new legal basis of the Union. Unlike this idea of a constitutional beginning, the Lisbon Treaty leaves all previous treaties in place and merely operates as their novelization.

The Constitutional Treaty's references to European 'law' and 'framework law' have been abandoned and the existing concepts of 'regulations', 'directives' and 'decisions' have been retained by drafters of the Lisbon Treaty.[16] Any possibility of jurisprudential assumptions of legal monism constructing the constitutional supremacy of the Union's legal system over legal systems of Member States has thus been ruled out and the current system of EU law continues to recognize the horizontal plurality of legal systems as well as of its own legal acts. The incorporation of the *Charter of Fundamental Rights of the European Union* and its limitation as regards the competences of the Union as well as the Union's accession to the *European Convention for the Protection of Human Rights and Fundamental Freedoms* serve as examples of this continuing legal pluralism within the EU.[17]

16 See *The Council of the European Union Note No. 11218/07*, 'IGC 2007 Mandate', Brussels, 26 June 2007, 3.

17 Article 6 of the Lisbon Treaty reads: '1. The Union recognises the rights, freedoms and principles set out in the Charter of Fundamental Rights of the European Union of 7 December 2000, as adapted at Strasbourg, on 12 December 2007, which shall have the same legal value as the Treaties. The provisions of the Charter shall not extend in any way the competences of the Union as defined in the Treaties. The rights, freedoms and principles in the Charter shall be interpreted in accordance with the general provisions in Title VII of the Charter governing its interpretation and application and with due regard to the explanations referred to in the Charter, that set out the sources of those provisions. 2. The Union shall accede to the European Convention for the Protection of Human Rights and Fundamental Freedoms. Such accession shall not affect the Union's competences as defined in the Treaties. 3. Fundamental rights, as guaranteed by the European Convention

Scrutinizing democratic principles of the EU in detail, Title II is an obvious starting point of any analysis. It is noteworthy that Article 9 of the Treaty opens by drafting the first principle of justice as fairness – the equal treatment of all citizens before EU laws – together with the legal construction of EU citizenship as additional and not replacing national citizenship. Drafters considered the principle of civic equality before the law as a constitutive principle of any supranational form of governance by European legality[18] and thus fully adopted what has been the most important precondition of the existence of any democratic polity.

The Lisbon Treaty presents the Union as a system of compound democracy,[19] with the twin representation of citizens and states. Further, it commits the Union to the founding principle of representative democracy, guaranteeing the right for EU citizens to be democratically represented at both EU and Member State levels. The democratic foundations of the Union are further extended by the citizens' right to participate in 'the democratic life of the Union' legislated for in the third section of Article 10 of the Treaty on European Union (TEU). The principle of representative democracy is supplemented by the concept of participatory democracy which is further elaborated by Article 11 of the TEU. Finally, the complexity of the EU's political structures and operations are manifested by closely associating representative democracy with public accountability and multi-party democracy operating at both the Member State and EU level and, therefore, shaping and 'expressing the will of citizens of the Union'.

Specific EU responses to the deficit of representative democracy are reflected in more general issues of the Union's legitimacy and functioning, accountability, multilevel governance and commitment to a supranational civic and democratic political culture. The Union's democratic foundation is inseparable from questions of who is represented and how, and which democratic checks and limitations of power apply to the Union.

Representative and Direct Democracy and its Adoption by the EU

It is hardly disputed that the Union's multilevel governance[20] is an historically and politically unique project which is irreducible to just another kind of international

---

for the Protection of Human Rights and Fundamental Freedoms and as they result from the constitutional traditions common to the Member States, shall constitute general principles of the Union's law'. One can speculate about the meaning of 'general principles', but this term hardly can challenge the pluralistic character of the EU legal system.

18 Consolidated Version of the Treaty on European Union, *Official Journal of the European Union*, 9th May 2008, C115/20.

19 Sergio Fabbrini, *Compound Democracies: Why the United States and Europe Are Becoming Similar* (Oxford: Oxford University Press, 2007).

20 Liesbet Hooghe and Gary Marks, *Multi-Level Governance and European Integration* (Oxford: Rowman & Littlefield, 2001).

organization. It involves economically, politically and legally experimental processes and elements.[21] However, the pressures to find a solution to the Union's deficits of democratic legitimacy became increasingly pressing in the post-Maastricht era.[22] Despite imaginative scholarly attempts to present the Union as demanding and deserving models of legitimacy that break with traditional ideas of representative democracy, the appeal of representative democracy survives.[23] An institutional design favouring the executive branch of government needed to be reformed to avoid further alienation and a growing gap between EU governing bodies and those governed by them. The original model of legitimacy of European integration through 'output' needed to be substantially supplemented by legitimacy through 'input' bringing on board more democratic representation and public accountability of the Union's institutions and their decision-making.[24]

The post-national constellation of the EU[25] called for its democratization to narrow the gap between the Union and its citizens and to deal with the Union's democratic deficit.[26] European political integration based on the limitation of Member State sovereignty[27] resulted in a need to enhance democratic governing and functioning of the post-sovereign Union.[28] As with the failed Constitutional Treaty,[29] the Lisbon Treaty sought to strike the right balance between administrative efficiency and democratic legitimacy by strengthening the democratic decision-making of the Union's institutions and increasing the contribution and participation of Member States' democratic institutions in EU decision-making.

---

21 Brigid Laffan, Rory O'Donnell and Michael Smith, *Europe's Experimental Union: Rethinking Integration* (London: Routledge, 2000).

22 Robert A. Dahl, 'A Democratic Dilemma: System Effectiveness versus Citizen Participation', *Political Science Quarterly* 109 (1994): 23.

23 Agustín J. Menéndez, 'The European Democratic Challenge: The Forging of a Supranational *Volonté Générale*', *European Law Journal 15 (2009):* 277.

24 William Wallace and Julie Smith, 'Democracy or Technocracy? European Integration and the Problem of Popular Consent', in *The Crisis of Representation in Europe*, ed. Jack Hayward (Oxford: Frank Cass, 1995), 137.

25 Jürgen Habermas, 'The Postnational Constellation and the Future of Democracy', in *The Postnational Constellation: Political Essays* (Cambridge: Polity Press, 2001), 58.

26 See, for instance, Beate Kohler-Koch and Berthold Rittberger, eds, *Debating the Democratic Legitimacy of the European Union* (Oxford: Rowman & Littlefield, 2007).

27 For the political and international context of the self-limitation of state sovereignty in the EU, see, for example, Jürgen Habermas and Jacques Derrida, 'February 15, or What Binds Europeans Together: A Plea for a Common Foreign Policy, Beginning in the Core of Europe', *Constellations* 10 (2003): 294.

28 Dimitris N. Chryssochoou, *Theorizing European Integration* (London: Sage, 2001), 136–146; see also Neil Walker, 'Late Sovereignty in the European Union', in *Sovereignty in Transition*, ed. Neil Walker (Oxford: Hart Publishing, 2003).

29 Ben Crum, 'Tailoring Representative Democracy to the European Union: Does the European Constitution Reduce the Democratic Deficit?', *European Law Journal* 11 (2005): 452.

Representative democracy is a form of government in which citizens elect their representatives and grant them political power for a limited period of time.[30] Throughout modern European history, it has been associated with government's respect for and protection of individual liberties (liberal democracy)[31] and parliamentarianism (the legislative body elected in the general election by the people and representing its popular sovereignty).[32] A parliament elected by the people consists of individual members generally organized in political parties or other formations. Parliamentarians are divided into a majority, which supports the executive, or government, and the minority, or opposition, which actively opposes government initiatives but still participates in parliamentary politics and enjoys representation in different parliamentary bodies.

Presently, representative democracy is absent from the EU institutional framework,[33] yet representative democracy is considered the political foundation of the Union. It is a precondition of EU membership, and all Member States are constitutional parliamentary democracies.

Before the end of Cold War and the collapse of the Soviet regimes of 'the people's democracies' in Central and Eastern Europe in 1989 and in the Soviet Union itself in 1991, representative democracy and parliamentarianism had been taken for granted within the Member States of the European Community. The accession of post-dictatorial Greece (1981), Portugal (1986) and Spain (1986) to the European Community confirmed that a constitutional parliamentary democracy was a *de facto* if not *de jure* condition of membership. However, it was not until 1993 and the Copenhagen criteria set up for post-communist emerging democracies when the rule of law and democracy standards were officially defined as conditions of EU membership.[34] Enlargements of EU membership in 2004, 2007 and 2013 thus demonstrate that the political model of representative democracy is now one of the most critical conditions for any state seeking membership. Democracy is a cornerstone of the EU's accession policy and contributes significantly to the belief that the EU is a 'democratic polity' promoting intrinsic democratic values in external relations and global politics.[35]

The EU Treaty lists democracy as one of the foundational values common to all Member States. The quality and standards of democratic politics in Member States

30 Giovanni Sartori, *The Theory of Democracy Revisited: The Contemporary Debate* (Chatham, NJ: Chatham House Publishers, 1987), 21.

31 Ibid., 367–398.

32 Klaus von Beyme, *Parliamentary Democracy: Democratization, Destabilization, Reconsolidation, 1789–1999* (Houndmills: Palgrave Macmillan, 2000).

33 Dimitris N. Chryssochoou, supra n. 28.

34 Wojciech Sadurski, 'Accession's Democracy Dividend: The Impact of the EU Enlargement upon Democracy in the New Member States of Central and Eastern Europe', *European Law Journal* 10 (2004): 371.

35 Richard Youngs, *The European Union and the Promotion of Democracy* (Oxford: Oxford University Press, 2001).

is consequently an intrinsic part of the EU's multilevel governance. However, Member States were originally assumed to be democratically governed and the principle of representative democracy did not inform the body of EU laws and functions of EU institutions. Only recently, in light of growing populist electoral successes in a number of Member States, did the Amsterdam Treaty establish formal mechanisms for guaranteeing the perpetuation of democratic government in Member States. In 2000, no recourse was made to the Amsterdam Treaty provisions despite the rise of the far-right Freedom Party in Austria. Instead, an 'early warning' amendment to the Treaty provisions, nicknamed 'Lex Austria', was subsequently introduced by the Nice Treaty. The 'Lex Austria' amendment allowed the European Council 'to suspend certain of the rights deriving from the application of the Treaties to the Member State' if actions of this state constitute 'a clear risk of a serious breach'[36] of the Union's values of 'human dignity, freedom, equality, democracy, the rule of law, and respect for human rights'.[37]

The concept of participatory democracy is usually defined against the background of more established notions of representative and direct democracy. Participatory democracy requires extending power and decision-making to a broad swathe of the population. Advocates of participatory democracy often criticize representational institutions for limiting democratic participation to voting processes and for insufficient means for voters to control their representatives or hold them accountable.[38] Although all forms of democratic government require public participation, participatory democracy involves an enhanced form of participation that allows those people affected by or interested in political decisions to contribute directly to the decision-making process. This heightened level of engagement is thought to strengthen democracy's general virtues of self-government, self-realization and self-education through public discussion and civil society.[39]

The EU embraced the concept of participatory democracy to deal with its perceived deficit of democratic representation[40] and to promote alternative forms democratic legitimacy.[41] The Union's commitment to post-national forms of

36 Article 7 of the Consolidated Version of the Treaty on European Union, *Official Journal of the European Union*, 9th May 2008, C115/19.

37 Article 2 of the Consolidated Version of the Treaty on European Union, *Official Journal of the European Union*, 9th May 2008, C115/17.

38 Carole Pateman, 'Participation and Democratic Theory', in *The Democracy Sourcebook*, eds Robert A. Dahl, Ian Shapiro and Jose Antonio Cheibub (Cambridge: MA, The MIT Press, 2003), 41–42.

39 Baogang He, 'Civil Society and Democracy', in *Democratic Theory Today: Challenges for the 21st Century*, eds April Carter and Geoffrey Stokes (Cambridge: Polity Press, 2002), 211–213.

40 For general comments, see Gráinne de Búrca, 'The Quest for Legitimacy in the European Union', *Modern Law Review* 59 (1996): 349.

41 Phillipe Schmitter, 'Democracy in Europe and Europe's Democratization', *Journal of Democracy* 14(4) (2003): 71.

participatory democracy draws on recent theories concerning political globalization and post-national democratization[42] as well as theories of governance that embrace policies of public accountability and the engagement of civil society.[43]

The Lisbon Treaty expands the Union's commitment to increasing political participation by adopting the *citizens' initiative* as a form of direct democracy.[44] The citizens' initiative is an attempt at closing the gap between rhetoric and reality in the Union's commitment to democracy. Until now, direct democracy has played virtually no role in the functioning of the Union. The exercise of direct democracy in EU matters was limited to the national referenda ratifying or rejecting the EU Treaties, and these referenda are entirely regulated by the Member States' constitutional systems, not EU law.[45]

In legal terms, the citizens' initiative requires the minimum number of one million of EU citizens. Furthermore, those citizens must be nationals of a significant number of Member States and the initiative has to be in matters of the European Commission's powers. Nevertheless, there is a more general goal associated with the citizens' initiative as an element of direct democracy applied at the EU level; namely, the evolution of a transnational European civil society.[46] By voicing and standing for the general interests of EU citizens, a transnational European civil society, which operates beyond the limits of nation states, is expected to act as a counterweight to the lobbying power of interest groups and their specific political goals.[47] Instead of the output-oriented and the interest aggregation-based legitimacy model, the citizens' initiative is part of an input-based procedural legitimacy model[48] which is intended to expand democratic deliberation in the post-national EU.

EU and Member State Democracy

Member States are assumed to be democratic nation states functioning through their representative political bodies. Furthermore, the Union itself guarantees

42 Michael T. Greven and Louis W. Pauly, eds, *Democracy Beyond the State: The European Dilemma and Emerging Global Order* (Oxford: Rowman & Littlefield, 2000).

43 Gary Marks et al., eds, *Governance in the European Union* (London: SAGE Publications, 1996).

44 Art 11(4) TEU.

45 'Direct democracy and the European Union … is that a threat or a promise', Editorial comments, *Common Market Law Review* 45 (2008): 930.

46 Olivier de Schutter, 'Europe in Search of its Civil Society', *European Law Journal* 8 (2002): 198.

47 Deirdre Curtin, 'Private Interest Representation or Civil Society Deliberation? A Contemporary Dilemma for European Governance', *Social & Legal Studies* 12 (2003): 55.

48 Carlo Ruzza and Vincent Della Sala, 'Conclusion: Deliberative Democracy, Input–Output Legitimacy and the Meaning of Civil Society', in *Governance and Civil Society in the European Union: Volume 2: Normative Perspectives*, eds Carlo Ruzza and Vincent Della Sala (Manchester: Manchester University Press, 2007), 136–137.

direct representation of EU citizens in the European Parliament.[49] The Parliament has only limited powers regarding the legislative process in the Union and certainly does not channel the political process in a manner comparable to parliaments of nation states. Furthermore, its members do not represent the democratic sovereign will of one European nation voting according to the principle 'one citizen, one vote' beyond their Member State constituencies. Nevertheless, while the Union does not exercise its power on the assumption of direct democratic legitimacy of its officials and legislator, EU citizens are not limited to channelling their public voice and collective will through political institutions of Member States. They equally can use the European Parliament as a forum of supranational political deliberation democratically representing citizens of EU Member States.

The EU thus emerges as a supranational organization guaranteeing the public voice of its citizens, yet denying their political will to be shaping EU political institutions in a system comparable to that of the democratic nation state. Compensating for this structural limitation, the Lisbon Treaty seeks to strengthen democratic controls of EU institutions by the alternative strategy of making national democratically elected parliaments part of its decision-making process and effectively turning them into agencies of the EU system of political checks and balances.

This move clearly shows that suggestions of introducing more expertise-oriented and deliberative concepts of legitimation as substitutes for democratic legitimation where representative democracy cannot be implemented at EU level have only limited validity.[50] Article 12 of the Lisbon Treaty, therefore, allocates more powers to national parliaments, especially their involvement in guaranteeing the EU principle of subsidiarity.[51] Due to the non-existence of the democratically elected legislator and democratically accountable government at EU level, the Union continues to be based on the principle of conferral, which is typical of international organizations. Enhancement of its democratic legitimacy, therefore, has been directly linked to the strengthening of the principles of subsidiarity and proportionality.[52]

49 Ibid.

50 Christian Joerges and Jürgen Neyer, 'From Intergovernmental Bargaining to Deliberative Political Processes: The Constitutionalisation of Comitology', *European Law Journal* 3(3) (1997): 273.

51 Consolidated Version of the Treaty on European Union, *Official Journal of the European Union*, 9th May 2008, C115/20.

52 Article 5 of the Treaty reads: '1. The limits of Union competences are governed by the principle of conferral. The use of Union competences is governed by the principles of subsidiarity and proportionality. 2. Under the principle of conferral, the Union shall act only within the limits of the competences conferred upon it by the Member States in the Treaties to attain the objectives set out therein. Competences not conferred upon the Union in the Treaties remain with the Member States. 3. Under the principle of subsidiarity, in areas which do not fall within its exclusive competence, the Union shall act only if and in so far as the objectives of the proposed action cannot be sufficiently achieved by the Member States, either at central level or at regional and local level, but can rather, by reason of the scale or effects of the proposed action, be better achieved at Union level'.

The process of progressive integration runs as a coeval process of power transfer to the EU and increasingly growing involvement of democratic institutions of Member States in EU policy and decision-making. This process is illustrated by two protocols attached to the Lisbon Treaty, namely the *Protocol on the role of national parliaments in the European Union* and the *Protocol on the application of the principles of subsidiarity and proportionality*. Both protocols give more influence to national legislators to potentially challenge the EU legislation and thus make democratically elected and representative institutions of Member States directly involved in operations of EU institutions. Indeed, this involvement recursively enhances limited democratic legitimacy of the European Parliament, the Council and the Commission.

The political system of the EU thus evolves through parallel processes of the Union's self-empowering and the continuing active involvement of sovereign Member States via their independent democratic political systems. While the Union benefits from the process of power transfer from the national level to the European level, its very existence depends on Member States and the system of their political negotiations and legal agreements. The organization of EU politics is not superior to those of Member States but rather coexists and benefits from them and internalizes their operations.

As regards democratic legitimation, this structural setting has significant consequences because it incorporates the system of international cooperation which commonly tends to compromise parliamentary power and control. Unable to actively participate in the creation of acts of legislation, it is ever more important that national parliaments can have monitoring powers over European legislation. Furthermore, bringing national parliaments on board EU decision-making significantly contributes to the improvement of accountability of both EU and Member State executive powers.[53]

The Union's External 'Democracy Dividend': a Comment on Recent EU Enlargements

Apart from provisions of the Lisbon Treaty's Title II, the democratic principle mainly appears in Title V, the Union's coordination of the common foreign and security policy. Under this title, Article 21 reads as follows:

> [T]he Union's action on the international scene shall be guided by the principles which have inspired its own creation, development and enlargement, and which it seeks to advance in the wider world: democracy, the rule of law, the universality and indivisibility of human rights and fundamental freedoms, respect for human

53 This problem was already discussed during the process of EU constitution-making. See, for instance, Ben Crum, supra n. 29, 460–465.

> dignity, the principles of equality and solidarity, and respect for the principles of the United Nations Charter and international law.
>
> The Union shall seek to develop relations and build partnerships with third countries, and international, regional or global organizations which share the principles referred to in the first subparagraph. It shall promote multilateral solutions to common problems, in particular in the framework of the United Nations.[54]

This article primarily reflects on the stabilizing and proselytizing roles of the Union. It enhances the Union's self-referentiality regarding its general commitment to a set of political and legal principles and values which determine both EU enlargement policies and the Union's international policies.

Self-reflection of the Union as an organization embodying and promoting peace among nations of the world, multilateralism in international relations, cosmopolitan values, universal humanity and social and economic progress of humankind is strongly present in the text of the Lisbon Treaty. This coeval promotion of democratic principles inside the Union, outside its borders and as preconditions of EU membership has been steadily progressing in the last two decades. Apart from internal transformation and increasing political integration of the EU after the Maastricht Treaty, the second reason for this transformation was the process of EU enlargement which dominated the Union's agenda in the 1990s and primarily involved post-communist countries undergoing fundamental social and democratic transitions at that time.[55]

These coeval processes of the Union's 'deepening' and 'widening' required both codification of the principle of democratic government and possible sanctions of those Member States which might breach it. The EU can thus demand its Member States and candidate states to be democratically governed and committed to the protection of human dignity, rights, equality and freedom. Focusing on the Union's external stabilizing role, it is clear that, historically, one of the most noticeable common benefits was the Union's *democratizing effect* on post-communist candidate states during their accession talks between 1993 and 2004.[56]

From the perspective of the candidate states, EU membership and conditionality process were equally legitimized by 'the national benefit' and received the public support. After the fall of communism, the process of Europeanization was always closely associated with the process of democratization. Some academics even wrote about the 'accession's democracy dividend'[57] when examining the force,

54 Consolidated Version of the Treaty on European Union, *Official Journal of the European Union*, 9th May 2008, C115/28.

55 For a more detailed analysis of the following issues, see especially, Jiří Přibáň, 'From "Which Rule of Law?" to "The Rule of Which Law?": postcommunist experiences of European legal integration', *Hague Journal on the Rule of Law* 1(2) (2009): 337.

56 Ibid., 119.

57 Wojciech Sadurski, supra n. 34, 371.

impact and limitations of the Union's external pressure on the accession countries. EU membership was considered the best protection of emerging constitutional democracies in Central and Eastern Europe against illiberal and authoritarian politics, corruption, arbitrary use of power by civil servants, lack of public accountability and many other sorts of political failures. In other words, EU institutions were expected to promote and police exactly the same goals which defined post-communist constitutional and political transformations. Weak national political and legal institutions, which suffered from insufficient resources and experience and were prone to political cronyism and corruption, were expected to be externally supported and stabilized during the transitional period by the EU.

EU institutions 'patronized' national politics and represented another check on standards and quality of constitutional and democratic transformations. In June 1993, the European Council enacted a set of EU membership conditions which became known as the 'Copenhagen criteria' and divided the EU accession conditions to three different categories – political, economic and legal. While economic conditions specified the need to establish a functioning market economy compatible with market pressures, competition and regulations within the EU, political conditions listed the need to guarantee institutional stability of emerging democracies and their constitutional systems, including the rule of law principles and human rights catalogues.[58] Political conditions even included respect for and protection of minorities for which there was no ground within the framework of European law.[59]

Until the Copenhagen Council, no formal democratic criteria for applicant countries were defined by the Union.[60] At the beginning of the EU accession process, the Commission's overall scrutiny and evaluation classified three different groups of candidate states: those already conforming to the democracy criterion (the Czech Republic, Estonia, Hungary, Poland and Estonia), those on their way to meeting the criterion (Lithuania, Latvia, Romania, Bulgaria) and Slovakia as a country failing to meet it and therefore excluded from accession talks. However, the Slovak parliamentary election of 1998 resulted in the end of the Mečiar government and the new government led by Prime Minister Dzurinda subsequently reopened accession talks in February 2000 and eventually succeeded in bringing the country to the EU in the first enlargement wave in May 2004.[61]

---

58 Manfred Novak, 'Human Rights 'Conditionality' in Relation to Entry to, and Full Participation in, the EU', in *The EU and Human Rights*, eds Phillip Alston, Mara R. Bustello and James Heenan (Oxford: Oxford University Press, 1999), 687.

59 Bruno De Witte and Gabriel N. Toggenburg, 'Human Rights and Membership of the European Union', in *The European Union Charter of Fundamental Rights: Politics, Law and Policy*, eds Steve Peers and Angela Ward (Oxford: Hart Publishing, 2004), 67–68.

60 Wojciech Sadurski, 'Charter and Enlagement', *European Law Journal* 8(3) (2002): 343.

61 Frank Schimmelfennig, Stefan Engert and Heiko Knobel, 'The Impact of EU Political Conditionality', in *The Europeanization of Central and Eastern Europe*, eds Frank Schimmelfennig and Ulrich Sedelmaier (Ithaca, NY: Cornell University Press, 2005), 37–42.

While the Slovak example persuasively shows the public mobilization and democratization potential of EU membership and the Union's stabilizing role in national politics,[62] conditionality criteria also strongly affected national political and legal agendas in countries classified as already having democratic governance in 1997. Indeed, the rule of law and democratic transformation originated in internal political changes in those countries. Political demands for free elections, multi-party political systems, the independent systems of justice, freedom of expression, local government and so on had been formulated by national democratic forces. Nevertheless, it is important to emphasize that those forces could always rely on the EU as a major point of reference and supranational organization of democratically governed liberal states based on the rule of law. The EU represented a 'normal state of things' towards which post-communist countries in transformation were heading and which, therefore, could and actually did have a strong synergistic effect in European politics.[63]

The candidate states' 'patronized status' did not change until the Union's engagement in the constitution-making process. During the Convention's work on the constitutional treaty, the candidate states were invited to contribute to its drafting but they could not block any consensus that could be established amongst Member States at the time. In other words, the post-communist states' status changed from passive recipients of EU laws to active participants in EU constitution-making and fully engaged members in the post-accession EU.

On the Functional Differentiation of European Society

The current state of the EU is a specific example of functionally differentiated supranational society politically searching and legally constituting its collective self-reflections beyond 'sacred' bonds of the modern nation state. In the absence of EU democratic statehood, technocratic governance paradoxically remains a major force behind the evolution and self-reflection of European polity and continues to facilitate its legitimation.

The constitution of a democratic polity is a product of the *classicist* Enlightenment period. However, the current EU is typical of *baroque* political institutional settings which can hardly generate representative democratic politics and inspire the emergence of the European *demos* from upside down. New checks and balances introduced by the Lisbon Treaty certainly make the Union more democratically accountable but they are far from the democratic state's constitution of popular sovereignty and power separation.

62 Geoffrey Pridham, 'EU Enlargement and Consolidating Democracy in Post-Communit States – Formality and Reality', *Journal of Common Market Studies* 40(5) (2002): 953.

63 See, for instance, Andrew Evans, 'Voluntary Harmonisation in Integration between the European Community and Eastern Europe', *European Law Review* 22 (1997): 201.

The process of democratic self-reflection and imagination of citizens of the EU cannot be governed by European comitology and self-administration. The European civic culture and the legislated EU charter of fundamental rights should not be mistaken for democratic government. Polity-building by legal means, such as European treaties and civil rights, is unable to fully substitute for self-reflections and political self-determination of EU populations. It even can have harmful effects and result in human rights consumerism rather than civic activism and democratic participation.

If European identity is imaginable as a legislated catalogue of civil rights and freedoms, it is more than obvious that this juridical expression of European identity further needs to be transformed to civil bonds and culture vital for any democratic statehood, especially in its supranational forms. The Lisbon Treaty enhances democratic accountability of the Union and increasingly supports EU institutions by democratically legitimate national institutions, but it cannot fulfil the task of constructing a democratic polity which stretches far beyond legal operations and depends on the *postmodern* architecture of the reflexive European public self-generation and political mobilization.

Democracy and technocracy are just two different pictures of the same modern political system. In this sense, the Lisbon Treaty merely has recognized the importance of mutual processes of politicization and depoliticization when it emphasized both 'democratic accountability' and 'efficiency'. European politics, rather than merely constituting new political organization and forms of deliberation and decision-making, thus replicates one of the general operations of the modern political system in which it is the job of politicians to enforce expert knowledge and to translate it to the language of popular sovereignty and will-formation. EU and Member State politicians can keep their decision-making power only if they persuade the public and make technocratic decisions that are democratically legitimate.

Modern semantics of democratic legitimacy persist at EU level. They also change the Union's description and the constitution of the political system operating beyond the nation state and/or international politics. At the same time, the EU's general commitment to democracy and human rights is not turned into a fully operational system comparable to the constitutional state and the democratic deficit continues to be partly compensated for by the surplus of the functioning system of EU law.

The complex process of making the EU both more efficient and democratic has implications for the very notion of European society as a society of functionally differentiated systems of economy, law, politics, education and so on without ultimate moral and cultural foundations and integration. This functionally differentiated European society is uncontainable by some form of statehood-/constitution-framing which would make it possible to think of European society as another form of modern national society typical of modern European history. One cannot imagine European society as a hierarchical unity of principles but only as a network of horizontally differentiated systems governed by their internal rationalities and communication codes. The project of the 'ever closer Union', therefore, needs to be reconceptualized as the 'ever more functionally differentiated European society'.

Postscript

Sovereignty of Popular Memories: A Critique of Political Existentialism

Modern democracy, whether local, national or supranational, does not need any transcendental source of legitimation and draws on the force of political negotiation, deliberation and representation. It generates legitimacy from within its political system and without recourse to the divine will or tradition. This historical and structural change means that popular sovereignty became a social rather than political question. Immanent problems of the conditions and quality of social life replaced transcendental notions of sovereignty as an external, unconditional and exclusive force constituting the political society. Permanently evolving self-referential political and legal procedures operate without this image of a transcendental sovereign ruling the rest of society by its laws.

Separation of power and the protection of human rights enhance functional differentiation and self-limitation of the political and legal systems. Separating different branches of power results in the proliferation of political procedures, conflicts and decision-making and, therefore, further functional differentiation of both politics and law in modern society. At the same time, the protection of human rights differentiates between the public and private spheres and constitutes further demarcations and limitations of democratic politics.

The notion of popular sovereignty as one self-governing sovereign polity of equal and free citizens is thus contrasted to the ever growing differentiation of political and legal procedures. The people is sovereign, yet only through self-limiting and permanently differentiating subsystems of constitutional rights and communication between different branches of constitutional power and their specific institutions.

Popular sovereignty, nevertheless, includes the normative idea of legitimate settlement between constituent and constituted power. This circular communication between governors and those who are governed by them is captured by the concept of sovereignty as polity incorporating self-descriptive normative images and holistic imaginations of society as cultural unity and totality. In this final and concluding chapter of the book, I, therefore, analyse the concept of sovereignty as part of cultural communication of collective symbolism and moral value foundationalism in both the national and post-national European or global contexts.

Following this analysis, I critically conclude that the semantics of sovereignty as the 'real' democratic polity representing the whole society is part of the specific cultural function of memory. All references to 'foundations' and 'constituting' moments of such polity use memory as operation, selecting between remembrance and forgetting which actually supports and enhances general operations of the systems of positive law and politics. While this specific selection does not make culture an autopoietic system of modern society, it further supplements the internal communication of the systems of positive law and politics and thus makes it possible to speak, for instance, of legal and/or political culture. However, this conceptualization of culture makes it an intrinsic part of different social systems which cannot be treated as their ultimate foundation.

Culture as the Foundation and Outcome of Sovereignty

Theories of popular sovereignty perceiving the people's existence as the substance of constitutional statehood and its ultimate legitimation often draw on the typically modern contrast between communal spontaneity and societal organization. The difference between the people and the state in the process of modernization was summarized, for instance, by Ferdinand Tönnies in the following words:

> In the same way as the individual natural will evolves into pure thinking and rational will, which tends to dissolve and subjugate its predecessors, the original collective forms of Gemeinschaft have developed into Gesellschaft and the rational will of the Gesellschaft. In the course of history, folk culture has given rise to the civilisation of the state.[1]

This sociological explanation of political evolution of modern statehood provides for the social and legitimation basis of the modern state and the importance of spontaneity of culture in legitimizing the rational state organization and its legal system. However, Tönnies equally emphasized the opposite capacity of the modern state to create its own culture and establish the morality rising above the state and fostering a new culture founded on the civilizing force of the state.[2]

Despite Tönnies's statement that '[L]aw is, in every respect, nothing but common will',[3] the relationship between the people and its state is circular, not foundational. The people's life and culture do not legitimize the state as its substance because they equally are outcomes of state organization and operations. The people as the natural substance and imagined community actually take the exclusive form of constitutional reasoning and social ordering.

Indeed, the classic concept of community adopted by Tönnies and other sociologists of his time involved a warning against social disintegration by emphasizing the need for social unity and integration. Community was considered 'the whole', contrasted to the society dissipating into different 'parts', such as

1 Ferdinand Tönnies, *Community and Society* (Mineola, NY: Dover Publications, 2002), 225.

2 Ibid., 230–231.

3 Ibid., 190.

economy, politics, law and so on. Nevertheless, the rational will and justification in public opinion involves the capacity to transform political legislation and conventions into a specific culture and order of mores and folkways. Politics of universal civilization symbolized by the modern democratic state and popular sovereignty has the social capacity to construct its particular polity and popular culture – a culture of shared symbols, identity and communal bonds.

Political legitimation, therefore, is a circular process of integrating a particular polity as cultural community by the state as a modern political organization and coevally shaping the polity's culture by political decision-making and authoritative definition of the polity's foundations through social and education policies, the state media, state sponsorship of historical science and the humanities and so on. The sovereign people is considered a collective entity both constituting and constituted by its state and therefore both exercising and endangered by its sovereign power.

The paradox of modern state constitutionalism is concentrated in the democratic polity self-constituting its sovereignty in the pre-political domain of 'real life' to which it, however, is subjected through the state constitution. Constitutional limitation of popular sovereignty is a source of political self-empowerment and juridical self-constitution of the 'real' democratic polity.

The paradoxical constitution of the sovereign state by the polity as an entity with common culture and collective selfhood which, nevertheless, comes into being exclusively through sovereign power of the state has only one solution – the separation of political self-determination from constitutional self-limitation of the polity through the permanent possibility of reformulating the political constitution as legal representation of the democratic polity and the legal constitution as political representation of the democratic state. Constitutional sovereignty thus constantly communicates the constituent power of the sovereign democratic polity as the constituted power of the sovereign state.

The meaning of popular sovereignty subsequently lies in the state sovereignty's reformulation as the self-determining command of the democratic polity extending to all citizens in general and dealing with general interests of the polity as a democratically self-constituted community. As Ulrich Preuss states, '[T]he turn from having power to being a power constitutes a polity'.[4] This shift, however, requires adjustment at the level of constitutional law because political constitutions are now required to operate as representative constitutions facilitating a normative framework of the democratic polity, its value foundations and political will.

The democratic polity of the people may be perceived and communicated by the system of culture and its symbols as a mysterious collectivity, turning the social multitude of individuals into the unity of general political will which historically used to be both exercised through and limited by the constitutional state. This state both organizes popular self-rule and makes it the subject of exclusive power of its

---

4 Ulrich K. Preuss, 'Disconnecting Constitutions from Statehood: Is Global Constitutionalism a Viable Concept?', in *The Twilight of Constitutionalism?*, eds Petra Dobner and Martin Loughlin (Oxford: Oxford University Press, 2010), 34.

institutions. Popular sovereignty and constitutional sovereignty are identical and explicable only through the metaphor of the people as the self-governed democratic polity organized within the democratic state. Without the democratic polity as the origin of public power, no system of government can meet the standards of the modern constitution.[5]

The original function of the democratic polity, therefore, is to guarantee legitimacy of the democratic constitutional system of authority and this system has found its most comprehensive institutional framework in the modern state – a framework impossible to simply replicate at any international, supranational or transnational societal level. Apart from political coercion, the state enhances the possibility of the polity's democratic self-organization and the capacity of free citizens to interact, deliberate and share common goals and responsibilities. The democratic polity thus needs to be perceived as a self-reflective concept enhancing the capacity of collective self-attribution[6] of political decisions and legal norms which turns the social multitude into one self-constituted and self-constituting polity.

As Hans Lindahl says, this act of self-constitution, however, may happen only retroactively as an act of self-identification of 'the members of a polity in constituent action by exercising the powers granted to them by a constitution'.[7] Lindahl's ontology of collective selfhood shows that an act of constituent power – the sovereign people can only retrospectively constitute a legal order because the constitutive act itself cannot be part of that order. The permanent question 'Who are we?' turns the paradox of constituent/constituted power into an ontology of the collective self that 'exists in the modes of *questionability* and, by way of its acts, of *responsiveness*'.[8]

No wonder political constitutions have become those *mysterious objects of desire* of modern nations in Europe and elsewhere. They became ultimate representations of 'the people' as political nations and thus completely changed the concept of the polity by identifying it with political nationhood. The modern constitutional state was thus originally differentiated from the body of social hierarchies, particularisms and loyalties and constituted a new body politic, yet through increasing modernization as democratization became ever more symbolically representative of the whole society and its sovereign power could be legitimized only by virtue of democratic authority.

---

5 Martin Loughlin, 'The Concept of Constituent Power', *European Journal of Political Theory* 13(2) (2014): 218.

6 Hans K. Lindahl, 'Constituent Power and Reflexive Identity: Towards an Ontology of Collective Selfhood', in *The Paradox of Constitutionalism: Constituent Power and Constitutional Form*, eds Martin Loughlin and Neil Walker (Oxford: Oxford University Press. 2007), 19.

7 Ibid.

8 Ibid., 21.

Nations and Nation States as *Obstacle Epistémologiques*?

Avoiding the plethora of normative claims and theoretical problems associated with the difference between the political and cultural notions of nation, the following section is to merely sketch an alternative understanding of nationhood and national sovereignty as part of evolution and systemic organization of modern society. The social systems' theoretical analysis of popular sovereignty and polity is thus to be further amended by a brief critique of the concept of nation as pre-political community, the real existence of which is the substance of sovereignty concentrated in the modern constitutional state.

Modern nationalisms have been living the dream in which the state as a political unit incorporates, determines and symbolizes the nation as a cultural unit. The problem of modern nationalism is the problem of political legitimacy requiring that ethnic boundaries should not cut across political ones and that there is ethnic unity between governors and those who are governed by them.[9] Legitimacy becomes a structural problem of social solidarity and collective beliefs shared by the whole national polity. The nation state takes care of culture because it guarantees its legitimation.[10] Culture replaces consensus as a legitimation formula and the modern state is reconstituted as the nation state.

Modern political constitution, backed by the sovereign power of the nation state, thus has had two important functions – limiting the exercise of sovereign power by means of a system of constitutional checks and balances and symbolically constituting polity as the whole of society. A sovereign act of popular constitution-making is both constitutive of the systems of politics and law as well as expressing the collective identity of the democratic polity governing itself by delegating its sovereign power to its representatives. The sovereign state is considered the 'container'[11] of emerging modern society which is delineated by territorial borders, supreme authority and laws. The expressive mode of collective identity stretches beyond the domain of law and politics and establishes the ethical and cultural self-reflections of the people as a real political force and a symbolically imagined community.

According to this holistic view, the order of society is guaranteed by sovereign power and state constitutions actually are the constitutions of society. The modern state presupposes a constitutive attribute of the pre-existent polity which pursues its political self-constitution and existence through the state and its sovereign power. Sovereignty may be the absolute and exclusive power of the state[12] but

9 Ernest Gellner, *Nations and Nationalisms* (Oxford: Blackwell, 1983), 1–3.

10 Otto von Gierke, *Community in Historical Perspective*, ed. Antony Black (Cambridge: Cambridge University Press, 1990), 160.

11 Peter J. Taylor, 'The State as Container: Territoriality in the Modern World-System', *Progress in Human Geography* 18 (1994): 151.

12 Gianfranco Poggi, *The State: Its Nature, Development and Prospects* (Stanford, CA: Stanford University Press, 1994).

only because it already is the power generated and constituted by a historically new form of polity – the sovereign democratic nation as a community of shared destiny of the whole people.

As Benedict Anderson famously stated, nations are 'imagined communities' politically organized in the nation state.[13] They are imagined, first of all, as *limited* because all nations, even the biggest ones, are defined by their boundaries, beyond which exist other nations. Furthermore, this us/them distinction is supported by the imagination of nations as politically *sovereign* entities self-governed within the nation state. Apart from this hierarchical political organization, nations finally are imagined as a *community* of a 'deep, horizontal comradeship' and fraternity.[14]

This imagination opens an entirely new description of popular sovereignty but also the possibility of endless comparisons of national cultures evolving in a unique manner, yet synchronically and in parallel to each other. Nations exist because of their unique history and present, yet they proceed along the same trajectory of modernity and their collective identities remain comparable.[15]

Popular sovereignty materialized in both the pre-political concept of nation and its nation state is part of this trajectory as well as the fact that modern nationalisms and national identities are split between past and future. Nations are new polities abolishing the old regimes and proclaiming the new collective future and political settlement. At the same time, this movement and 'new time' recursively constitutes national history and genealogy, so that political rupture coincides with the invention of historical traditions, popular memories and collective continuities. The political future of modern nations thus coincided with historical 'national reawakening' and the new time of modernity required the imagination of the 'old time' of predecessors.[16]

In this respect, the difference between civic and ethnic nationhood, so vital for formulating different political ideals and defining normative limits and principles of inclusion in and exclusion from the polity,[17] is just another manifestation of the expressive symbolism of the concept of the sovereign national polity. Expectations of social unification and political integration were an intrinsic part of the modern concept of nation and the establishment of such unity was facilitated by the modern state organization. Particularisms of ethnically and territorially defined communities coincided with the universalism of the state as a modern political organization and the concept of the nation state effectively managed to symbolize both cultural differences and societal unity. In the modern state, the people transformed from a particular social estate to the general symbol of polity

13 Benedict Anderson, *Imagined Communities: Reflections on the Origin and Spread of Nationalism* (London: Verso, 1983).

14 Ibid., 7.

15 Ibid., 188.

16 Ibid., 194–195.

17 Craig Calhoun, 'Nationalism and Ethnicity', *Annual Review of Sociology* 19 (1993): 211.

and the sovereign transcending the very realm of politics. National culture became a reservoir of collective popular memories and practices differentiating 'us' from 'them' in both societal and political terms.

Collective identity and communal bonds are possible to establish and communicate as long as there is parallel reference to those who are different from our polity, its sense of commonality and cultural heritage. In the language of systems theory, self-reference of the national polity coincides with other-reference to different polities. Commenting on this historical coexistence of the cultural concept of nation and the political concept of state, Niklas Luhmann states:

> [T]he idea of nation obviously belongs to the set of short-lived semantics that can exercise a fascination for a transitional period without betraying what societal system they refer to. It can therefore be assumed that this idea is now on the wane, a phase in which it does more harm than good and from a sociological point of view constitutes one of those *obstacle épistémologiques* [hypothesized by Gaston Bachelard] that for reason of past plausibilities block urgently needed insights.[18]

The conceptual difference between universalism and particularism could be reconciled by the nation's political theology in theories of popular sovereignty and modern democratic statehood. However, the concept of the nation as constitutional polity appears just one of many semantic forms dealing with the paradox of the constitutional unity of sovereign power symbolically representing the multitude of citizens.

If nations are imagined communities brought to their historical existence from sleep and preserved by collective memories, they logically can be imagined as merely historical and biographical communities of limited persistence which, sooner or later, will be forgotten by modern society. Their existence and political organization of the nation state are the subject of social evolution like any other outcome of social imagination and structural differentiation.

Sovereignty of the Cosmopolitan Good Beyond a Nation

The whole history of national reawakening and the self-creation of modern nations also may be treated as just one form of Rousseau's original combination of a sociological and moralist perspective according to which the corrupt political state can be saved by the moral goodness associated with the general will. The golden age of humanity may be recovered from history and redeem the present corrupt state of politics.

---

18 Niklas Luhmann, *Theory of Society, Volume 2* (Stanford, CA: Stanford University Press, 2013), 289.

The sovereign will of the nation is good by definition and any conflicts emerging in the state's legislative domain, for instance, may only be conflicts of particular interests but not conflicts as regards the common good. Political leaders must be committed to this moral transformation of politics and, rather than the commanding particular will, represent the collective will of the nation. The general will forms a legitimate basis of the laws of the sovereign, free and equal people. Unconditional submission to this will creates a state of solidarity and unity of all citizens sharing the same substantive political virtues and mores.

This image of society as solidarity and unity of values and pre-politically shared cultural experiences, already criticized in other chapters of this book, persists in the context of Europeanization and globalization. It recently has been transformed into a question of the capacity of supranational and transnational politics to redesign and recreate the republican democratic politics historically associated with the nation state and reinvent self-creative legitimacy of supranational and transnational power. Different scholars discuss the universal virtues of popular sovereignty which can materialize in a globalized world if exclusive *demoi* mainly residing in nation states are replaced by all-inclusive *demos* governed as a cosmopolitan polity by the cosmopolitan democratic rule of law.[19] The basic norm of cosmopolitan law is expected to replace politics of territorially segmented nation states and their sovereignty[20] and 'cooperative transnationality and transsovereignty'[21] is to emerge between sovereign nation states at global level.

Similarly, the EU political and legal sovereignty debate, which has been exponentially growing since the Maastricht Treaty and subsequent constitution-making and post-constitutional integrative efforts, is a legitimacy debate[22] drawing on 'the legal imagination'.[23] It is informed by the question whether the constitution of European society relies on functional differentiation of social systems, or it needs to be constituted by the strong communal bonds and pre-political social solidarity of an 'imagined community'.[24]

---

19 David Held, *Democracy and the Global Order: from the Modern State to Cosmopolitan Governance* (Cambridge: Polity, 1995), 221.

20 David Held, 'Principles of Cosmopolitan Order', in *The Political Philosophy of Cosmopolitanism*, eds Gillian Brock and Harry Brighouse (Cambridge: Cambridge University Press, 2005), 26.

21 Ulrich Beck, *Power in the Global Age: A New Global Political Economy* (Cambridge: Polity, 2006), 168.

22 See, for instance, Ralf Rogowski and Charles Turner, 'Europe: Law, Politics, History, Culture', in *The Shape of the New Europe*, eds Ralf Rogowski and Charles Turner (Cambridge: Cambridge University Press, 2006), 7, 17.

23 Bruno De Witte, 'Sovereignty and European Integration: The Weight of Legal Tradition', *Maastricht Journal of European and Comparative Law* 2 (1995): 145.

24 For the elaboration of the notorious concept of 'imagined community' in the context of Europe, see Ulrich Haltern, 'Pathos and Patina: The Failure and Promise of Constitutionalism in the European Imagination', *European Law Journal* 9(1) (2003): 28.

Calls for creating a 'cosmopolitan Europe' and the adoption of European cosmopolitan law,[25] indeed, indicate that Europe may be reflected as an imagined community that can be shaped in many different ways, from fantasies of Kant's world republic to the pan-European humanism of Erasmus, Althusius and Leibniz.[26] In these images of Europe, social constructivism becomes normative constructivism entirely related to the symbolic political universe, and the ethics discourse becomes fully differentiated from the systems of European law and politics. Political imagination transcends both everyday power politics and formal legality and the EU becomes a metaphor of what may be described as 'the sovereignty of good'.[27]

A number of theories of European or global polity thus surprisingly get stuck in the same conceptual dichotomies and paradoxes like state theories of political and constitutional sovereignty. Enhancement of public accountability and democratization of international, supranational and transnational political and legal institutions is considered the best solution for democratic deficits accompanying processes of political and legal globalization.[28] Similarly, a simple fact that authority in European or global society is often exercised independently of state authority invites equally simple normative aspirations regarding supranational and transnational justice and human rights as the cosmopolitan basic norm and/or ethical foundations of a cosmo-polity.

Nevertheless, the very idea of sovereign polity as community of cosmopolitan laws and values is challenged by the same ambiguity like nation state polities, and theorists contemplate whether the prior existence of a world community of cosmopolitan values is a necessary precondition of the institutionalization of global justice and human rights, or whether it is exactly this institutionalization itself that eventually may constitute global cosmo-polity.

Like popular sovereignty, sovereignty of cosmopolitan community as the ultimate authority for which the EU is sometimes used as a model may be part of political and moral rhetoric, yet it does not have any operative sense. Irrespective of their ethical, juridical or political form, the foundations of national, supranational and transnational polities may only be speculated on and actually replicate the paradox of state constitutionalism as the impossibility to determine the precedence and supremacy of either legal or political sovereignty.

Visions of world community as the ultimate authority over and above sovereign states legitimized by global justice and rights draw on the image of a

25 See, for instance, Pavlos Eleftheriadis, 'Cosmopolitan Law', *European Law Journal* 9(2) (2003): 241.

26 For the latter call for European political and communal self-reflection, see Ian Ward, 'Beyond Constitutionalism: The Search for a European Political Imagination', *European Law Journal* 7(1) (2001): 32–37.

27 Iris Murdoch, *Sovereignty of Good* (London: Routledge, 2001).

28 Andrew Kuper, *Democracy Beyond Borders* (Oxford: Oxford University Press, 2004).

self-constituting and self-governing polity of the shared destiny and foundational values. Advocates of this cosmopolitan community use the same Rousseau-like formula identifying authority with the totality of polity when they expect that 'authority and community ideally ought to be congruent'[29] in global polity.

Though it may seem logical that the evolution of the global economic system should coincide with the evolution of a similarly complex global political system, a global democratic polity of cosmopolitan values,[30] nevertheless, continues to be just a utopian project. International human rights treaties may be considered a normative force for the globalization of law, unifying state constitutions and subjecting them to a supreme, legally binding interpretation,[31] but cosmopolitan democracy, human rights and a global political constitution are just a legalistic dream.

The concepts, paradoxes, formulas and ambiguities regarding sovereignty in the democratic constitutional state re-enter the supranational and transnational systems of globalized law and politics. The specific self-description of society as sovereign polity, therefore, is generally valid and applicable to the nation states as well as supranational and transnational organizations which invite the self-description of European or global society as polity of values.

Democratic Polity as the Unity of Collective Memory and Imagination: on Culture as a System of Symbolic Communication

The notion of polity is clearly different from nationhood and the nation state because supranational or transnational legal networks and regimes, such as the EU, can constitute their supranational and transnational polities – communities self-constituted by supranational and transnational law and politics, including symbolic communication of shared values and images of the collective selfhood. The semantics of popular sovereignty as national unity is part of modern societal symbolism, and nationhood certainly is not the ultimate form of social integration and the exclusive image of societal unity.

Responding to the history of nationalism and conflicts between sovereign nation states, the supranational project of European economic, legal and political integration has been normatively driven by a critique of ethnic and cultural nationalism and genuine ambitions to both reconstruct democratic nation states in Europe and construct a post-national European polity. Nevertheless, the constitution of such a post-national polity faces the same paradoxes and semantic

29 Jens Bartelson, *Visions of World Community* (Cambridge: Cambridge University Press, 2009), 179.

30 David Held, supra n. 19, 267–283.

31 Jürgen Habermas, 'The Constitutionalization of International Law and the Legitimation Problems of a Constitution for World Society', *Constellations* 15(4) (2008): 448–449.

challenges like the concept of popular sovereignty originally evolving within the nation state political and legal framework, yet constituting its specific culture and symbolism of social unity as the shared destiny.

In modernity, all societal ways of life, including the life in law and politics, have or are culture and therefore may be observed from the comparative perspective.[32] The Romantic paradox of patriotically and nationally differentiated cosmopolitanism of political ideals of the Enlightenment, which still dominates the political and legal imagination, actually serves as the best example of both the expressive symbolism of modern culture and comparative methodology of social science applicable in the context of law and politics.

The semantics of culture makes it possible to keep the image of society as unity which, nevertheless, can be contrasted and compared to other culturally defined communities as specific units of modern society.[33] What can be contrasted and compared remains experienced as different in cultural practices and symbolized in critical self-reflections of different communities.

Because culture has different forms in different societies, specific cultures can be compared to other cultures experienced, enjoyed and learned elsewhere. Cultural comparisons between different habits, practices, systems of beliefs and power struggles illuminated the concepts of modern nationhood and statehood. Constant political and social appeals to culture and cultural identity symbolically express the common realm of political society. The concept of polity as the politically and culturally differentiated self-description of society significantly depends on the possibility of comparing historical and regional differences.

Regarding culture as a specific system of modern society with distinct forms of social communication, Niklas Luhmann, for instance, states that '[O]nly in modern societies has a sufficiently general concept of culture developed that is suitable for distinguishing social memory from other social functions'.[34] He praises Parsons for having a ground-breaking intuition that social memory should be distinguished from other social functions and that this function consists of 'latent-pattern maintenance'. This latency is the task of the cultural subsystem but it is necessary to ask 'why society invents a concept of culture to describe its memory'.[35]

National memory and culture have always been a matter of both remembering national origins and reinventing them through shared collective practices and experiences, such as national memorial days and festivities. Memory, whether national or cosmopolitan, is thus always constructed by present uses of the past.

---

32 Niklas Luhmann, supra n. 18, 225.

33 Geoffrey Cubitt, ed., *Imagining Nations* (Manchester: Manchester University Press, 1998).

34 Niklas Luhmann, *Theory of Society, Volume 1* (Stanford, CA: Stanford University Press, 2012), 354.

35 Ibid.

Nations and other polities are constituted by such present uses of the past and their collective memories are subject to different uses by the political and legal systems.

By definition, social memory is selective. It, rather than the archive imperative indiscriminately collecting evidence of the past events, is modelled on the selective logic of historical narratives and myths. It is not primarily interested in the society's past but its history – present stories about the past constantly selecting specific events and differentiating between the glorious and inglorious past. The function of memory consists of turning past events into present histories.

Culture consists of parallel processes of remembering and forgetting. According to Luhmann, 'culture is indeed nothing other than the memory of society, hence the filter of forgetting/remembering and the appropriation of the past to determine the variation framework of the future'.[36] Political identity as imagined unity, therefore, needs this temporalization of collective existence which had to be brought to life from its historical 'sleep' and can proceed towards the bright future as a historically unique polity sharing the same destiny.

However, this collective memory and shared history is at permanent risk of being forgotten. *Historiographies* of modern nations subsequently need to be supplemented by their *biographies* which treat nations as persons with distinct identity.[37] The same relationship between historiographies and biographies applies to any supranational and transnational polity. Culture consists of this permanent imagination of the past and present in which historiographies are as important as present and future biographies of collective identity. Numerous 'biographies' of European integration highlighting its historical role and moral meaning are strong evidence of this supranational imagination which, furthermore, often identifies with the spirit of cosmopolitanism.

The general concept of culture as a reflection on self-descriptions of modern society and its national or supranational and transnational contextualization, rather than simply drawing on moral and civilizational universalism, opens radically new possibilities of social observation and self-identifications.[38] The concepts of culture and collective identity, therefore, should be considered as specific forms of societal differentiation and comparisons conducted within specific social subsystems, and the semantics of sovereignty as the democratic polity is one of its examples. It makes it possible to differentiate between democratic and undemocratic political systems, compare different democratic 'cultures' and regimes, analyse their historical evolution and so on.

---

36 Ibid., 355.

37 Benedict Anderson, supra n. 13, 204.

38 Niklas Luhmann, supra n. 18, 176.

From an Ontology of the Collective Self to the Social Systems Theory of Sovereignty: Concluding Remarks on Culture, Memory and Polity

Modern democracy is not unmediated political action by the people because

> ... there can be no such action; it is the form of political organization that, appealing to the rule of law, postpones acts of attribution by establishing the minimal conditions under which such acts may be viewed, ever provisionally, as acts of the people.[39]

This ontology of collective selfhood of the democratic polity is more evidence that the concept of polity cannot operate as a foundational concept of modern society guaranteeing its cultural unity or moral integration.[40] It is constituted by operations of social memory and merely reconstructs the image of society but cannot justify its unity, centralization or political hierarchization and constitution of ultimate social authority.

Contrary to the political and legal intuitions and epistemologies, functionally differentiated modern society cannot be identified with territory, collective identity, shared experiences, value foundations and destiny. It is not a collective entity living within territorial boundaries of the nation state or other territorially organized (local, regional, supranational and so on) political units. Simple normative oppositions between nation state and supranational or international political organizations, such as the EU and the UN, need to be criticized and abandoned. For instance, the EU with its territorial boundaries and system of governance of European population is a mere supranational segment of globally functioning society. It, therefore, hardly can be treated as a political avant-garde acting as a centre of cosmopolitan ethics and political ideals for various peripheries of global society.

The interplay of political centres and peripheries, typical of modern European empires, has come to its close and the EU cannot appropriate the role of a global political and social centre spreading the message of political multilateralism and ethical universalism of human rights and values binding all humans as members of one *all-inclusive cosmo-polity*.

The heterarchy of global society coincides with the universalism of functional systems, such as economy, politics, law, science and education, operating in it. Indeed, European society and other supranational territorially segmented organizations, such as the African Union, NATO, ASEAN and national or subnational societies around the world, constitute important particularisms in these universally functioning and globally operating and self-constituting systems

39 Hans Lindahl, supra n. 6, 24.

40 Hans Lindahl, 'The Paradox of Constituent Power. The ambiguous self-constitution of the European Union', *Ratio Juris: An International Journal of Jurisprudence and Philosophy of Law* 20(4) (2007): 485.

of law, politics, economy and so on. However, it has to be emphasized that it is the functional systems of global society that select from different particularisms and traditions while abandoning the operative importance of territorial oppositions or the opposition between traditional communities and modern society.

Political constitutions evolving within modern nation states and beyond their organizational limitations at supranational and transnational level, rather, are specific products of societal evolution facilitating the structural coupling between the systems of politics and law. They, therefore, are not a general mirror of the totality of society and social solidarity. Their polities are merely fragmented semantic reflections of political and legal evolution. For instance, attempts at constructing the European democratic polity – *demos* – by the act of constitution-making and adoption of a formal constitutional document for the EU were doomed to fail because of their unrealistic expectation of legally and politically constituting a general European society for particular EU institutions and specific operations of the functionally differentiated systems of EU law and politics.

Society is neither polity, nor any other form of civic community constituted and shared by human beings as citizens and political agents. It is a much more complex unity of differences and distinctions of functionally differentiated and specifically organized, yet universally operating social systems and their self-descriptive modes of communication.

The concept of popular sovereignty, therefore, is not a simple metaphor of social unity and totality. The paradoxical process of general societal structures of modern law and politics constructing its specific culture actually represents a persuasive argument against all kinds of holistic theories of popular sovereignty and nationalist ideologies of the modern state and society. Political modernization as democratization and functional differentiation of the systems of positive law and politics effectively means that popular sovereignty and democratic government cannot determine their substantive foundations. The sovereign state and its laws cannot be perceived as embodiment of collective consciousness, identity and existence of a particular polity.

Constitutional polity may only be described as the political and legal systems' internal construction of the concept of society. Political identity and the fiction of collective selfhood are constructed from the remembered past that is meaningful as present and can be linked to future operations of the system. The distinction between past and future constitutes both the present polity and its memory. However, this memory is not collective memory in the sense of individuals sharing the same 'real' state of affairs and past. In the case of sovereign polity, it is a social memory communicated by the systems of positive law and politics to generate and actualize determinate meaning of the systems' operations.

To conclude, the complex semantics of sovereign constitutional polity as society constructed by the political system and juridically communicated through political constitutions is part of the specific function of collective memory and culture. It is a systemic construct which cannot guarantee the overall social integration. All 'foundations' and 'constituting' moments of polity, therefore, merely use memory as an operation selecting between what needs to be remembered and forgotten to facilitate the function of the political system – collectively binding decision-making at local, national, supranational or transnational levels – and its juridical form of constitutions with their specific legal operations.

Bibliography

Abbott, Kenneth and Duncan Snidal, 'Hard and Soft Law in International Governance', *International Organization* 54 (2000): 421–456.

Agamben, Giorgio, *Homo Sacer: Sovereign Power and Bare Life* (Stanford, CA: Stanford University Press, 1998).

Agamben, Giorgio, *Potentialities: Collected Essays in Philosophy* (Stanford, CA: Stanford University Press, 1999).

Agamben, Giorgio, *State of Exception* (Chicago, IL: The University of Chicago Press, 2005).

Albi, Anneli, *EU Enlargement and the Constitutions of Central and Eastern Europe* (Cambridge: Cambridge University Press, 2005).

Albi, Anneli, 'Ironies in Human Rights Protection in the EU: Pre-Accession Conditionality and Post-Accession Conundrums', *European Law Journal* 15(1) (2009): 46–69.

Alter, Karen J., *Establishing the Supremacy of European Law: The Making of an International Rule of Law in Europe* (Oxford: Oxford University Press, 2001).

Amstutz, Marc, 'Global (Non-)Law: The Perspective of Evolutionary Jurisprudence', *German Law Journal* 9 (2008): 465–476.

Andersen, Svein and Kjell Eliassen, eds, *The European Union: How Democratic Is It?* (London: Sage, 1996).

Anderson, Benedict,*Imagined Communities: Reflections on the Origin and Spread of Nationalism* (London: Verso, 1983).

Arato, Andrew, 'Constitutionalism and the Founding of Constitutions: Carl Schmitt and the Revival of the Doctrine of the Constituent Power in the United States', *Cardozo Law Review* 21 (2000): 1739–1747.

Arato, Andrew and Jean Cohen, *Civil Society and Political Theory* (Cambridge, MA: The MIT Press, 1992).

Armstrong, Kenneth, 'Legal Integration: Theorizing the Legal Dimension of European Integration', *Journal of Common Market Studies* 36 (1998): 155–174.

Ashenden, Samantha, 'The Problem of Power in Luhmann's Systems Theory', in *Luhmann on Law and Politics: Critical Appraisals and Applications*, eds Michael King and Chris Thornhill (Oxford: Hart Publishing, 2006), 127–144.

Aziz, Miriam, 'Sovereignty Lost, Sovereignty Regained? Some Reflections on the Bundesverfassungsgericht's Banana Judgment', *Columbia Journal of European Law* 9 (2002): 109–140.

Aziz, Miriam, *The Impact of European Rights on National Legal Cultures* (Oxford: Hart Publishing, 2004).

Banchoff, Thomas and Mitchell P. Smith, eds, *Legitimacy and the European Union: The Contested Polity* (London: Routledge, 1999).
Barnard, Frederick M., 'National Culture and Political Legitimacy: Herder and Rousseau', *Journal of the History of Ideas* 44(2) (1983): 231–253.
Bartelson, Jens, *A Genealogy of Sovereignty* (Cambridge: Cambridge University Press, 1995).
Bartelson, Jens, *The Critique of the State* (Cambridge: Cambridge University Press, 2004).
Bartelson, Jens, *Visions of World Community* (Cambridge: Cambridge University Press, 2009).
Bayart, Jean Francois, *Global Subjects: A Political Critique of Globalization* (Cambridge: Polity Press, 2007).
Beaumont, Paul and Neil Walker, eds, *Legal Framework of the Single European Currency* (Oxford: Hart, 1999).
Beck, Anthony, 'Foucault and Law: The Collapse of Law's Empire', *Oxford Journal of Legal Studies* 16 (1996): 489–502.
Beck, Ulrich, *What Is Globalization?* (London: Polity, 2000).
Beck, Ulrich, *Power in the Global Age: A New Global Political Economy* (Cambridge: Polity Press 2005).
Beck, Ulrich, *The Cosmopolitan Vision* (Cambridge: Polity Press, 2006).
Beetham, David, *Max Weber and the Theory of Modern Politics. 2nd revised edition* (Cambridge: Polity, 1985).
Beiner, Ronald, *Civil Religion: A Dialogue in the History of Political Philosophy* (Cambridge: Cambridge University Press, 2011).
Bellamy, Richard, *Political Constitutionalism: A Republican Defence of the Constitutionality of Democracy* (Cambridge: Cambridge University Press, 2007).
Bellamy, Richard and Dario Castiglione, eds, *Constitutionalism in Transformation: European and Theoretical Perspectives* (Oxford: Blackwell, 1996).
Bellamy, Richard and Dario Castiglione, 'Building the Union: The Nature of Sovereignty in the Political Architecture of Europe', *Philosophy and Law* 16 (1997): 421–445.
Benda-Beckmann, Franz von, 'Who Is Afraid of Legal Pluralism?', *Journal of Legal Pluralism and Unofficial Law* 47 (2002): 37–82.
Bengoetxea, Jorge-Ramon, 'Legal System as a Regulative Ideal', *Archiv für Rechts- und SozialPhilosophie [ARSP]* 53 (1994): 65–79.
Benoit, Bertrand, *Social-Nationalism: An Anatomy of French Euroscepticism* (Aldershot: Ashgate, 1997).
Bentham, Jeremy, 'Anarchical Fallacies', in *The Works of Jeremy Bentham*, Vol. II, ed. John Bowring (Edinburgh: Tait, 1843), 491–524.
Berger, Peter L. and Thomas Luckmann, *The Social Construction of Reality* (Harmondsworth: Penguin, 1966).
Bergström, Carl F., *Comitology: Delegation of Power in the European Union and the Committee System* (Oxford: Oxford University Press, 2005).

Berman, Paul S., *Global Legal Pluralism: A Jurisprudence of Law Beyond Borders* (Cambridge: Cambridge University Press, 2012).

Bernstorff, Jochen von, *The Public International Law Theory of Hans Kelsen: Believing in Universal Law* (Cambridge: Cambridge University Press, 2010).

Beulac, Stephane, *The Power of Language in the Making of International Law* (Leiden: Nijhoff Publishers, 2004).

Beyme, Klaus von, *Parliamentary Democracy: Democratization, Destabilization, Reconsolidation, 1789–1999* (Houndmills: Palgrave Macmillan, 2000).

Bicker, Hans, Tina Otten and Laura Chelsea Weymann, 'The financial crisis in the German and English press: Metaphorical structures in the media coverage on Greece, Spain and Italy', *Discourse & Society* 25(4) (2014): 424–445.

Biondi, Andrea, Piet Eeckhout and Stephanie Ripley, eds, *EU Law after Lisbon* (Oxford: Oxford University Press, 2012).

Bobbio, Norberto, *The Future of Democracy* (Minneapolis, MN: The University of Minnesota Press, 1987).

Bobbio, Norberto, *Thomas Hobbes and the Natural Law Tradition* (Chicago, IL: University of Chicago Press, 1993).

Bobbio, Norberto and Danilo Zolo, 'Hans Kelsen, The Theory of Law, and the International Legal System: A Talk', *European Journal of International Law* 9 (1998): 355–367.

Bodin, Jean, *Six Books of the Commonwealth* (Oxford: Blackwell, 1955).

Bodin, Jean, *On Sovereignty* (Cambridge: Cambridge University Press, 1992).

Bogdandy, Armin von and Stephan Schill, 'Overcoming Absolute Primacy: Respect for National Identity under the Lisbon Treaty', *Common Market Law Review* 48 (2011): 1417–1453.

Bonth, Margreth H.M. de, 'Sovereignty Revisited', in *Flexibility in Constitutions: Forms of closer cooperation in federal and non-federal settings; post Nice edition*, ed. Annette Schrauwen (Groningen: Europa Law Publishing, 2002), 97–105.

Borowski, Martin, 'Legal Pluralism in the European Union', in *Law and Democracy in Neil MacCormick's Legal and Political Theory: The Post-Sovereign Constellation*, eds Agustín J. Menendez and John E. Fossum (Dordrecht: Springer, 2011), 185–210.

Bunck, Julie Marie, *Law, Power and The Sovereign State: The Evolution and Application of the Concept of Sovereignty* (University Park, PA: The Pennsylvania State University Press, 1995).

Búrca, Gráinne de, 'The Quest for Legitimacy in the European Union', *Modern Law Review* 59 (1996): 349–376.

Búrca, Gráinne de, 'Legal Principles as an Instrument of Differentiation? The Principles of Proportionality and Subsidiarity', in *The Many Faces of Differentiation in EU Law*, eds Bruno De Witte, Dominik Hanf and Ellen Vos (Antwerpen: Intersentia, 2001), 131–144.

Burger, Thomas, 'Talcott Parsons: The Problem of Order in Society', *American Journal of Sociology* 83 (1978): 320–339.

Burrow, John, *A History of Histories* (London: Allen Lane, 2007).
Calhoun, Craig, 'Nationalism and Ethnicity', *Annual Review of Sociology* 19 (1993): 211–239.
Calleo, David P., *Rethinking Europe's Future* (Oxford: Oxford University Press, 2001).
Callies Gralf P. and Peer Zumbansen, *Rough Consensus and Running Code: A Theory of Transnational Private Law* (Oxford: Hart Publishing, 2010).
Cameron, Fraser, 'Widening and Deepening', in *The Future of Europe: Integration and Enlargement*, ed. Fraser Cameron (London: Routledge, 2004), 1–17.
Caparoso, James A., 'The European Union and the Forms of State: Westphalian, Regulatory or Post-modern', *Journal of Common Market Studies* 34 (1996): 29–52.
Carter, Caitriona and Andrew Scott, 'Legitimacy and Governance Beyond the European Nation State: Conceptualising Governance in the European Union', *European Law Journal* 4(4) (1998): 429–445.
Carty, Anthony, 'Interwar German Theories of International Law: The Psycho-analytical and Phenomenological Perspectives of Hans Kelsen and Carl Schmitt', *Cardozo Law Review* 16(3&4) (1994–1995): 1235–1292.
Carty, Anthony, 'Sovereignty in International Law: A Concept of Eternal Return', in *Reclaiming Sovereignty*, eds Laura Brace and John Hoffman (London: Pinter, 1997), 101–116.
Chalmers, Damian, 'European Restatements of Sovereignty', in *Sovereignty and the Law: Domestic, European and International Perspectives*, eds Richard Rawlings, Peter Leyland and Alison Young (Oxford: Oxford University Press, 2013), 186–212.
Checkel, Jeffrey T., 'Social Construction and European Integration', in *The Social Construction of Europe*, eds Thomas Christiansen, Knud E. Jorgensen and Antje Wiener (London: Sage, 2001), 50–64.
Christiansen, Thomas, Knud E. Joergensen and Antje Wiener, eds, *The Social Construction of Europe* (London: Sage, 2001).
Chryssochoou, Dimitris N., *Theorizing European Integration* (London: Sage, 2001).
Claes, Monica, *The National Courts' Mandate in the European Constitution* (Oxford: Hart Publishing, 2006), 723–724.
Clarke, John, 'Reconstituting Europe: governing a European people?' in *Remaking Governance: Peoples, Politics and the Public Sphere*, ed. Janet Newman (Bristol: The Policy Press, 2005), 17–37.
Cohen, Antonin, 'Constitutionalism Without Constitution: Transnational Élites Between Political Mobilization and Legal Expertise in the Making of a Constitution for Europe (1940s–1960s)', *Law & Social Inquiry* 32 (2007): 109–135.
Cohen, Jean, 'Whose Sovereignty? Empire Versus International Law', *Ethics & International Affairs* 18 (2004): 1–23.

Cohen, Jean L., 'Sovereignty in the Context of Globalisation: A Constitutional Pluralist Perspective', in *The Philosophy of International Law*, eds Samantha Besson and John Tasioulas (Oxford: Oxford University Press, 2010), 261–280.

Cohen, Jean L., *Globalization and Sovereignty. Rethinking Legality, Legitimacy and Constitutionalism* (Cambridge: Cambridge University Press 2012).

Collins, Hugh, 'European Private Law and the Cultural Identity of Member States', *European Review of Private Law* 3 (1995): 353–365.

Colliot-Thelene, Catherine, 'Carl Schmitt versus Max Weber: Juridical Rationality and Economic Rationality', in *The Challenge of Carl Schmitt*, ed. Chantal Mouffe (London: Verso, 1999), 138–154.

Constant, Benjamin, 'The Liberty of the Ancients and the Moderns', in *French Liberalism in the 19th Century: An Anthology*, eds Robert Leroux and David M. Hart (Oxon: Routledge, 2012), 68–82.

Conway, Gerard, *The Limits of Legal Reasoning and the European Court of Justice* (Cambridge: Cambridge University Press, 2012).

Cotterrell, Roger, 'Legality and Political Legitimacy in the Sociology of Max Weber', in *Legality, Ideology and the State*, ed. D. Sugarman (London: Academic Press, 1983), 69–93.

Cotterrell, Roger, *Law's Community: Legal Theory in Sociolegal Perspective* (Oxford: Clarendon Press, 1995).

Cotterrell, Roger, 'Images of Europe in Sociolegal Traditions', in *European Ways of Law*, eds Volkmar Gessner and David Nelken (Oxford: Hart Publishing, 2007), 21–39.

Cotterrell, Roger, 'Transnational Communities and the Concept of Law', *Ratio Juris* 21 (2008): 1–18.

Craig, Paul, 'Constitutions, Constitutionalism, and the European Union', *European Law Journal* 7 (2001): 125–150.

Craig, Paul, 'Integration, Democracy, and Legitimacy', in *The Evolution of EU Law. 2nd edition*, eds Paul Craig and Gráinne de Búrca (Oxford: Oxford University Press, 2011), 13–40.

Craig, Paul and Carol Harlow, eds, *Lawmaking in the European Union* (Dordrecht: Kluwer, 1998).

Cram, Laura, 'The European Commission as a Multi-Organization: Social Policy and IT in the EU', *Journal of European Public Policy* 1 (1994): 195–217.

Cremona, Marise, ed., *The Enlargement of the European Union* (Oxford: Oxford University Press, 2003).

Crouch, Colin, *Post-democracy (Themes for the 21st Century)* (Oxford: Polity, 2004).

Crum, Ben, 'Tailoring Representative Democracy to the European Union: Does the European Constitution Reduce the Democratic Deficit?', *European Law Journal* 11 (2005): 452–467.

Cubitt, Geoffrey, ed., *Imagining Nations* (Manchester: Manchester University Press, 1998).

Curtin, Deirdre, 'The Constitutional Structure of the Union: A Europe of Bits and Pieces', *Common Market Law Review* 30 (1993): 17–69.

Curtin, Deirdre, 'Private Interest Representation or Civil Society Deliberation? A Contemporary Dilemma for European Governance', *Social & Legal Studies* 12 (2003): 55–75.

Czarnota, Adam, Martin Krygier and Wojciech Sadurski, eds, *Spreading Democracy and the Rule of Law: The Impact of EU Enlargement on the Rule of Law, Democracy, and Constitutionalism in Post-communist Legal Orders* (Dordrecht: Springer 2006).

Dahl, Robert A., 'A Democratic Dilemma: System Effectiveness versus Citizen Participation', *Political Science Quarterly* 109 (1994): 23–34.

Dahrendorf, Ralf, *Der Wiederbeginn der Geschichte. Vom Fall der Mauer zum Krieg im Irak* (München: C.H. Beck, 2004).

Dannhauser, Werner J., 'Some Thoughts on Liberty, Equality and Tocqueville's *Democracy in America*', *Social Philosophy and Policy* 2(1) (1984): 141–160.

Delacroix, Sylvie, 'Schmitt's Critique of Kelsenian Normativism', *Ratio Juris* 18(1) (2005): 30–45.

Delanty, Gerard, *Social Theory in a Changing World: Conceptions of Modernity* (Cambridge: Polity Press, 1999).

Delanty, Gerard, *Citizenship in a Global Age* (Buckingham: Open University Press, 2000).

Deleuze, Gilles, *Spinoza, Practical Philosophy* (San Francisco, CA: City Lights Books, 1988).

Delhey, Jan, 'Do Enlargements Make the European Union Less Cohesive? An Analysis of Trust between EU Nationalities', *Journal of Common Market Studies* 45 (2007): 253–279.

Delmas-Marty, Mireille, *Ordering Pluralism. A Conceptual Framework for Understanding the Transnational Legal World* (Oxford: Hart Publishing, 2009).

Den Boer, Monica, Alain Guggenhühl and Sophie Vanhoonacker, eds, *Coping with Flexibility and Legitimacy after Amsterdam* (Maastricht: European Institute of Public Administration, 1998).

Derrida, Jacques, *Rogues: Two Essays on Reason* (Stanford, CA: Stanford University Press, 2005).

Derrida, Jacques, *The Beast and the Sovereign. Volume I.* (Chicago, IL: The University of Chicago Press, 2009).

De Schutter, Olivier, 'Anchoring the European Union to the European Social Charter: the Case for Accession', in *Social Rights in Europe*, eds Gráinne de Búrca, Bruno De Witte and Larissa Ogertschnig (Oxford: Oxford University Press, 2005), 111–152.

De Witte, Bruno, 'Sovereignty and European Integration: The Weight of Legal Tradition', *Maastricht Journal of European and Comparative Law* 2 (1995): 145–173.

De Witte, Bruno, 'Future Path of Flexibility: enhanced cooperation, partial agreements and pioneer groups', in *The European Union: An Ongoing Process of Integration*, eds Jaap W. de Zwaan, Jan H. Jans, Frans A. Nelissen and Steven Blockmans (Cambridge: Cambridge University Press, 2005), 141–152.

De Witte, Bruno and Gabriel N. Toggenburg, 'Human Rights and Membership of the European Union', in *The European Union Charter of Fundamental Rights: Politics, Law and Policy*, eds Steve Peers and Angela Ward (Oxford: Hart Publishing, 2004), 59–82.

Dijn, Annelien de, *French Political Thought from Montesquieu to Tocqueville: Liberty in a Levelled Society?* (Cambridge: Cambridge University Press, 2008).

Djelic, Marie-Laure and Kerstin Sahlin-Andersson, eds, *Transnational Governance: Institutional Dynamics of Regulation* (Cambridge: Cambridge University Press, 2006).

Domingo, Rafael, *The New Global Law* (Cambridge: Cambridge University Press, 2010).

Dunsire, Andrew, 'Tipping the Balance: Autopoiesis and Governance', *Administration & Society* 28 (1996): 299–334.

Durkheim, Emile, *Professional Ethics and Civic Morals* (London: Routledge, 1957).

Dyzenhaus, David, *Legality and Legitimacy: Carl Schmitt, Hans Kelsen and Hermann Heller in Weimar* (Oxford: Oxford University Press, 1997).

Dyzenhaus, David, 'Hobbes and the Legitimacy of Law', *Law and Philosophy* 20 (2001): 461–498.

Dyzenhaus, David, 'The Politics and the Question of Constituent Power', in *The Paradox of Constitutionalism: Constituent Power and Constitutional Form*, eds Martin Loughlin and Neil Walker (Oxford: Oxford University Press, 2007), 136–137.

Editorial Comments, CMLR, 'Direct democracy and the European Union ... is that a threat or a promise', *Common Market Law Review* 45 (2008): 929–940.

Edwards, Michael, *Civil Society* (Cambridge: Polity Press, 2009).

Ehrlich, Eugen, *Fundamental Principles of the Sociology of Law* (New York: Arno Press, 1975) [Originally published in 1936].

Eleftheriadis, Pavlos, 'Cosmopolitan Law', *European Law Journal*, 9(2) (2003): 241–263.

Eleftheriadis, Pavlos, 'Law and Sovereignty', *Law and Philosophy* 29 (2010): 535–569.

Elliott, Mark, 'United Kingdom: Parliamentary Sovereignty under Pressure', *International Journal of Constitutional Law* 2(3) (2004): 545–627.

Eriksen, Erik O., ed., *Making the European Polity: Reflexive Integration in the EU* (London: Routledge, 2005).

Estella, Antonio, *The EU Principle of Subsidiarity and its Critique* (Oxford: Oxford University Press, 2002).

Evans, Andrew, 'Voluntary Harmonisation in Integration between the European Community and Eastern Europe', *European Law Review* 22 (1997): 201–220.

Ewald, Francois, 'A Concept of Social Law', in *Dilemmas of Law in the Welfare State*, ed. Gunther Teubner (Berlin: Walter de Gruyter, 1988), 40–75.

Ewald, Francois, 'The Law of Law', in *Autopoietic Law: A New Approach to Law and Society*, ed. Gunther Teubner (Berlin: Walter de Gruyter, 1988), 36–50.

Ewald, Francois, 'Norms, Discipline, and the Law', in *Law and the Order of Culture*, ed. Robert Post (Berkeley, CA: University of California Press, 1991), 138–161.

Fabbrini, Sergio, *Compound Democracies: Why the United States and Europe Are Becoming Similar* (Oxford: Oxford University Press, 2007).

Falk, Richard, *Law in an Emerging Global Village: A Post-Westphalian Perspective* (Ardsley: Transnational Publishers, 1998).

Fassbender, Bardo, 'Sovereignty and Constitutionalism in International Law', in *Sovereignty in Transition*, ed. Neil Walker (Oxford: Hart Publishing, 2003), 115–143.

Featherstone, Kevin, 'Jean Monnet and the "Democratic Deficit" in the European Union', *Journal of Common Market Studies* 32 (1994): 149–170.

Fichera, Massimo, 'The European Arrest Warrant and the Sovereign State: A Marriage of Convenience?', *European Law Journal* 15(1) (2009): 70–97.

Fischer-Lescano, Andreas, *Globalverfassung: Die Geltungsbegründung der Menschenrechte* (Weilerwist: Velbruck, 2005).

Fischer-Lescano, Andreas and Günther Teubner, 'Regime-Collisions: The Vain Search for Legal Unity in the Fragmentation of Global Law', *Michigan Journal of International Law* 25 (2004): 999–1046.

Fitzpatrick, Peter, *Mythology of Modern Law* (London: Routledge, 1992).

Follesdal, Andreas and Simon Hix, 'Why There is a Democratic Deficit in the EU: A Response to Majone and Moravcsik', *Journal of Common Market Studies* 44 (2006): 533–562.

Foucault, Michel, *The Will to Knowledge: The History of Sexuality, Vol. 1* (Harmondsworth: Penguin, 1979).

Foucault, Michel, 'Truth and Power', in *Power/Knowledge: Selected Interviews and Writings 1972–1977,* ed. Colin Gordon (New York: Pantheon, 1980), 109–133.

Foucault, Michel, 'Omnes et Singulatim: towards a Criticism of "Political Reason"', *The Tanner Lectures on Human Values 1981* (Salt Lake City, UT: University of Utah Press, 1981), 221–254.

Foucault, Michel, *Discipline and Punish: The Birth of the Prison* (Harmondsworth: Penguin, 1991; the original English translation published by Pantheon Books in 1977).

Foucault, Michel, 'Sex, Power, and the Politics of Identity', in *Essential Works of Foucault 1954–1984, Vol. 1: Ethics*, ed. Paul Rabinow (London: Penguin, 2000), 163–173.

Foucault, Michel, 'Governmentality', in *Power. Essential works of Foucault 1954–1984, volume 3*, ed. James D. Faubion (London: Penguin, 2000), 201–222.

Foucault, Michel, *'Society Must Be Defended'. Lectures at the College de France, 1975–76* (New York: Picador, 2003).

Foucault, Michel, *Security, Territory, Population. Lectures at the College de France, 1977–78* (Basingstoke: Palgrave Macmillan, 2007).

Fowler, Michael and Julie Marie Bunck, *Law, Power and The Sovereign State: The Evolution and Application of the Concept of Sovereignty* (University Park, PA: The Pennsylvania State University Press, 1995).

Gaja, Giorgio, 'How Flexible is Flexibility under the Amsterdam Treaty?', *Common Market Law Review* 35 (1998): 855–870.

Galanter, Marc, 'Justice in Many Rooms: Courts, Private Ordering and Indigenous Law', *Journal of Legal Pluralism and Unofficial Law* 19 (1981): 1–47.

Gauthier, David, 'Hobbes's Social Contract', in *The Social Contract Theories: Critical Essays on Hobbes, Locke, and Rousseau*, ed. Christopher Morris (Oxford: Rowman & Littlefield, 1999), 59–71.

Gellner, Ernest, *Nations and Nationalisms* (Oxford: Blackwell, 1983).

George, Stephen, *Politics and Policy in the European Union* (Oxford: Oxford University Press, 3rd edition, 1996).

Giddens, Anthony, *The Constitution of Society: Outline of the Theory of Structuration* (Berkeley, CA: University of California Press, 1982).

Giddens, Anthony, *The Nation-State and Violence: Volume Two of A Contemporary Critique of Historical Materialism* (Berkeley, CA: University of California Press, 1985).

Giddens, Anthony, *Politics, Sociology and Social Theory: Encounters with Classical and Contemporary Social Thought* (Cambridge: Polity Press, 1995).

Giddens, Anthony, *Runaway World: How Globalization is Reshaping Our Lives* (London: Routledge, 2003).

Gierke, Otto von, *Community in Historical Perspective*, ed. Antony Black (Cambridge: Cambridge University Press, 1990).

Goulder, Ben and Peter Fitzpatrick, *Foucault's Law* (Oxon: Routledge, 2009).

Grande, Edgar and Louis W. Pauly, eds, *Complex Sovereignty: Reconstituting Political Authority in the Twenty-first Century* (Toronto: Toronto University Press, 2005).

Greenfeld, Leah, *Nationalism: Five Roads to Modernity* (Cambridge, MA: Harvard University Press, 1992).

Greer, Scott L., *Nationalism and Self-Government: Politics of Autonomy in Scotland and Catalonia* (Albany, NY: SUNY Press, 2008).

Greven, Michael T. Greven and Louis W. Pauly, eds, *Democracy Beyond the State: The European Dilemma and Emerging Global Order* (Oxford: Rowman & Littlefield, 2000).

Griffiths, Anne, 'Legal Pluralism', in *An Introduction to Law and Social Theory*, eds Reza Banakar and Max Travers (Oxford: Hart Publishing 2002), 289–310.

Griffiths, John, 'What is Legal Pluralism?', *Journal of legal pluralism and Unofficial Law* 24 (1986): 1–55.

Griffiths, John, 'Legal Pluralism and the Theory of Legislation: With Special Reference to the Regulation of Euthanasia', in *Legal Polycentricity: Consequences of Pluralism in Law*, eds Hanne Petersen and Henrik Zahle (Aldershot: Dartmouth, 1998), 201–234.

Griffiths, Richard T., *Europe's First Constitution: The European Political Community, 1952–1954* (London: Federal Trust, 2000).
Griller, Stefan et al., *The Treaty of Amsterdam: Facts, Analysis, Prospects* (Wien: Springer, 2000).
Grimm, Dieter, 'Defending Sovereign Statehood Against Transforming the European Union into a State', *European Constitutional Law Review* 5 (2009): 353–373.
Gstöhl, Sieglinde, 'The European Union after Amsterdam: Towards a Theoretical Approach to (Differentiated) Integration', in *The State of the European Union Vol. 5: Risks, Reform, Resistance, and Revival*, eds Maria G. Cowles and Michael Smith (Oxford: Oxford University Press, 2000), 42–63.
Haas, Ernst B., *The Uniting of Europe: Political, Social and Economic Forces 1950–1957* (Stanford, CA: Stanford University Press, 1958).
Haas, Ernst B., 'Does Constructivism Subsume Neo-functionalism?', in *The Social Construction of Europe*, eds Thomas Christiansen, Knud E. Jorgensen and Antje Wiener (London: Sage, 2001), 22–31.
Habermas, Jürgen, *Moral Consciousness and Communicative Action* (Cambridge, MA: The MIT Press, 1990).
Habermas, Jürgen, 'Reconciliation through the Public Use of Reason: Remarks on John Rawls's Political Liberalism', *Journal of Philosophy* 92(3) (1995): 109–113.
Habermas, Jürgen, *Postnational Constellation: Political Essays* (Cambridge: Polity, 2001).
Habermas, Jürgen, 'Does Europe Need a Constitution?', in *Time of Transitions*, Jürgen Habermas (Cambridge: Polity Press, 2006), 89–109.
Habermas, Jürgen, *Divided West* (Cambridge: Polity, 2006).
Habermas, Jürgen, 'The Constitutionalization of International Law and the Legitimation Problems of a Constitution for World Society', *Constellations* 15(4) (2008): 444–455.
Habermas, Jürgen and Jacques Derrida, 'February 15, or What Binds Europeans Together: A Plea for a Common Foreign Policy, Beginning in the Core of Europe', *Constellations* 10 (2003): 291–297.
Halberstam, Daniel and Christoph Möllers, 'The German Constitutional Court says "Ja zu Deutschland"', *German Law Journal* 10 (2009): 1241–1258.
Haltern, Ulrich, 'Pathos and Patina: The Failure and Promise of Constitutionalism in the European Imagination', *European Law Journal* 9(1) (2003): 14–44.
Hardt, Michael and Antonio Negri, *Empire* (Harvard, MA: Harvard University Press, 2000).
Harris, James W., 'Kelsen's Concept of Authority', *The Cambridge Law Journal* 36 (1977): 353–363.
Harrison, Ross, *Hobbes, Locke and Confusion's Masterpiece: An Examination of Seventeenth Century Political Philosophy* (Cambridge: Cambridge University Press, 2003).

Hartley, Trevor C., *European Union Law in a Global Context: Text, Cases and Materials* (Cambridge: Cambridge University Press, 2004).

Haughton, Tim, 'When Does the EU Make a Difference? Conditionality and the Accession Process in Central and Eastern Europe', *Political Studies Review* 5 (2007): 233–246.

Hayward, Jack and Rüdiger Wurzel, eds, *European Disunion: Between Sovereignty and Solidarity* (London: Palgrave, 2012).

He, Baogang, 'Civil Society and Democracy', in *Democratic Theory Today: Challenges for the 21st Century*, eds April Carter and Geoffrey Stokes (Cambridge: Polity Press, 2002), 203–227.

Held, David, *Democracy and the Global Order: From the Modern State to Cosmopolitan Governance* (Cambridge: Polity, 1995).

Held, David, 'Principles of Cosmopolitan Order', in *The Political Philosophy of Cosmopolitanism*, eds Gillian Brock and Harry Brighouse (Cambridge: Cambridge University Press, 2005), 10–38.

Heller, Hermann, 'Politische Demokratie und soziale Homogenität' [1928], in Hermann Heller, *Gesammelte Schriften, vol. 2*, ed. Christoph Müller (Leiden: Sijthoff, 1971).

Heller, Hermann, *Staatslehre, 6th edition* (original print Leiden: Sijthoff, 1934; Tubingen: JCB Mohr, 1983).

Hensel, Howard, ed., *Sovereignty and the Global Community: The Quest for Order in the International System* (Aldershot: Ashgate, 2004).

Herdegen, Matthias, 'Maastricht and the German Constitutional Court: Constitutional Restraints for an "Ever Closer Union"', *Common Market Law Review* 31(1994): 235–249.

Hertogh, Marc, 'From "Men of Files" to "Men of the Senses": A Brief Characterisation of Eugen Ehrlich's Sociology of Law', in *Living Law: Reconsidering Eugen Ehrlich*, ed. Marc Hertogh (Oxford: Hart Publishing 2009), 1–17.

Herzog, Roman and Lüder Gerken, *Stop the European Court of Justice* manifesto, EU Observer, 10 September 2008.

Hillion, Christophe, ed., *EU Enlargement: A Legal Approach* (Oxford: Hart Publishing 2004).

Hoffman, John, *Beyond the State: An Introductory Critique* (Cambridge: Polity Press, 1995).

Holton, Robert J., *Globalization and the Nation State* (Palgrave: MacMillan1998).

Honneth, Axel, 'Foucault's Theory of Society: A Systems-Theoretic Dissolution of the *Dialectic of Enlightenment*', in *Critique and Power: Recasting the Foucault/Habermas Debate*, ed. Michael Kelly (Cambridge, MA: The MIT Press, 1994), 157–184.

Hooghe, Liesbet, ed., *Cohesion Policy and European Integration: Building Multi-level Governance* (Oxford: Oxford University Press, 1996).

Hooghe, Liesbet and Gary Marks, *Multi-Level Governance and European Integration* (Oxford: Rowman & Littlefield, 2001).

Hoy, David Couzens and Thomas McCarthy, *Critical Theory* (Oxford: Blackwell, 1994).

Hunt, Alan, 'Foucault's Expulsion of Law: Toward a Retrieval', *Law & Social Inquiry* 17(1) (1992): 1–38.

Hunt, Alan and Gary Wickham, *Foucault and Law: Toward a Sociology of Law as Governance* (London: Pluto Press, 1994).

Hurrell, Andrew, *On Global Order: Power, Values, and the Constitution of International Society* (Oxford: Oxford University Press, 2007).

Jachtenfuchs, Markus and Beate Kohler-Koch, 'Governance and Institutional Development', in *European Integration Theory*, eds Antje Wiener and Thomas Diez (Oxford: Oxford University Press, 2004), 97–115.

Jackson, John, 'Sovereignty-Modern: A New Approach to an Outdated Concept', *The American Journal of International Law* 97(4) (2003): 782–802.

Jackson, Robert H., *Quasi-States: Sovereignty, International Relations and the Third World* (Cambridge: Cambridge University Press, 1990).

Jacobs, Francis, 'Judicial Dialogue and the Cross-Fertilization of Legal Systems: The European Court of Justice', *Texas International Law Journal* 38 (2003): 547–556.

Jacobsen, Michael and Stephanie Lawson, 'Between Globalization and Localization: A Case Study of Human Rights versus State Sovereignty', *Global Governance* 5 (1999): 203–219.

James, Alan, 'The Practice of Sovereign Statehood in Contemporary International Society', *Political Studies* 47(3) (1999): 457–473.

Jayasuriya, Kanishka, 'Globalization, Sovereignty, and the Rule of Law: From Political to Economic Constitutionalism?', *Constellations* 8 (2001): 442–460.

Jellinek, Georg, *Die Lehre von den Staatenverbindungen* (Vienna: Alfred Holder, 1882), 34. The translation quoted from Rafael Domingo, *The New Global Law* (Cambridge: Cambridge University Press, 2010).

Jessop, Bob, 'Governance and meta-governance: on reflexivity, requisite variety and requisite irony', in *Governance as Social and Political Communication*, ed. Henrik P. Bang (Manchester: Manchester University Press, 2003), 142–172.

Joerges, Christian, 'Good Governance through Comitology?', in *EU Committees: Social Regulation, Law and Politics*, eds Christian Joerges and Ellen Vos (Oxford: Hart Publishing, 1999), 311–338.

Joerges, Christian, 'The Law in the Process of Constitutionalizing Europe', in *Constitution-Making and Democratic Legitimacy, Arena Report 5/2002*, eds Erik O. Eriksen, John E. Fossum and Agustín J. Menendez (Oslo, Arena, 2002), 13–48.

Joerges, Christian, 'Constitutionalism and Transnational Governance: Exploring a Magic Triangle', in *Transnational Governance and Constitutionalism*, eds Christian Joerges, Inger-Johanne Sand and Günther Teubner (Oxford: Hart Publishing, 2004), 339–375.

Joerges, Christian and Renaud Dehousse, eds, *Good Governance in Europe's Integrated Market* (Oxford: Oxford University Press, 2002).

Joerges, Christian and Jürgen Neyer, 'From Intergovernmental Bargaining to Deliberative Political Processes: The Constitutionalisation of Comitology', *European Law Journal* 3(3) (1997): 273–299.

Jouvenel, Bertrand de, *On Power. Its Nature and the History of Its Growth* (Boston, MA: Beacon Press, 1962).

Jouvenel, Bertrand de, *On Sovereignty. An Inquiry into the Political Good* (Indianapolis, IN: Liberty Fund, 1997), 218.

Kaldor, Mary, *Global Civil Society: An Answer to War* (London: Polity Press, 2003).

Kammerhofer, Jörg, *Uncertainty in International Law: a Kelsenian Perspective* (Oxon: Routledge, 2011).

Keating, Michael, *Plurinational Democracy: Stateless Nations in a Post-Sovereignty Era* (Oxford: Oxford University Press, 2001).

Kellerman, Alfred E. et al., eds, *The Impact of EU Accession on the Legal Orders of New Member States and (Pre-)Candidate Countries* (Dordrecht: Springer 2006).

Kelsen, Hans, *Das Problem der Souveranität und die Theorie des Völkerrechts: Beitrag zu einer reinen Rechtslehre* [*The Problem of Sovereignty and the Theory of International Law: A Contribution towards a Pure Theory of Law*] (Tübingen: Mohr, 1920).

Kelsen, Hans, *Peace Through Law* (Chapel Hill, NC: The University of North Carolina Press, 1944).

Kelsen, Hans, 'The Principle of Sovereign Equality of States as a Basis for International Organisation', *Yale Law Journal* 53 (1944): 207–220.

Kelsen, Hans, *General Theory of Law and State* (Cambridge, MA: Harvard University Press, 1945).

Kelsen, Hans, *Society and Nature: A Sociological Inquiry* (London: Kegan, Trench, Trubner & Comp, 1946).

Kelsen, Hans, *Principles of International Law* (New York: Rinehart & Comp., 1952).

Kelsen, Hans, 'The Natural-Law Doctrine Before the Tribunal of Science', in *What is Justice? Justice, Law, and Politics in the Mirror of Science*, Hans Kelsen (Berkeley, CA: University of California Press, 1957), 137–173.

Kelsen, Hans, *General Theory of Law and State* (New York: Russell&Russell, 1961).

Kelsen, Hans, *The Pure Theory of Law* (2nd edition, Berkeley, CA: University of California Press, 1970, orig. 1960).

Kelsen, Hans, *Introduction to the Problems of Legal Theory: A Translation of the First Edition of the Reine Rechtslehre or Pure Theory of Law* (Oxford: Oxford University Press, 1992).

Kelsen, Hans, 'Sovereignty', in *Normativity and Norms: Critical Perspectives on Kelsenian Themes*, ed. Stanley L. Paulson (Oxford: Oxford University Press, 1999; the essay originally published in 1962).

Kelsen, Hans, 'On the Essence and Value of Democracy' [1927], in *Weimar: A Jurisprudence of Crisis*, eds Arthur Jacobson and Bernhard Schlink (Berkeley, CA: University of California Press, 2000), 84–109.

Kelsen, Hans, 'Eine Grundlegung des Rechtssoziologie', in *Rechtssoziologie und Rechtswissenschaft. Eine Kontroverse (1915–1917)*, Hans Kelsen and Eugen Ehrlich (Baden Baden: Nomos, 2003), 3–54.

Kennedy, Ellen, *Constitutional Failure: Carl Schmitt in Weimar* (Durham, NC: Duke University Press, 2004).

Keohane, Robert O. and Joseph Nye, *Power and Interdependence: World Politics in Transition* (Boston, MA: Little, Brown, 1977).

Keohane, Robert O., *Power and Governance in a Partially Globalized World* (London: Routledge, 2002).

Keohane, Robert O. and Stanley Hoffmann, 'Institutional Change in Europe in the 1980s', in *The New European Community: Decisionmaking and Institutional Change*, eds Robert Keohane and Stanley Hoffman (Boulder, CO: Westview Press, 1991), 1–40.

King, Michael and Chris Thornhill, *Niklas Luhmann's Theory of Politics and Law* (Houndmills: Palgrave Macmillan, 2006).

King, Preston, *The Ideology of Order: A Comparative Analysis of Jean Bodin and Thomas Hobbes* (London: Allen and Unwin, 1974).

Kis, János, 'From the 1989 Constitution to the 2011 Fundamental Law', in *Constitution for a Disunited Nation: on Hungary's 2011 Fundamental Law*, ed., Gábor Attila Tóth (Budapest: CEU Press, 2012), 1–21.

Kohler-Koch, Beate and Berthold Rittberger, eds, *Debating the Democratic Legitimacy of the European Union* (Oxford: Rowman & Littlefield, 2007).

Kommers, Donald P. and Russell A. Miller, *The Constitutional Jurisprudence of the Federal Republic of Germany. 3rd edition, revised and expanded* (Durham, NC: Duke University Press, 2012).

Koskenniemi, Martti, 'The Future of Statehood', *Harvard International Law Journal* 32 (1991): 397–410.

Koskenniemi, Martti and Päivi Leino, 'Fragmentation of International Law? Postmodern Anxieties', *Leiden Journal of International Law* 15 (2002): 553–579.

Koskenniemi, Martti, *The Gentle Civilizer of Nations: The Rise and Fall of International Law 1870–1960* (Cambridge: Cambridge University Press, 2004).

Koskenniemi, Martti, *From Apology to Utopia: The Structure of International Legal Argument* (Cambridge: Cambridge University Press, 2006).

Krasner, Stephen D., *Sovereignty, Organized Hypocrisy* (Princeton, NJ: Princeton University Press, 1999).

Krasner, Stephen D., ed., *Problematic Sovereignty: Contested Rules and Political Possibilities* (New York: Columbia University Press, 2001).

Krasner, Stephen D., 'Sharing Sovereignty: New Institutions for Collapsed and Failing States', *International Security* 29(2) (2004): 85–120.

Krisch, Nico, *Beyond Constitutionalism: The Pluralist Structure of Postnational Law* (Oxford: Oxford University Press, 2010).

Krisch, Nico, 'Who Is Afraid of Radical Pluralism? Legal Order and Political Stability in the Postnational Space', *Ratio Juris* 24(4) (2011): 386–412.

Kumm, Matthias, 'Who is the Final Arbiter of Constitutionality in Europe?: Three Conceptions of the Relationship Between the German Federal Constitutional Court and the European Court of Justice', *Common Market Law Review* 36(2) (1999): 351–386.

Kundera, Milan, *The Art of the Novel* (London: Faber and Faber, revised edition 2005).

Kuper, Andrew, *Democracy Beyond Borders* (Oxford: Oxford University Press, 2004).

Laffan, Brigid, 'The European Union: A Distinctive Model of Internationalization', *Journal of European Public Policy* 5(2) (1998): 235–253.

Laffan, Brigid, Rory O'Donnell and Michael Smith, *Europe's Experimental Union: Rethinking Integration* (London: Routledge, 1999).

Lamers, Karl, 'Strenthening the Hard Core', in *The Question of Europe*, eds Peter Gowan and Perry Anderson (London: Verso, 2000), 104–116.

Lamers, Karl and Wolfgang Schäuble, 'Reflections on European Policy', The Christian Democratic Union/Christian Social Union Group, Bonn, 1 September 1994.

Lash, Scott, *Sociology of Postmodernism* (Oxon: Routledge, 1990).

La Torre, Massimo, *Constitutionalism and Legal Reasoning: A New Paradigm for the Concept of Law* (Dordrecht: Springer, 2007).

La Torre, Massimo, *Law as Institution: Normative Language between Power and Values* (Dordrecht: Springer, 2010).

Leibfried, Stephan and Paul Pierson, eds, *European Social Policy: Between Fragmentation and Integration* (Washington, DC: Brookings Institution Press, 1995).

Lenaerts, Koen, 'Interlocking Legal Orders in the European Union and Comparative Law', *International and Comparative Law Quarterly* 52(4) (2003): 873–906.

Lepenies, Wolf, *Between Literature and Science: The Rise of Sociology* (Cambridge: Cambridge University Press, 1988).

Lessig, Lawrence, 'Post-Constitutionalism', *Michigan Law Review* 94 (1996): 1422–1470.

Levy, Daniel, Max Pensky and John Torpey, eds, *Old Europe, New Europe, Core Europe* (London: Verso, 2005).

Levy, Daniel and Natan Sznaider, 'Sovereignty Transformed: a sociology of human rights', *The British Journal of Sociology* 57(4) (2006): 657–76.

Lincoln, Abraham, *Speeches and Writings: Volume 2: 1859–1865* (New York, NY: Library of America, 1989).

Lindahl, Hans, 'European Integration: Popular Sovereignty and a Politics of Boundaries', *European Law Journal* 6(3) (2000): 239–256.

Lindahl, Hans, 'Dialectic and Revolution: Confronting Kelsen and Gadamer on Legal Interpretation', *Cardozo Law Review* 24 (2003): 769–798.

Lindahl, Hans, 'Constituent Power and Reflexive Identity: Towards an Ontology of Collective Selfhood', in *The Paradox of Constitutionalism: Constituent Power and Constitutional Form*, eds Martin Loughlin and Neil Walker (Oxford: Oxford University Press, 2007), 9–24.

Lindahl, Hans, 'The Paradox of Constituent Power. The ambiguous self-constitution of the European Union', *Ratio Juris: An International Journal of Jurisprudence and Philosophy of Law* 20(4) (2007): 485–505.

Lindahl, Hans, 'Societal Constitutionalism as Political Constitutionalism: Reconsidering the Relation between Politics and Global Legal Orders', *Social and Legal Studies* 20(2) (2011): 230–237.

Lindberg, Leon and Stewart Scheingold, *Europe's Would-be-Polity: Patterns of Change in the European Community* (Upper Saddle River, NJ: Prentice-Hall, 1970).

Lipset, Seymor M., ed., *Social Science and Politics* (Oxford: Oxford University Press, 1969).

Loughlin, Martin, *The Idea of Public Law* (Oxford: Oxford University Press, 2003).

Loughlin, Martin, 'The Concept of Constituent Power', *European Journal of Political Theory* 13(2) (2014): 218–237.

Luhmann, Niklas, *Gesellschaftsstruktur und Semantik. Studien zur Wissenssoziologie der modernen Gesellschaft*, vol. 1 (Frankfurt: Suhrkamp, 1980).

Luhmann, Niklas, *Gesellschaftsstruktur und Semantik. Studien zur Wissenssoziologie der modernen Gesellschaft*, vol. 2 (Frankfurt: Suhrkamp, 1981).

Luhmann, Niklas, *Gesellschaftsstruktur und Semantik. Studien zur Wissenssoziologie der modernen Gesellschaft*, vol. 3 (Frankfurt: Suhrkamp, 1989).

Luhmann, Niklas, *Essays on Self-Reference* (New York: Columbia University Press, 1990).

Luhmann, Niklas, *Political Theory in the Welfare State* (Berlin: Walter de Gruyter, 1990).

Luhmann, Niklas, *Social Systems* (Stanford, CA: Stanford University Press, 1995).

Luhmann, Niklas, *Observations on Modernity* (Stanford, CA: Stanford University Press, 1998).

Luhmann, Niklas, *Die Politik der Gesellschaft* (Frankfurt: Suhrkamp, 2002).

Luhmann, Niklas, *Theories of Distinction: Redescribing the Descriptions of Modernity* (Stanford, CA: Stanford University Press, 2002).

Luhmann, Niklas, *Law as a Social System* (Oxford: Oxford University Press, 2004).

Luhmann, Niklas, *Theory of Society. Volume 1* (Stanford, CA: Stanford University Press, 2012).

Luhmann, Niklas, *Theory of Society. Volume 2.* (Stanford, CA: Stanford University Press, 2013).

Lukes, Steven, *Power: A Radical View. Second Edition* (Houndmills: Palgrave Macmillan, 2005).

MacCormick, Neil, 'Law as Institutional Fact', *Law Quarterly Review* 90 (1974): 102–129.

MacCormick, Neil and Ota Weinberger, *An Institutional Theory of Law: New Approaches to Legal Positivism* (Dordrecht: D. Reidel, 1986).

MacCormick, Neil, 'Beyond the Sovereign State', *The Modern Law Review* 56(1) (1993): 1–18.
MacCormick, Neil, 'Sovereignty, Democracy and Subsidiarity', in *Democracy and Constitutional Culture in the Union of Europe*, eds Richard Bellamy, V. Bufacchi and Dario Castiglione (London: Lothian Foundation, 1995), 95–104.
MacCormick, Neil, 'Risking Constitutional Collision in Europe?', *Oxford Journal of Legal Studies* 18 (1998): 517–532.
MacCormick, Neil, *Questioning Sovereignty: Law, State, and Nation in the European Commonwealth* (Oxford: Oxford University Press, 1999).
MacCormick, Neil, 'Questioning Post-Sovereignty', *European Law Review* 29 (2004): 852–863.
Maduro, Miguel P., 'Europe and constitution: what if this is as good as it gets?', in *European Constitutionalism Beyond the State*, eds Joseph H.H. Weiler and Marlene Wind (Cambridge: Cambridge University Press, 2003), 74–102.
Maduro, Miguel, 'Contrapunctual Law: Europe's Constitutional Pluralism in Action', in *Sovereignty in Transition,* ed. Neil Walker (Oxford: Hart Publishing, 2003), 501–537.
Maduro, Miguel, 'The Importance of Being Called a Constitution: Constitutional authority and the authority of constitutionalism', *International Journal of Constitutional Law* 3 (2005): 332–356.
Maduro, Miguel, 'Courts and Pluralism: Essay on a Theory of Judicial Adjudication in the Context of Legal and Constitutional Pluralism', in *Ruling the World? Constitutionalism, International Law and Global Governance*, eds Jeffrey L. Dunoff and Joel P. Trachtman (Cambridge: Cambridge University Press, 2009), 356–380.
Maiolo, Francesco, *Medieval Sovereignty: Marsilius of Padua and Bartolus of Saxoferrato* (Delft: Eburon Publishers 2007).
Majone, Giandomenico, 'Europe's 'Democratic Deficit': The Question of Standards', *European Law Journal* 4 (1998): 5–28.
Mancini, Federico G., 'The Making of a Constitution for Europe', *Common Market Law Review* 26 (1989): 595–614.
Mancini, Federico G., *Democracy and Constitutionalism in the European Union* (Oxford: Hart Publishing, 2000).
Marks, Gary, Liesbet Hooghe and Kermit Blank, 'European Integration since the 1980s: State-Centric versus Multi-Level Governance', *Journal of Common Market Studies* 34 (1996): 341–378.
Marks, Gary, Fritz W. Scharpf, Philippe C. Schmitter and Wolfgang Streeck, eds, *Governance in the European Union* (London: Sage, 1996).
Marshall, James, *Swords and Symbols: The Technique of Sovereignty* (Oxford: Oxford University Press, 1939).
Martin, Rex, 'Hobbes and the Doctrine of Natural Rights: The Place of Consent in His Political Philosophy', *Western Political Quarterly* 33 (1980): 380–392.
McCarthy, Thomas, *Ideals and Illusions: On Reconstruction and Deconstruction in Contemporary Critical Theory* (Cambridge, MA: The MIT Press, 1993).

McCormick, John P., 'The Dilemmas of Dictatorship: Carl Schmitt and Constitutional Emergency Powers' *The Canadian Journal of Law & Jurisprudence* 10 (1997): 163–187.

McCormick, John P., *Carl Schmitt's Critique of Liberalism: Against Politics as Technology* (Cambridge: Cambridge University Press, 1998).

McCormick, John P., *Weber, Habermas, and Transformation of the European State: Constitutional, Social, and Supranational Democracy* (Cambridge: Cambridge University Press, 2007).

Mehta, Pratap B., 'The Rise of Judicial Sovereignty', *Journal of Democracy* 18(2) (2007): 70–83.

Meier, Heinrich, *Carl Schmitt and Leo Strauss: The Hidden Dialogue* (Chicago, IL: The University of Chicago Press, 1995).

Meier, Heinrich, *The Lesson of Carl Schmitt: Four Chapters on the Distinction Between Political Theology and Political Philosophy* (Chicago, IL: The University of Chicago Press, 1998).

Mellisaris, Emmanuel, *Ubiquitous Law: Legal Theory and the Space for Legal Pluralism* (Aldershot: Ashgate, 2009).

Menéndez, Agustín J., 'The European Democratic Challenge: The Forging of a Supranational *Volonté Générale*', *European Law Journal 15 (2009):* 277.

Merry, Sally E., 'Legal Pluralism', *Law and Society Review* 22(5) (1998): 869–896.

Meyer, John W., John Boli, George M. Thomas and Francisco O. Ramirez, 'World Society and the Nation State', *The American Journal of Sociology* 103(1) (1997): 144–181.

Milward, Alan, *The European Rescue of the Nation State* (Berkeley, CA: University of California Press, 1992).

Mingers, John, *Self-Producing Systems: Implications and Applications of Autopoiesis* (Dordrecht: Springer, 1994).

Minkkinen, Panu, 'Why is Law a Normative Discipline? On Hans Kelsen's "Normology"', *Res Publica* 11(3) (2005): 235–249.

Monar, Jörg, 'Schengen and Flexibility in the Treaty of Amsterdam: Opportunities and Risks of Differentiated Integration in EU Justice and Home Affairs', in *Schengen, Judicial Cooperation and Policy Cooperation*, ed. Monica de Boer (Maastricht: European Institute of Public Administration, 1997), 9–28.

Monar, Jörg, 'Justice and Home Affairs in the Treaty of Amsterdam: Reform and Price of Fragmentation', *European Law Review* 23 (1998): 320–335.

Montesquieu, Charles de, *The Spirit of the Laws* (Cambridge: Cambridge University Press, 1989).

Moore, Sally F., *Law as Process: An Anthropological Approach* (London: Routledge, 1978).

Moravcsik, Andrew, 'Preferences and Power in the European Community: A Liberal Intergovernmentalist Approach', *Journal of Common Market Studies* 31 (1993): 473–524.

Moravcsik, Andrew, *The Choice for Europe: Social Purpose and State Power from Messina to Maastricht* (Ithaca, NY: Cornell University Press, 1998).

Moravcsik, Andrew, 'In Defence of the "Democratic Deficit": Reassessing Legitimacy in the European Union', *Journal of Common Market Studies* 40 (2002): 603–624.
Moravcsik, Andrew, 'The Myth of Europe's Democratic Deficit', *Intereconomics: Review of European Economic Policy* 43 (2008): 331–340.
Morawa, Alexander H.E. and Kyriaki Topidi, eds, *Constitutional Evolution in Central and Eastern Europe: Expansion and Integration into the EU* (Aldershot: Ashgate 2011).
Morgenthau, Hans, 'The Problem of Sovereignty Reconsidered', *Columbia Law Review* 58(3) (1948): 341–365.
Mörth, Ulrika, ed., *Soft Law in Governance and Regulation: An Interdisciplinary Approach* (Cheltenham: Edward Elgar, 2004).
Murdoch, Iris, *Sovereignty of Good* (London: Routledge, 2001).
Nasstrom, Sofia, 'What Globalization Overshadows', *Political Theory* 31 (2003): 808–834.
Negri, Antonio, *Il potere costituente: Saggio sulle alternative del moderno* (Milan: SugarCo, 1992).
Nelken, David, 'An Email from Global Bukowina', *International Journal of Law in Context* 3(3) (2007): 189–202.
Nelken, David, 'Ehrlich's Legacies: Back to the Future in the Sociology of Law?', in *Living Law: Reconsidering Eugen Ehrlich*, ed. Marc Hertogh (Oxford: Hart Publishing 2009), 237–272.
Neunreither, Karlheinz and Antje Wiener, eds, *Amsterdam and Beyond: Institutional Dynamics and Prospects for Democracy in the European Union* (Oxford: Oxford University Press, 2000).
Novak, Manfred, 'Human Rights "Conditionality" in Relation to Entry to, and Full Participation in, the EU', in *The EU and Human Rights*, eds Phillip Alston, Mara R. Bustello and James Heenan (Oxford: Oxford University Press, 1999), 687–698.
Nussberger, Angelika, 'The Poland: the Constitutional Tribunal on the implementation of the European Arrest Warrant', *International Journal of Constitutional Law* 6(1) (2008): 162–170.
Oakeshott, Michael, *Rationalism in Politics and Other Essays* (Indianapolis, IN: Liberty Fund, 1991).
Offe, Claus, *Reflections on America: Tocqueville, Weber and Adorno in the United States* (Cambridge: Polity Press, 2005).
Olivecrona, Karl, *Law as Fact* (London: Stevens, 1971).
Orr, Andrew C., 'Unmanned, Unprecedented, and Unresolved: The Status of American Drone Strikes in Pakistan under International Law', *Cornell International Law Journal* 44 (2011): 729–752.
Parsons, Talcott, 'On the Concept of Political Power', *Proceedings of the American Philosophical Society* 107(3) (1963): 232–262.
Pascal, Blaise, *Pensée* (New York: Dutton, 1958).

Pateman, Carole, 'Participation and Democratic Theory', in *The Democracy Sourcebook*, eds Robert A. Dahl, Ian Shapiro and Jose Antonio Cheibub (Cambridge: MA, The MIT Press, 2003), 40–47.

Paulson, Stanley J., 'The Weak Reading of Authority in Hans Kelsen's Pure Theory of Law', *Law and Philosophy* 19 (2000): 131–171.

Pernice, Ingolf, 'Multilevel Constitutionalism and the Treaty of Amsterdam, European Constitution Making Revisited', *Common Market Law Review* 36 (1999): 703–750.

Pernice, Ingolf, 'Multi-level Constitutionalism in the European Union', *European Law Review* 27 (2002): 511–529.

Peters, Guy and Jon Pierre, 'Multi-level Governance and Democracy: A Faustian Bargain?', in *Multi-level Governance*, eds Ian Bache and Matthew Flinders (Oxford: Oxford University Press, 2004), 74–89.

Philippopoulos-Mihalopoulos, Andreas, *Niklas Luhmann. Law, Justice, Society* (London: Routledge-GlassHouse, 2010).

Philpott, Daniel, *Revolutions in Sovereignty: How Ideas Shaped Modern International Relations* (Princeton, NJ: Princeton University Press, 2001).

Piana, Daniela, 'An Evolutionary Approach to the Constitutionalism of an Enlarged EU: Why will Cognitive and Cultural Boundaries Matter?', in *Spreading Democracy and the Rule of Law? The Impact of EU Enlargement on the Rule of Law, Democracy and Constitutionalism in Post-communist Legal Orders*, eds Wojciech Sadurski, Adam Czarnota and Martin Krygier (Dordrecht, Springer, 2006), 219–235.

Pinneli, Cesare, 'The Kelsen/Schmitt Controversy and the Evolving Relations between Constitutional and International Law', *Ratio Juris* 23(4) (2010): 493–504.

Pogge, Thomas W., 'Cosmopolitanism and Sovereignty', *Ethics* 103 (1992): 48–75.

Poggi, Gianfranco, *The State: Its Nature, Development and Prospects* (Stanford, CA: Stanford University Press, 1994).

Pospíšil, Leo, *Anthropology of Law: A Comparative Perspective* (New York: Harper and Row, 1971).

Preuss, Ulrich, 'Constitutional Powermaking for the New Polity: Some Deliberations on the Relations between Constituent Power and the Constitution', *Cardozo Law Review* 14 (1992–1993): 639–660.

Preuss, Ulrich K., 'Disconnecting Constitutions from Statehood: Is Global Constitutionalism a Viable Concept?', in *The Twilight of Constitutionalism?*, eds Petra Dobner and Martin Loughlin (Oxford: Oxford University Press, 2010), 23–46.

Přibáň, Jiří, *Legal Symbolism: On Law, Time and European Identity* (Aldershot: Ashgate, 2007).

Přibáň, Jiří, 'From "Which Rule of Law?" to "The Rule of Which Law?": post-communist experiences of European legal integration', *Hague Journal on the Rule of Law* 1(2) (2009): 337–358.

Přibáň, Jiří, 'Multiple Sovereignty: On Europe's Self-Constitutionalization and Legal Self-Reference', *Ratio Juris* 23(1) (2010): 41–64.
Přibáň, Jiří and David Nelken, eds, *Law's New Boundaries: The Consequences of Legal Autopoiesis* (Aldershot: Ashgate, 2001).
Pridham, Geoffrey, 'EU Enlargement and Consolidating Democracy in Post-Communist States – Formality and Reality', *Journal of Common Market Studies* 40(5) (2002): 953–73.
Rajagopal, Balakrishnan, 'The Role of Law in Counter-Hegemonic Globalization and Global Legal Pluralism: Lessons from the Narmada Valley Struggle in India', *Leiden Journal of International Law* 18 (2005): 345–387.
Ranciere, Jacques, 'Does Democracy Mean Something?', in *Dissensus*, Jacques Ranciere (London: Continuum, 2010), 45–61.
Rasch, William, *Niklas Luhmann's Modernity: The Paradoxes of Differentiation* (Stanford, CA: Stanford University Press, 2000), 151.
Rasch, William, *Sovereignty and Its Discontents: On the Primacy of Conflict and the Structure of the Political* (London: Birkbeck Law Press, 2004).
Rawls, John, 'Political Liberalism: Reply to Habermas', *Journal of Philosophy* 92(3) (1995): 132–180.
Rawls, John, *The Law of Peoples* (Cambridge, MA: Harvard University Press (1999).
Rheinstein, Max, 'Sociology of law, apropos Moll's translation of Eugen Ehrlich's Grundlegung der soziologie des Rechts', *Journal of Ethics* 48 (1983): 232–239.
Rhodes, Carolyn and Sonia Mazey, eds, *The State of the European Union, Vol. 3: Building a European Polity?* (Boulder, CO: Lynne Rienner Publishers, 1995).
Rhodes, Roderick A.W., 'The Hollowing Out of the State', *The Political Quarterly* 65 (1994): 138–151.
Rhodes, Roderick A.W., 'The New Governance: Governing without Government', *Political Studies* 44 (1996): 652–667.
Rico, Guillem, 'The 2010 Regional Election in Catalonia: A Multilevel Account in an Age of Economic Crisis', *South European Society and Politics* 17(2) (2012): 217–238.
Riekmann, Sonja P., Monika Mokre and Michael Latzer, eds, *The State of Europe: Transformations of Statehood from a European Perspective* (Cambridge: Cambridge University Press, 2005).
Riley, Patrick, *The General Will before Rousseau: The Transformation of the Divine into the Civic* (Princeton, NJ: Princeton University Press, 1986).
Roberts, Simon A., *Order and Dispute* (New York: St Martin's Press, 1979).
Roberts, Simon A., 'Against Legal Pluralism', *Journal of Legal Pluralism and Unofficial Law* 42 (1998): 95–106.
Roermund, Bert van, *Law, Narrative and Reality: An Essay in Intercepting Politics* (Dordrecht: Kluwer, 1997).
Roermund, Bert van, 'Authority and Authorisation', *Law and Philosophy* 19 (2000): 201–222.

Rogowski, Ralf and Charles Turner, 'Europe: Law, Politics, History, Culture', in *The Shape of the New Europe*, eds Ralf Rogowski and Charles Turner (Cambridge: Cambridge University Press, 2006), 1–22.
Rorty, Richard, 'Post-Democracy', *London Review of Books* 26(7) (2004): 1 April 2004.
Rose, Nikolas and Peter Miller, 'Political Power Beyond the State: Problematics of Government', *British Journal of Sociology* 43(2) (1992): 173–205.
Rose, Nikolas and Mariana Valverde, 'Governed by Law?', *Social & Legal Studies* 7 (1998): 541–551.
Rosenau, James, *Along the Domestic-Foreign Frontier: Exploring Governance in a Turbulent World* (Cambridge: Cambridge University Press, 1997).
Rosenfeld, Michel, *The Identity of the Constitutional Subject: Selfhood, Citizenship, Culture, and Community* (London: Routledge 2009).
Rousseau, Jean-Jacques, *Discourse on Political Economy and the Social Contract* (Oxford: Oxford University Press, 1994).
Rubin, Edward L., *Beyond Camelot: Rethinking Politics and Law for the Modern State* (Princeton, NJ: Princeton University Press, 2005).
Ruzza, Carlo and Vincent Della Sala, 'Conclusion: Deliberative Democracy, Input–Output Legitimacy and the Meaning of Civil Society', in *Governance and Civil Society in the European Union: Volume 2: Normative Perspectives*, eds Carlo Ruzza and Vincent Della Sala (Manchester: Manchester University Press, 2007), 134–139.
Sabine, George H., 'The Concept of the State as Power', *Philosophical Review* 29(4) (1920): 301–318.
Sadurski, Wojciech, 'Charter and Enlagement', *European Law Journal* 8(3) (2002): 340–362.
Sadurski, Wojciech, 'Accession's Democracy Dividend: The Impact of the EU Enlargement upon Democracy in the New Member States of Central and Eastern Europe', *European Law Journal* 10(4) (2004): 371–401.
Sadurski, Wojciech, '"Solange, chapter 3": Constitutional Courts in Central Europe – Democracy – European Union', *European Law Journal* 14(1) (2008): 1–35.
Sadurski, Wojciech, *Constitutionalism and the Enlargement of Europe* (Oxford: Oxford University Press, 2012).
Salmon, J.H.M., 'The Legacy of Jean Bodin: absolutism, populism, or constitutionalism?', *History of Political Thought* 17(4) (1996): 500–522.
Sartori, Giovanni, *The Theory of Democracy Revisited: The Contemporary Debate* (Chatham, NJ: Chatham House Publishers, 1987).
Sassen, Saskia, *Losing Control? Sovereignty in an Age of Globalization* (New York: Columbia University Press, 1996).
Scharpf, Fritz W., *Governing in Europe: Effective and Democratic?* (Oxford: Oxford University Press, 1999).
Schelsky, Helmut, *Recht und Institution* (Berlin: Duncker und Humblot, 1985).

Scheuerman, William E., *Between the Norm and the Exception: the Frankfurt School and the Rule of Law* (Cambridge, MA: The MIT Press, 1994).

Scheuerman, William E., *Carl Schmitt: the End of Law* (Oxford: Rowman & Littlefield, 1999).

Schimmelfennig, Frank, Stefan Engert and Heiko Knobel, 'The Impact of EU Political Conditionality', in *The Europeanization of Central and Eastern Europe*, eds Frank Schimmelfennig and Ulrich Sedelmaier (Ithaca, NY: Cornell University Press, 2005), 29–50.

Schmitt, Carl, 'Die Wendung zum totalen Staat' (1931), in *Positionen und Begriffe im Kampf mit Weimar-Genf-Versailles: 1923–1939* (Hamburg: Hanseatische Verlagsanstalt, 1940), 146–157.

Schmitt, Carl, *Politische Theologie II* (Berlin: Duncker und Humblot, 1969).

Schmitt, Carl, *Political Theology: Four Chapters on the Concept of Sovereignty* (Chicago, IL: The University of Chicago Press, 1985).

Schmitt, Carl, *The Nomos of the Earth in the International Law of the Jus Publicum Europaeum* (New York: Telos Press, 2003).

Schmitt, Carl, *Legality and Legitimacy* (Durham: Duke University Press, 2004).

Schmitt, Carl, *The Concept of the Political. Expanded Edition* (Chicago, IL: .The University of Chicago Press, 2007).

Schmitt, Carl, *Constitutional Theory* (Durham, NC: Duke University Press, 2008).

Schmitt, Carl, *The Leviathan in the State Theory of Thomas Hobbes: Meaning and Failure of a Political Symbol* (Chicago, IL: The University of Chicago Press, 2008).

Schmitter, Phillipe, 'Democracy in Europe and Europe's Democratization', *Journal of Democracy* 14(4) (2003): 71–85.

Schreuer, Christoph, 'The Waning of the Sovereign State: Towards a New Paradigm of International Law?', *European Journal of International Law* 4 (1993): 447–471.

Schutter, Olivier de, 'Europe in Search of its Civil Society', *European Law Journal* 8 (2002): 198–217.

Sciulli, David, *Theory of Societal Constitutionalism: Foundations of a Non-Marxist Critical Theory* (Cambridge: Cambridge University Press, 1992).

Scott, Joanne and David M. Trubek, 'Mind the Gap: Law and New Approaches to Governance in the European Union', *European Law Journal* 8 (2002): 1–18.

Searle, John, *The Construction of Social Reality* (London: Penguin 1995).

Searle, John, *Making the Social World: The Structure of Human Civilization* (Oxford: Oxford University Press, 2010).

Senden, Linda, *Soft Law in European Community Law* (Oxford: Hart Publishing, 2004).

Senden, Linda and Sacha Prechal, 'Differentiation in and through Community Soft Law', in *The Many Faces of Differentiation in EU Law*, eds Bruno De Witte, Dominik Hanf and Ellen Vos (Antwerpen: Intersentia, 2001), 181–199.

Shaw, Jo, 'Postnational Constitutionalism in the European Union', *Journal of European Public Policy* 6 (1999): 579–597.

Shaw, Jo and Antje Wiener, 'The Paradox of the "European Polity"', in *The State of the European Union Vol. 5: Risks, Reform, Resistance, and Revival*, eds Maria G. Cowles and Michael Smith (Oxford: Oxford University Press, 2000), 64–89.

Shaw, Jo and Antje Wiener, eds, *Evolving Norms of Constitutionalism: Special Issue of European Law Journal* (Oxford: Blackwell, 2003).

Shils, Edward, *The Constitution of Society* (Chicago, IL: The University of Chicago Press, 1972).

Shiner, Larry, 'Reading Foucault: Anti-Method and the Genealogy of Power-Knowledge', *History and Theory*, 21(3) (1982): 382–398.

Simmons, Beth A., *Mobilizing for Human Rights: International Law in Domestic Politics* (Cambridge: Cambridge University Press, 2009).

Skinner, Quentin, 'Hobbes on Representation', *European Journal of Philosophy* 13(2) (2005): 155–184.

Skocpol, Theda, *States and Social Revolutions* (Cambridge: Cambridge University Press, 1979).

Slaughter, Anne-Marie, Alec Sweet Stone and Joseph H.H. Weiler, Joseph, eds, *The European Court and National Courts: Doctrine and Jurisprudence. Legal Change in its Social Context* (Oxford: Hart Publishing, 1998).

Smith, Carole, 'The Sovereign State v Foucault: Law and Disciplinary Power', *The Sociological Review* 48 (2000): 283–306.

Smith, Jackie, Charles Chatfield and Ron Pagnucco, eds, *Transnational Social Movements and Global Politics: A Solidarity Beyond the State* (Syracuse, NY: Syracuse University Press, 1997).

Snyder, Francis, *New Directions in European Community Law* (London: Weidenfeld & Nicholson, 1990).

Snyder, Francis, 'Soft Law and Institutional Practice in the European Community', in *The Construction of Europe – Essays in honour of Emil Noel*, ed. Stephen Martin (Dordrecht: Kluwer, 1993), 197–225.

Snyder, Francis, 'Soft Law and Institutional Practice in the European Community', in *The Construction of Europe: Essays in honour of Mile Noel*, ed. Stephen Martin (Dordrecht: Kluwer, 1994), 197–225.

Snyder, Francis, 'Governing Economic Globalisation: Global Legal Pluralism and European Law', *European Law Journal* 5 (1999): 334–374.

Sousa Santos, Boaventura de, *Towards a New Legal Common Sense. 2nd edition* (London: Butterworths, 2002).

Spencer, Herbert, *The Man Versus the State: With Six Essays on Government, Society, and Freedom* (Indianapolis, IN: Liberty Fund, 1982).

Spruyt, Hendrik, *The Sovereign State and its Competitors: an Analysis of Systems Change* (Princeton, NJ: Princeton University Press, 1994).

Starke, Joseph G., 'Monism and Dualism in the Theory of International Law', in *Normativity and Norms: Critical Perspectives on Kelsenian Themes*, ed. Stanley L. Paulson (Oxford: Oxford University Press, 1999; the essay originally published in 1938).

Steffek, Jens, 'Sources of Legitimacy Beyond the State: A View from International Relations', in *Transnational Governance and Constitutionalism*, eds Christian Joerges, Inger-Johanne Sand and Gunther Teubner (Oxford: Hart Publishing, 2004), 81–101.

Stein, Eric, 'Toward Supremacy of Treaty-Constitution by Judicial Fiat: On the Margin of the Costa Case', *Michigan Law Review* 63 (1965): 491–518.

Stein, Eric, 'Lawyers, Judges, and the Making of a Transnational Constitution', *American Journal of International Law* 75 (1981): 1–27.

Stone Sweet, Alec and Wayne Sandholtz, 'Integration, Transnational Governance and the Institutionalization of the European Polity', in *European Integration and Supranational Governance*, eds Alec Stone Sweet and Wayne Sandholtz (Oxford: Oxford University Press, 1998), 1–26.

Strauss, Leo, 'Notes on Carl Schmitt's Concept of the Political', in Carl Schmitt, *The Concept of the Political. Expanded Edition* (Chicago, IL: .The University of Chicago Press, 2007), 97–122.

Streeck, Wolfgang, 'Neo-voluntarism: A New European Social Policy Regime', in *Governance in the European Union*, eds Gary Marks et al. (London: Sage, 1996), 64–94.

Stubb, Alexander, *Negotiationg Flexibility in the European Union* (Basingstoke: Palgrave, 2002).

Suganami, Hidemi, 'Understanding Sovereignty Through Kelsen/Schmitt', *Review of International Studies* 33 (2007): 511–530.

Tadros, Victor, 'Between Governance and Discipline: The Law and Michel Foucault', *Oxford Journal of Legal Studies* 18 (1998): 75–103.

Takis, Tridimas, *The General Principles of EU Law* (Oxford: Oxford University Press, 2006).

Tamanaha, Brian, 'The Folly of the "Social Scientific" Concept of Legal Pluralism', *Journal of Law and Society* 20 (1993): 192–217.

Tamanaha, Brian, *A General Jurisprudence of Law and Society* (Oxford: Oxford University Press, 2001).

Tamanaha, Brian, *On the Rule of Law: History, Politics, Theory* (Cambridge: Cambridge University Press, 2004).

Taylor, Charles, 'Foucault on Freedom and Truth', *Political Theory* 12(2) (1984): 152–183.

Taylor, Paul, *The European Union in the 1990s* (Oxford: Oxford University Press, 1996).

Taylor, Peter J., 'The State as Container: Territoriality in the Modern World-System', *Progress in Human Geography* 18 (1994): 151–162.

Teubner, Gunther, 'How the Law Thinks: Toward a Constructivist Epistemology of Law', *Law & Society Review* 23(5) (1989): 727–757.

Teubner, Gunther, 'The Two Faces of Janus: Rethinking Legal Pluralism', *Cardozo Law Review* 13 (1992): 1443–1462.

Teubner, Gunther, *Law as an Autopoietic System* (Oxford: Blackwell, 1993).

Teubner, Gunther, ed., *Global Law Without a State* (Aldershot: Dartmouth, 1997).

Teubner, Gunther, '"Global Bukowina": Legal Pluralism in the World Society', in *Global Law Without a State*, ed. Gunther Teubner (Aldershot: Dartmouth, 1997), 3–28.

Teubner, Gunther, 'Breaking Frames: Economic Globalisation and the Emergence of Lex Mercatoria', *European Journal of Social Theory* 5 (2002): 199–217.

Teubner, Gunther, 'Societal Constitutionalism: Alternatives to State-Centred Constitutional Theory?', in *Transnational Governance and Constitutionalism*, eds Christian Joerges, Inger-Johanne Sand and Gunther Teubner (Oxford: Hart Publishing, 2004), 3–28.

Teubner, Gunther, 'Constitutionalizing Polycontexturality', *Social and Legal Studies* 20(2) (2011): 210–229.

Teubner, Gunther, *Constitutional Fragments: Societal Constitutionalism and Globalization* (Oxford: Oxford University Press, 2012).

Teubner, Gunther and Andreas Fischer-Lescano, 'Regime Collisions: The Vain Search for Legal Unity in the Fragmentation of Global Law', *Michigan Journal of International Law* 25(4) (2004): 999–1046.

Thornhill, Chris, *Political Theory in Modern Germany: an Introduction* (Cambridge: Polity, 2000).

Thornhill, Chris, 'Carl Schmitt after the Deluge', *History of European Ideas* 26 (2001): 225–240.

Thornhill, Chris, 'Niklas Luhmann, Carl Schmitt and the Modern Form of the Political', *European Journal of Social Theory* 10(4) (2007): 499–522.

Thornhill, Chris, 'Constitutional Law from the Perspective of Power: A Response to Gunther Teubner', *Social and Legal Studies* 20(2) (2011): 244–247.

Thornhill, Chris, *A Sociology of Constitutions: Constitutions and State Legitimacy in Historical-Sociological Perspective* (Cambridge: Cambridge University Press, 2011).

Thym, Daniel, 'In the Name of Sovereign Statehood: A Critical Introduction to the Lisbon Judgement of the German Constitutional Court', *Common Market Law Review* 46 (2009): 1795–1822.

Tindemans, Leo, 'European Union. Report by Mr Leo Tindemans, Prime Minister of Belgium, to the European Council', *Bulletin of the European Communities*, Supplement 1/76 (1976).

Tindemans, Leo, 'Dreams come true, gradually: The Tindemans Report a quarter of a century on', in *The European Union beyond Amsterdam: New Concepts of European Integration*, ed. Martin Westlake (London: Routledge, 1998), 130–141.

Tocqueville, Alexis de, *Democracy in America* (Chicago, IL: University of Chicago Press, 2000).

Tönnies, Ferdinand, *Community and Society* (Mineola, NY: Dover Publications, 2002).

Trubek, David and Louise Trubek, 'Hard and Soft Law in the Construction of Social Europe: the Role of the Open Method of Co-ordination', *European Law Journal* 11 (2005): 343–364.

Trubek, David, Patrick Cottrell and Mark Nance, '"Soft Law", "Hard Law" and EU Integration', in *Law and New Governance in the EU and the US*, eds Gráinne de Búrca and Joanne Scott (Oxford: Hart Publishing, 2006), 65–94.

Tsagourias, Nicholas K., ed., *Transnational Constitutionalism: International and European Perspectives* (Cambridge: Cambridge University Press, 2007).

Tsakatika, Myrto, 'The European Union and the democratic limits of governance', in *Governance and Civil Society in the European Union, volume 1: Normative Perspectives*, eds Carlo Ruzza and Vincent Della Sala (Manchester: Manchester University Press, 2007), 30–54.

Tully, James, 'Wittgenstein and Political Philosophy: Understanding Practices of Critical Reflection', *Political Theory* 17(2) (1989): 172–204.

Tully, James, *Constitutionalism in an Age of Diversity* (Cambridge: Cambridge University Press, 1995).

Tuori, Karlo, *Ratio and Voluntas: The Tension Between Reason and Will in Law* (Aldershot: Ashgate, 2010).

Turner, Bryan S., 'Outline of a Theory of Human rights', *Sociology* 27(3) (1993): 489–512.

Tuytschaever, Filip, *Differentiation in European Union Law* (Oxford: Hart Publishing, 1999).

Unger, Roberto M., *Law in Modern Society: Toward a Criticism of Social Theory* (New York: Free Press, 1976).

Usher, John A., 'Enhanced Cooperation or Flexibility in the Post-Nice Era', in *Accountability and Legitimacy in the European Union*, eds Anthony Arnull and Dan Wincott (Oxford: Oxford University Press, 2002), 97–112.

Van Mill, David, *Liberty, Rationality, and Agency in Hobbes's Leviathan* (Albany, NY: SUNY Press, 2001).

Vesting, Thomas, 'The Network Economy as a Challenge to Create New Public Law', in *Public Governance in the Age of Globalization*, ed. Karl-Heinz Ladeur (Aldershot: Ashgate, 2004), 247–288.

Vinx, Lars, *Hans Kelsen's Pure Theory of Law: Legality and Legitimacy* (Oxford: Oxford University Press, 2007).

Wagner, Peter, *A Sociology of Modernity: Liberty and Discipline* (London: Routledge, 1994).

Walby, Kevin, 'Contributions to a Post-Sovereigntist Understanding of Law: Foucault, Law as Governance, and Legal Pluralism', *Social & Legal Studies* 16 (2007): 551–571.

Walker, Neil, 'Sovereignty and Differentiated Integration in the European Union', *European Law Journal* 4 (1998): 355–388.

Walker, Neil, 'Theoretical Reflections on Flexibility and Europe's Future', in *Constitutional Change in the EU: From Uniformity to Flexibility*, eds Gráinne de Búrca and Joanne Scott (Oxford: Hart Publishing, 2000), 9–30.

Walker, Neil, 'The Idea of Constitutional Pluralism', *Modern Law Review* 65 (2002): 317–359.

Walker, Neil, 'Late Sovereignty in the European Union', in *Sovereignty in Transition*, ed. Neil Walker (Oxford: Hart Publishing, 2003), 3–32.

Walker, Neil, ed., *Sovereignty in Transition* (Oxford: Hart Publishing, 2003).

Walker, Neil, 'Europe's Constitutional Engagement', *Ratio Juris* 18 (2005): 387–399.

Walker, Neil, 'EU Constitutionalism and New Governance', in *Law and New Governance in the EU and the US*, eds Gráinne de Búrca and Joanne Scott (Oxford: Hart Publishing, 2006), 15–36.

Walker, Neil, 'Post-Constituent Constitutionalism? The Case of the European Union', in *The Paradox of Constitutionalism: Constituent Power and Constitutional Form*, eds Martin Loughlin and Neil Walker (Oxford: Oxford University Press, 2007), 247–267.

Walker, R.B.J., 'Sovereignty, Identity, Community: Reflections on the Horizons of Contemporary Political Practice', in *Contending Sovereignties: Redefining Political Community*, eds R.B.J. Walker and Saul H. Mendlovitz (Boulder, CO: Lynne Rienner, 1990), 159–185.

Wallace, William, 'The Sharing of Sovereignty: The European Paradox', *Political Studies* 47 (1999): 503–521.

Wallace, William, 'Europe after the Cold War: interstate order or postsovereign regional system?', *Review of International Studies* 25(5) (1999): 201–223.

Wallace, William and Julie Smith, 'Democracy or Technocracy? European Integration and the Problem of Popular Consent', in *The Crisis of Representation in Europe*, ed. Jack Hayward (London: Frank Cass, 1995), 137–157.

Wallerstein, Immanuel, *World-Systems Analysis: An Introduction* (Durham NC: Duke University Press, 2004).

Walzer, Michael, *Spheres of Justice: A Defense of Pluralism and Equality* (New York: Basic Books, 1983).

Ward, Ian, 'Beyond Constitutionalism: The Search for a European Political Imagination', *European Law Journal* 7(1) (2001): 24–37.

Waters, Melissa A., 'Creeping Monism: The Judicial Trend toward Interpretive Incorporation of Human Rights Treaties', *Columbia Law Review* 107 (2007): 628–705.

Weale, Albert, 'Democratic Legitimacy and the Constitution of Europe', in *Democracy and Constitutional Culture in the Union of Europe*, eds Richard Bellamy, Vittorio Bufacchi and Dario Castiglione (London: Lothian Foundation Press, 1995), 81–94.

Weber, Max, *Economy and Society: An Outline of Interpretive Sociology. Vols I and II* (Berkeley, CA: University of California Press, 1978; originally published in 1968).

Weber, Max, 'The Nation State and Economic Policy', in *Political Writings*, Max Weber (Cambridge: Cambridge University Press, 1994), 1–28.

Weiler, Joseph H.H., 'Does Europe Need a Constitution? Demos, Telos and the German Maastricht Decision', *European Law Journal* 1(3) (1995): 219–258.

Weiler, Joseph H.H., 'In defence of the status quo: Europe's constitutional *Sonderweg*', in *European Constitutionalism Beyond the State*, eds Joseph H.H. Weiler and Marlene Wind (Cambridge: Cambridge University Press, 2003), 7–23.

Weiler, Joseph H.H. and Marlene Wind, 'Introduction: European constitutionalism beyond the state', in *European Constitutionalism Beyond the State*, eds Joseph H.H. Weiler and Marlene Wind (Cambridge: Cambridge University Press, 2003), 1–4.

Weinberger, Ota, *Law, Institution and Legal Politics: Fundamental Problems of Legal Theory and Social Philosophy* (Dordrecht: Kluwer, 1991).

Wellens, Karel C. and Gustaaf M. Borchart, 'Soft Law in EC Law', *European Law Review* 14 (1989): 267–321.

Wendel, Mattias, 'Comparative reasoning and the making of a common constitutional law: EU-related decisions of national constitutional courts in a transnational perspective', *International Journal of Constitutional Law* 11(4) (2013): 981–1002.

Wendt, Alexander, 'Collective Identity Formation and the International State', *American Political Science Review* 88(2) (1994): 384–396.

Wessels, Wolfgang, 'An Ever Closer Fusion? A Dynamic Macropolitical View on Integration Processes', *Journal of Common Market Studies* 35(2) (1997): 267–299.

Westlake, Martin, 'The European Union's 'blind watchmakers': The process of constitutional change', in *The European Union Beyond Amsterdam: New Concepts of European Integration*, ed. Martin Westlake (London: Routledge, 1998), 14–30.

Wickham, Gary, 'Foucault, Law, and Power: A Reassessment', *Journal of Law and Society* 33(4) (2006): 596–614.

Wickham, Gary and George Pavlich, eds, *Rethinking Law, Society and Governance: Foucault's Bequest* (Oxford: Hart Publishing, 2001).

Wiener, Antje, 'The Embedded Acquis Communautaire: Transmission Belt and Prism of New Governance', *European Law Journal* 4 (1998): 294–315.

Wiener, Antje, 'Editorial: Evolving Norms of Constitutionalism', *European Law Journal* 9 (2003): 1–13.

Wind, Marlene, 'The European Union as a polycentric polity', in *European Constitutionalism Beyond the State*, eds Joseph H.H. Weiler and Marlene Wind (Cambridge: Cambridge University Press, 2003), 103–131.

Wintgens, Luc J., 'Sovereignty and Representation', *Ratio Juris* 14(3) (2001): 272–280.

Wolin, Richard, 'Carl Schmitt, Political Existentialism, and the Total State', *Theory and Society* 19(4) (1990): 389–416.

Wolin, Richard, *Heidegger's Children: Hannah Arendt, Karl Lowith, Hans Jonas and Herbert Marcuse* (Princeton, NJ: Princeton University Press, 2001).

Wolin, Sheldon S., *Tocqueville Between Two Worlds: The Making of a Political and Theoretical Life* (Princeton, NJ: Princeton University Press, 2001).

Yack, Bernard, 'The Myth of the Civic Nation', in *Theorizing Nationalism*, ed. Ron Beiner (Albany, NY: State University of New York Press, 1998), 103–118.
Yack, Bernard, 'Popular Sovereignty and Nationalism', *Political Theory* 29(4) (2001): 517–536.
Youngs, Richard, *The European Union and the Promotion of Democracy* (Oxford: Oxford University Press, 2001).
Ziegert, Klaus A., 'Introduction to the Transaction Edition', in *Fundamental Principles of the Sociology of Law*, Eugen Ehrlich (New Brunswick, NJ: Transaction, 2002), xli, xlv.
Ziegert, Klaus A., 'World Society, Nation State and Living Law in the Twenty-first Century', in *Living Law: Reconsidering Eugen Ehrlich*, ed. Marc Hertogh (Oxford: Hart Publishing 2009), 223–236.
Zielonka, Jan, *Europe as Empire* (Oxford: Oxford University Press, 2006).
Zumbansen, Peer, 'Semantics of European Law', *European Law Journal* 5 (1999): 114–126.
Zumbansen, Peer, 'Transnational Legal Pluralism', *Transnational Legal Theory* 10(2) (2010): 141–189.
Zürn, Michael and Christian Joerges, eds, *Governance and Law in Post-National Constellations: Compliance in Europe and Beyond* (Cambridge: Cambridge University Press, 2005).

Legal and Political Documents

The European Union and the Venice Commission:

The Treaty of Lisbon amending the Treaty on European Union and the Treaty establishing European Community, CIG 14/07, Brussels, 3 December 2007.
Consolidated Version of the Treaty on European Union, *Official Journal of the European Union*, 9th May 2008, C115.
The Council of the European Union Note No. 11218/07, 'IGC 2007 Mandate', Brussels, 26 June 2007.
Presidency Conclusions of the Council of the European Union, CONCL 4, No. 14368/08, 16 October 2008.
Opinion on the New Constitution of Hungary: European Commission for Democracy Through Law (Venice Commission), in *Constitution for a Disunited Nation: on Hungary's 2011 Fundamental Law*, ed., Gábor Attila Tóth, (Budapest: CEU Press, 2012), 491–536.

Constitutional Justice of the EU Member States:

The Czech Constitutional Court's judgment of 8 March 2006, Pl. ÚS 50/04, (the Sugar Quota III Judgement).

The Czech Constitutional Court's judgement of 26 November 2008, Pl ÚS 19/08, (The Treaty of Lisbon I Judgement).

The German Federal Constitutional Court's judgement of 12 October 1993, BVerfGE 89, 155. (The Maastricht Treaty Judgement).

The German Federal Constitutional Court's judgement of 30 June 2009, BVerfG, 2 BvE 2/08; (The Lisbon Treaty Judgement).

The Polish Constitutional Tribunal's Judgement of 11 May 2005, K 18/04, (The Accession Treaty Judgement).

The Polish Constitutional Tribunal's Procedural Decision of 19 December 2006, no. 176/11/A/2006, (The Excise Duty Tax Decision).

The Polish Constitutional Tribunal's Judgement of 27 April 2005, P 1/05, (The European Arrest Warrant Judgement)., Official Collection of the Constitutional Tribunal Jurisdiction, OTK ZU, No. 4/A/2005.

Constitutional Court of Spain, *Sentencia* STC 031/2010, de 28 de junio de 2010 (BOE núm. 172, de 16 de julio de 2010).

Index

For Product Safety Concerns and Information please contact our EU representative GPSR@taylorandfrancis.com Taylor & Francis Verlag GmbH, Kaufingerstraße 24, 80331 München, Germany